WILD CARD QUILT

WILD CARD QUILT

TAKING A CHANCE ON HOME

JANISSE RAY

MILKWEED
EDITIONS

"One Wrong Turn," from *The Poet Game* by Greg Brown. Copyright © 1994 by Greg Brown, published by Hacklebarney Music (ASCAP). Reprinted with permission.

Mary Oliver, "In Blackwater Woods," from *American Primitive.* Copyright © 1978, 1979, 1980, 1981, 1982, 1983 by Mary Oliver. First appeared in *Yankee Magazine.* Used by permission of Little, Brown and Company, (Inc.).

"Gott spricht zu jedem . . . / God Speaks to Each of Us," from *Rilke's Book of Hours: Love Poems to God* by Rainer Maria Rilke, translated by Anita Barrows and Joanna Macy. Copyright © 1996 by Anita Barrows and Joanna Macy. Used by permission of Riverhead Books, an imprint of Penguin Putnam Inc.

Published 2003 by Milkweed Editions
Printed in Canada
Jacket and interior design by Christian Fünfhausen
Jacket and interior photographs provided by the author
Endsheets map by Raven Burchard
Author photograph on jacket flap by Raven Burchard
The text of this book is set in ACaslon
03 04 05 06 07   5 4 3 2 1
First Edition

Special underwriting for this book was generously
provided by DeL Corazón Family Fund.

Milkweed Editions, a nonprofit publisher, gratefully acknowledges support from the Bush Foundation; Joe B. Foster Family Foundation; Furthermore, a program of the J. M. Kaplan Fund; General Mills Foundation; Jerome Foundation; Dorothy Kaplan Light; Lila Wallace-Reader's Digest Fund; Marshall Field's Project Imagine with support from the Target Foundation; McKnight Foundation; Minnesota State Arts Board through an appropriation by the Minnesota State Legislature; National Endowment for the Arts; Kate and Stuart Nielsen; Deborah Reynolds; St. Paul Companies, Inc.; Ellen and Sheldon Sturgis; Surdna Foundation; Target Foundation; Gertrude Sexton Thompson Charitable Trust; James R. Thorpe Foundation; Toro Foundation; United Arts Fund of COMPAS; Lois Ream Waldref; Brenda Wehle and John C. Lynch; and Xcel Energy Foundation.

Library of Congress Cataloging-in-Publication Data

Ray, Janisse, 1962–
    Wild card quilt : taking a chance on home / Janisse Ray.— 1st ed.
    p. cm.
ISBN 1-57131-272-2 (acid-free paper)
1. Ray, Janisse, 1962– 2. Baxley (Ga.)—Biography. 3. Ray family. 4. Baxley (Ga.)—Social life and customs. 5. Country life—Georgia—Baxley. 6. Baxley (Ga.)—Rural conditions. 7. Women naturalists—Georgia—Baxley—Biography. 8. Longleaf pine—Georgia—Baxley Region. 9. Forest conservation—Georgia—Baxley Region. I. Title.
    F294.B39 R398 2003
    975.8'784—dc21

                                                                            2002152810

FOR MY FATHER
AND MOTHER,

Franklin Delano Ray and
Lee Ada Branch Ray,

AND FOR
Susan

WILD CARD QUILT

You, sent out beyond your recall,
go to the limits of your longing.
Embody me.

Flare up like flame
and make big shadows I can move in.

Let everything happen to you: beauty and terror.
Just keep going. No feeling is final.
Don't let yourself lose me.

Nearby is the country they call life.
You will know it by its seriousness.

Give me your hand.

> —RAINER MARIA RILKE,
> "God Speaks to Each of Us"

Introduction

M any years after I left the place I was born, I returned to the family farm in rural south Georgia,
hoping to find there a home I had been looking for all my
full-grown life.

These stories are from those years on the farm. All
of them relate to coming back and making a life in a place
that held my past, a place that as a young woman I had
gladly left behind. In this book I rejoin with place, land,
kin, history, and neighbors in an attempt to gather the
pieces of my life. I wanted to live in a less fragmented, less
broken, more meaningful way, to have more of what I
loved around me, to say with my body, "This is what matters." I was looking for wholeness.

The stories are examinations of personal, family, and
community history. They are observations on rural living,
accounts of my efforts to find society, and essays about the
landscape around me. Only by inspecting each piece could
I come to a conclusion about whether my life belonged
there.

Instead of a tribe, what I found in my south Georgia
home was an erosion of human bonds—both to each other
and to the land. Those elements I sought, such as community and sense of place, had been compromised one way
or another. I saw a way of life that once had made sense
pitched into failure.

During the past century, our country suffered a rural exodus; current figures estimate that 80 percent of the United States population now live in cities. The result is that agrarian communities are diminished. Nowhere in recent human history are our tribal, interdependent natures more realized than in farming communities; although these social units are not without dysfunction, ostracism, and strife, here the human spirit seems to thrive. I wanted to inhabit that life.

Perhaps stories keep us as a people in place glued together. As the stories vanish or are lost—as people depart homeplaces, as the landscapes are destroyed—no new stories form to replace them. Without the stories that fasten us each to each, the web that is community commences to unravel, its threads flapping in the wind, finally tearing loose completely and wafting away.

A life constructed of stories can be had. A simple, wonderful existence is possible in the country, one full of beauty and meaningful work and shared resources. It is possible, though many forces of the twenty-first century would tear it apart, to live in community.

I am clinging to a shaking cobweb strung between a leaky house and a wind-torn barn. I am spinning like crazy to reconstruct it, conversing with the ghosts of the pine flatwoods to weave their old stories in with the new ones. Here and there across the web, others are working hard, laying thread on top of sticky thread, to catch and bind us anew. People are spinning night and day, adding the bright colors of their dreams. We may make a beautiful net yet.

WILD CARD QUILT

Kitchen side of the house, spring.

Long Road Home

W hen I shoved open the door of my grandmother Beulah's farmhouse, shut tight and
neglected many heavy-hearted years, I entered a history
that stretched backward not simply to the limits of my
memory but to the farthest point of my family's memory,
although the people who knew that beginning are no
longer known.

It was night when we arrived, my son and I. Mama and
Daddy met us at the place, and Uncle Percy strolled over,
the tip of his cigarette a pinpoint of orange ash. A security
light on its tall pole cast pearly shadows across humps of
bushes in the yard, lighting the concrete steps. The screen
of the porch reflected the light, as if a huge moon were
shining, so that the screening appeared silver and not deep
rust, and translucent, as it would by daylight. The screen
door, loosed at its joints, sagged against the porch floor,
whose gray paint was tarnished by a thick layer of dust
the umber of the road running east of the house.

Then we were standing on the porch, trying to get in
through a door that had not been opened in years. In the
dim light, I recognized a plant stand in the corner that
Granddaddy had made out of a tree for Grandmama's
flowers. He chose a cedar with many branches, and each
branch, planed level, now held an empty clay flowerpot.
Spiderwebs constructed around the porch corners, having

collected the reddish gray dust that blanketed everything, dangled like old rags.

Uncle Percy fiddled with the door. The eldest son who had never left the homeplace, Percy lived in a trailer across the yard. "This key ain't wanting to turn," he said. "I believe I've bent it."

"Can you get it out?" Daddy asked. Uncle Percy fiddled some more, then handed the freed key to my father. "Looks like it's cracked," Daddy said. "Percy, you mind if I try it? We'll be in a fix if it was to break off." My head hurt from a terrible blend of fear and excitement, and from a long day driving east, pulling our possessions behind the truck. I sat down in one of Grandmama's rocking chairs.

The incandescent bulb lit one side of Daddy's face, which was the face of concentration. With a great deal of jiggling, Daddy forced the lock's tumblers into position and the doorknob turned. The door groaned as it separated from its frame. My father can make anything mechanical work—his heyday was the era of machines.

When I rose, the back of my shorts and shirt were stained with dust. Mama tried to brush it off. "Can't sit down until we clean," I said.

"It's that road," Mama said. "The summer's been so dry. When cars pass, the dust boils over the house."

Daddy did not enter the unlit doorway but instead relocked the lock. He jiggled again, and again the door heaved loose from its frame. "You got to back the key out about an eighth inch," Daddy said to me, "and turn it counterclockwise. That key's cracked and could break anytime. You got to be careful." He returned the key to Uncle Percy ceremoniously, and my mother's brother, who had inherited the house, turned to me.

"You're the one gone be needing this," he said.

I wouldn't, as it turned out. In the years that I occupied the house, it would almost never be locked from the outside.

"I'd take that key down to the hardware first thing tomorrow and make a copy," Daddy said emphatically. "We need to replace this doorknob. I'll look on the yard for one." By "the yard" he meant the junkyard he owned, seven miles away, where I was raised.

Daddy stood back. Mama too. I moved past them and hesitantly stepped through the open door into the interior darkness. Behind me, Uncle Percy fumbled for a set of light switches on the wall by the door.

What I recognized first was the smell. Despite having been closed up for years, the house had the same rush of pine and cedar it had always had, a fragrance I have never smelled anywhere else, ever—one of absolute belonging.

A light came on, then another.

Almost nothing had altered since I'd last been inside, nine or ten years before. Grandmama had been alive then, and one could think now that she wasn't far away. Her belongings—vinyl sofa and chairs bought in the early '70s, pictures of her children's families, gilded lamps, the same candy dishes—were a study in life interrupted. Whatnots, including a ceramic bluebird on a limb and an ashtray shaped in the form of a coiled snake, lined the low wall between the two living rooms. A life-size ceramic owl hung from the ceiling. Husks of dead insects that had been trapped inside littered the rust-colored carpet. Every exposed surface was coated with a film of dust, including the lacy drapes, which would not survive a washing. When I reached for one of the plastic yellow roses in a vase on the end table, it disintegrated at the touch.

"The old house needs a lot of work," Uncle Percy said then, affectionately. "Nobody's even been in here in I don't know how many years."

∞

I never thought I'd return to south Georgia to live, to my hometown of Baxley (population 4,150), to a farm seven miles from town on a dirt road. I had left Baxley seventeen years earlier, because it was expected that I would leave—mine was the first generation to attempt college— if I was to make anything of myself, and because I could not entertain the idea of living in a place where the people knew so much of each other's history. The world was infinite, full of possibility, and anonymous; Baxley was small, which to me meant limited and constricting.

My mother had been raised on this respectable farm, but my father was a town boy, a ruffian. He came from bad blood—his father was a ne'er-do-well, a brawling boaster, a lunatic woodsman. Daddy never remembers my grandfather sleeping a peaceable night with his wife and eight children; he never remembers a normal evening with his family. Instead, his father came and went, almost invariably in a rage, and in terror his children gave him wide berth. Daddy was eleven when his father abandoned the family for good.

My grandmother on that side worked in the fields, cooked in cafes and bootlegged whiskey to feed her family, who never had shoes on their feet or more than a set or two of clothes, and who never had enough food. Those were hard times. Mama, on the farm, hadn't known hunger. She told stories of opening watermelons and cutting out the heart to eat, then throwing the rest to the chickens.

My mother's parents disapproved of her association with my father, an objection that forced their daughter to elope. Part of their worry was justified in the years to come, for my mother chose a hard-working life for herself. That life, however, was founded on a bedrock of love, which makes most anything not only possible to withstand but also unalterable.

When they married, my father opened a junkyard, just outside the city limits, which barely sustained them and the young'uns they begat one after the other. I was the second child. Kay was first, four years older than me; my brother Dell was born a year later, and Stephen a year after Dell. A brilliant, tormented man, my father quested for the meaning of life; he became very dogmatic in his religious beliefs and started a church in a warehouse he bought downtown. Mama gave away her shorts and high heels, and quit wearing jewelry and lipstick. She began to go about with her head covered, in dresses dark and calf length. Daddy banished the television from the house.

Then, with four small children, my father succumbed to the mental illness that had plagued the Ray name for generations, the illness Mama's parents had worried about when he showed up at their door to court their middle daughter. During a three-year span, Daddy was hospitalized a number of times at the state mental institution. Later, my father would temper his brilliant fire, and use it to create and invent and repair and make do. Through it all, somehow, Mama kept her family fed, clothed, and together.

Longing had characterized my existence in this homeland. We were ever poor and very different from other
townspeople—proud, fervently religious, marred by lunacy,
suspicious. We were doomed to isolation. As a girl I longed
for a different life, a peaceful, forgiving one, a life such
as other people lived, such as I read about in books. I
longed to be away, or for things to be different. I longed
for lovers, before and after I had them. Growing up with
so many yearnings, I became both their progeny and
their maker, so that longing trailed me into adulthood.
Everywhere I turned, I wanted the world to be the way
I had imagined it could be.

Looking back from far away, that childhood seemed
remote and unreal, any shame lessened by the knowledge
that always, during and after childhood, both our parents
loved us—would die for us, in fact. They acted in what
they considered to be our best interest. But my apostasy
was real, and I felt there was no going back, not to the
whereabouts of my sorrowful origin. I remembered too
clearly how cramped life had been there.

Southern Georgia had been the country of longing.
Could I make it, now, the country of gratification?

ꙅꙅ

Surely I am not the only human who wakes up one
day, having left home, and finds herself slave to a patria,
imprinted with its memory, wanting to return. Maybe
it's true of humanity that we carry our nativity inside us
forever. We have witnessed time and again people's spirits
tugging at their bodies, trying to go home: emigrants pin-
ing, tears rolling at the thought of fjords or steppes or

lochs. In my years away from south Georgia, I had not been able to forget it. After all, even my bones were ossified from that locale, formed of it as surely as the tupelo and cypress are. My blood, its blood.

The landscape of my childhood was one of fierce occupation by trees. When we rode country roads on Sunday afternoons on the back of Daddy's truck, the woods crowded in on all sides, thick and cool, the trees intimate and sensual in ways we could not understand. Above, their interlacing branches made canopies we rode slowly beneath. In the bottoms, where the roads rose on bridges and above culverts, we passed through swamp chestnut oak, beech, and magnolia, the hard, red clay of the earth offering us clear passage. Along the high sand ridges we rode through longleaf pine flatwoods, where the last sunlight, as it cast through the tall and silent pines, made of the grass a kind of lace.

Even then, new methods of logging and the row-cropping of trees had begun, but I was too young to see this. I saw only a wall of forest as the truck chugged up a slight rise, then the pines, then a white-painted house sitting amid fields planted in cotton. I saw pecan trees shading the house, and Confederate roses in the yard. Barefoot children played in the dry ditch, gathering knobby pebbles of ferric oxide, rain rocks, to toss gingerly and carefully after us. As dark came on, we watched for foxes and deer to dash out, watched for snakes, watched for anything, our bright lights piercing before us as if into a dark-green tunnel. The music of choirs trailed out of country churches.

My life had not been the movement toward grace and happiness I had dreamed as a young woman it would be. After seventeen years away, I had arrived at the knowledge

that I no longer felt at home on the earth, riven as I was
from our predominant culture—cities with hordes of
strangers, a gluttony for material things, loss of nature
and family farms, general disconnection to land. I hun-
gered to be part of a rural community defined by land and
history and blood. The sap that ran from my roots to my
branches mingled with the sap of my neighbors: this person
a third cousin, this a fifth, that a sister-in-law, this a dead
uncle's wife. Couldn't I plop down among them and be
surrounded by meaning, and finally happy? I desired the
jubilance of the place for my son, who was nine years old.
I wanted him to run barefoot and pick blackberries and
climb magnolias and play with his cousins.

I knew by then I had to write, and my grandmother's
farmhouse had lain empty not only the two years she'd
been dead, but since she and Uncle Percy had moved over
to the trailer, for comfort's sake, nine years before. I hoped
it would be a quiet abode where I could write.

I was a grown daughter, a single mother, a naturalist,
and a writer. Could I resolve the troubles of childhood,
since I would no longer be a child in a childhood place?
Could life be functional here this time? Could I find a
voice where I had not had one?

South Georgia had invented me, sent me away for an
education. Even if it was an undistinguished, ill-fitting
embarrassment of a place, what right did I, one of its own,
have to abandon it? Could one person make a difference
to a homeland? Could I be a tongue for a whittled and be-
leaguered landscape? What was my responsibility toward
honor, and toward my convictions, and toward my family,
who had not left south Georgia for seven generations?

The last time I'd been here was the day we put my

grandmother, Beulah, with the dead, who live not so far away, less than a mile down the road, in a grassy cemetery.

She had died very quietly, one leg already an inky blue-black from a blood clot, with a final tremor of breath. My mother had been at her side. Mama had stepped into the nursing home corridor and summoned a nurse.

"Baby, she's gone," the nurse said.

Viewing of the body took place the day after Grandmama died. All afternoon I sat within a fluctuating ring of people under the water oaks in her swept yard, listening to stories while neighbors brought chicken and dumplings, pans of rolls, pound cakes. No one cried. We sat in the presence of death and did not mention it. Family flocked in from Chattanooga, Orlando, Jacksonville, Chicago, kinfolk I rarely saw, and while we dug our chair legs into the ground with our squirming, we stared into the faces of our kin, updating pictures in our minds. Late afternoon I ironed a nice dress, used a smudge of Grandmama's blush and lipstick, and rode to the funeral home with my cousin Jimmy.

Grandmama's casket had been wheeled to the front of the chapel. It was shining silver and gold, surrounded by roses and huge pots of white lilies. The casket was open, with the top of Grandmama's head, lying against pink satin, visible. I thought it looked as if any moment she would raise herself and ask what on earth she was doing in such a ridiculous box. "Help me out of here," she'd say, and I would. Her eyeglasses rested on her lifeless face. What need did a body have of glasses?

The few people in the chapel were immediate family, contemplative and somber on the benches. Slowly I walked past them to the front of the parlor and stood

beside Grandmama, looking down at her. Aunt Coot joined
me. We had often stood together beside Grandmama's
bed, especially during the last fortnight, when I'd helped
take care of her. Most of that time she wasn't able to even
speak. My aunt reached down and touched Grandmama,
smoothed her hair, fingered her elfin ears. The undertaker
had fixed her hair in precise, neat curls like a short-haired
doll might wear, and my grandmother would've liked the
way it looked. I touched the curls, my hand following my
aunt's. Grandmama's hair felt the same as when she was
alive, rough and wiry. Her ear was cold, frozen and un-
bending. Her hands were stiff and bloodless, and holding
one of them I remembered with satisfaction that a few
days before I'd removed fingernail polish a nurse had
painted on. Grandmama never in her life enameled her
nails.

We sat and sat. People started to arrive at the funeral
parlor: neighbors from Spring Branch Community who'd
known Grandmama all their lives. Nieces and nephews.
Distant kin. "You have to be Lee Ada's daughter," someone said. "You look exactly like her." I tried to meet them
all, following genealogical lines until I was exhausted,
fitting people into a framework of history and place that
embraced me.

During the last rites the next day, I sat beside Uncle
Percy. Most of the time, he twiddled his thumbs round
and round, motion without purpose, but once I looked
over to see a tiny spring flowing from his eye. On my left,
Aunt Fonida's body rocked and shook with silent tears.
Uncle James, a Baptist minister, recited Grandmama's
favorite verse, Ruth 1:16. "And Ruth said, Entreat me not
to leave thee, or to return from following after thee: for

whither thou goest, I will go, and where thou lodgest,
I will lodge: thy people shall be my people, and thy God
my God."

I rode with Aunt Fonida in the slow burial procession, following a glossy black hearse from Spring Branch
Church along a clay road that turned toward Carter
Cemetery. Behind us, a snake of cars crept past farms that
Grandmama had passed all her life, houses where she'd
stopped to visit. This was her world, and now she made
her last journey through it, back to a clay hill where we
would bury her beside Granddaddy, among the dead of
that country. At ninety-three, the matriarch of my mother's
side of the family, my last living grandparent, the elder of
the clan, was gone.

After the interment, after everyone had proceeded
back to the house and eaten the last helpings of chicken-
and-rice and pineapple cake, and then fled to their new
cars and left the history that was no longer relevant to
their lives, I drove away to graduate school in Montana
with my young son.

"You won't be back," friends said. "You'll fall in love
with the West, and one of those cowboys."

"I'll be back," I replied.

One night on the Montana prairie, I dreamed of my
grandmother. All night the coyotes had been singing. They
had two camps, one to the east and one to the west, and
their songs passed back and forth: bays, trills, barks. The
wild dogs seemed to never stop howling. Theirs was a
night tongue, calling interdependence and belonging. I
lay awake listening and understanding none of it.

Toward morning I dreamed I was haying a field on my
grandmother's land. I was riding the vintage John Deere

and the sun was close and brilliant, but not oppressive
the way it usually is in late summer in the South. I was
practically flying, bare armed, over this field. I knew that
although my grandmother was dead, she was watching
from the line of water oaks at the edge of the pasture. Yet
her body seemed to be the hayfield itself. I dreamed this
so wholly that when I woke I thought I was there, in my
grandmother's grassy arms.

The morning I urged the U-Haul out of Montana,
I dashed into the sidewalk cafe we frequented to grab a
bagel, and there was my friend Davy, drinking coffee and
waiting, newspaper scattered about.

"Sweetmeats," he greeted me. Davy is easy in his
body, slim, his neck-length hair plowed by finger lines.
Although he is openly gay, we are very flirtatious.

"Babydoll," I answered, jovial. "I'm on my way out."
He knew I was homeward bound.

"Know how women in the South wear blue jeans cut
off short, and they sew lace to the hem?" Davy asked with
false innocence. He's a Charleston native, so he knows only
too well the poignant stereotypes and untruths of the rural
South.

"They got big hair and when they walk their pantyhose
go swish, swish, swish," he drawled. "And the men, they
drive around with Confederate flags stuck all over their
trucks and there's a dead deer lying in the back they've
poached. And they live in house trailers with a pile of beer
cans in the yard that they've thrown out the window as
they emptied them. And it's 'nigger this' and 'nigger that.'"

He paused, looked directly at me.

"Girl, you gone come out the house and there's a big
ole rattlesnake coiled up on your front porch showing its

teeth at you." Davy opened his mouth wide, somehow managing a vulgar, lustful expression. He has the most expressive lips ever put on a man.

"Wild pigs come out in the morning from the swamp— watch out when you go rambling or they'll get you, get your boy, and get your little dog, too. Don't go swimming in no river, ole alligator'll drag you under." He drew in a quick breath. I dropped head to hands.

"And it's so hot down there you'll have to shave your legs." Davy took a sip of coffee and banged his mug down, coolly picking up a section of paper. I sat in the sweet sunshine, feeling behind me the beautiful people drinking their organic, hazelnut-flavored, songbird-friendly coffee, and beyond them the lovely enlightened town, and even beyond, the majestic mountains washed in green, rising past the cafe window.

"What you want to go back down there for?" Davy asked.

౭౷

How can one explain the potency of the past? Like a shad finning toward the certain muskiness of birthplace, or a homing pigeon with a message around its neck, I went home. Mostly I went home because I was afraid of losing what could have been mine. I don't mean property. I mean the fat drops of dew that fall from the maple. I mean two brilliant redbirds, both male, in a nearby holly, and the red-shouldered hawk, whose very ancestors perhaps had circled high over the branch, whistling, causing my own ancestors to raise their faces.

I was of two minds about the return: either I would

fail and leave after a year or two or I would revitalize my grandmother's farm, buying it piece by piece from aunts and uncles, and I would die where seven generations of grandmothers had died before me. Maybe, just maybe, if I could slay the demons of childhood memory, knowing what I now knew, I could carve out a life that would be courageous, and gratifying, and of a piece.

In August of 1997, seventeen years after I fled my home-town for good, eager to quit its smallness and its unfor-givingness, my son and I moved into my grandmother's heart-pine house, amid tobacco fields and cow pastures in Spring Branch, a farming section of northern Appling County, Georgia.

Restoration

T he day after we arrived was the first day of school. I
enrolled Silas in third grade and set to work, packing Grandmama's dusty and cobwebbed past into boxes
marked "linens" or "kitchen." During the last hot, dry,
sun-searing days of August, I emptied her things from
cabinets and cupboards and replaced them with ours. The
water to the house was off because of busted lines, so I
hauled water from an outside spigot to clean. Within a
couple of days, Daddy came and helped me fix the water
line, so we had running water.

For a week I washed shelves, walls, and ceilings. I
relined the kitchen cabinets with fresh newspaper, and
laundered curtains and linens. I vacuumed the dead wasps.
Before a week was out, I set up the computer and dared,
with a house in chaos, to write in the mornings.

The first weeks were hard. I was alternately full of fear
and full of peace. Afternoons, when I heard the school bus
struggle to a stop to let off Silas, I turned off the computer,
unplugging it and shutting the window behind it against
a chance of sudden thunderstorms. Daddy would show up
with Mama to work in the ninety-five-degree heat while
Silas positioned his plastic action toys on battlegrounds
of weedy flower beds. Uncle Percy would emerge from his
trailer to join the activity—the proposing of solutions, the
fetching of tools, the repair—even if he mostly watched.

Mama took care of Silas and helped with the renovation if her arthritis pain would allow it.

We replaced a corroded section of copper pipe that ran to the gas space heaters—"we" being Daddy and me. What we discovered on the way to fixing the gas leak was a spray-bottle-size leak in a hot water line, then another leak in the gas line, then we (mostly Daddy, thank goodness) wrenched a fitting apart while screwing in the new section of line. The lines were under the house in the dirt, with the black widow spiders and the rattlesnakes. We had to cut off the water and the gas and drive seven miles to town for new fittings.

"Can you do without water tonight?" Daddy asked.

"Is there a choice?"

"Not really. It's too dark to fix this now."

"I did without it the first two days. I can again."

"We'll get on it first thing in the morning."

"I need to write in the morning. Can you come in the afternoon? I'll do without water."

"Better go draw up some jugs, then."

"Why don't you and Silas come eat with us tonight?" Mama asked. "You can take baths at our house, too."

"Thank you, Mama. We'll get by here. I can make sandwiches, and sponge off."

∞

After five days of cooking on a camping stove, I fixed the real stove by cleaning out its orifices. Daddy and I got the hot water heater working again. Mama and I swept and mopped. We fixed busted water pipes and cleared blocked drains. We repainted and rescreened the front porch, where Grandmama's two rockers sat alongside our canoe paddles and walking sticks. We tidied flower beds and planted hens-and-chickens—Mama had given me cuttings of the succulent—in concrete pots on either side of the front steps.

After nine years of neglect, a hundred tasks jostled for our attention: repair the oven, paint the kitchen, rake pine straw around the blueberries, prune the fruit trees, saw up the fallen tree, clear away the smokehouse it fell on. Uncle Percy and I set about rebuilding the kitchen screen door, which was rotted and rusted. The jamb needed replacing, and the inner door was deteriorating as well. "If the termites weren't holding hands," I heard someone say, "the house would fall down." The railing along the kitchen stoop needed paint. We worked at the tasks, pegging away, a little every day toward a new home. Slowly we made the house ours.

Despite how my heart was wrenched, faced as I was with the hardest reminders of childhood (being where the memories happened was making them raw again), I'd never been more content than at the farm, as if I'd lived my whole life to come back. Those August days the air was thickly green, waterlogged, and charged with heat. It smelled of fallen pine needles clumped in the grass, and decaying water oak limbs, and also of deeply wet earth. Tough fists of sand pears dropped from the trees and rotted on the ground until my father came in his dilapidated pickup and gathered washtubs full for the wild hogs penned in his junkyard. Scuppernongs, which I had reminisced so often about, ripened on the vines, carrying fall's pungency, a scent different from the sweetness of the tangled pasture, where Uncle Bill boarded cows. The days were longer than days had been in years. They were long and eerily quiet.

How can I say "quiet" when frogs were honking and cicadas yea-saying and the fan whirring continuously on low and fat drops of rain smacking catalpa leaves? Quiet, with the distant grumble of thunder and determination of cars on the highway? The magnolia shading the bedroom window clattered its noisy castanets, discarding them on the ground. Yet a vast silence lay upon the land; wide as gauze, it enveloped me and drifted away with me. The long, quiescent days were vessels for an odd freedom, like wearing overalls instead of a Sunday suit. One can move inside silence, like air moves inside overalls.

I loved the farm.

I'd promised Silas a puppy for our new life, and we searched for one among those abandoned at dumpsters, or along roadsides.

"What about him?" I would ask. The dog would be too mangy or too big. Near Lane's Bridge we spotted a short-haired, brown-and-white pup with little legs and perky ears, ranging through wrappers.

"OK," Silas said eagerly. I pulled over, bumping to a halt. The dog spotted us and took off like a rocket, legs streaking. Because it seemed to be running sideways we burst out laughing.

"Let's follow it," I said, but the dog cut across a field and disappeared into woods.

We procured a free puppy from a neighbor who already had four or five unspayed dogs. Silas picked the runt of the latest litter not because he was small or sported a white tip on his black tail but because that dog, of them all, came up and licked his hand. He named him Enoch, after a carouser in *The Education of Little Tree*, a book we'd been reading aloud.

You should have seen my son's joy as they tore around the yard, racing between the aged pines, coming upon the feel of swiftness, that elation you get only from running hard. As Silas sprinted from pine to pine, he wanted me to count how many seconds it took. My boy and his long-tongued pup seemed to have run straight off the canvas of a Rockwell painting.

Silas figured out a way to race Enoch, with me as judge, but it was hard to tell who'd won.

"Mom," Silas called, maybe for the second or third time, "you're absentminded again, aren't you?" He's patient.

I admitted that I had been distracted and hadn't heard whatever he'd said. The work needing to be done, especially that beyond the farm, the needs of community and region, had besieged my head. On every side, I saw a landscape resembling ruin.

"Who won that time?" Silas said.

"You did."

Thus days passed at the farm, and the form of a life became evident.

ɷ

I'd been home about a month the afternoon I met my cousin Sue. Daddy and I were unclogging the septic tank drain. The commode had stopped flushing—one more malfunction in the declining house. I'd had to use the woods the past week; Silas, refusing the woods, waited until he got to school. The drain needed fixing badly.

We had the concrete tank lid levered up with Uncle

Percy's heavy-duty Handyman jack, and then we propped
it with cement blocks, hoping it wouldn't fall and kill us.
I reached down into that smelly richness and tore loose
the massive root systems of grass that clung there, then
I uncoiled a long metal snake up the six-inch PVC pipe
that ran underneath the house. Within ten feet I hit something that felt like rock. Whatever it was had blocked the
toilet drain.

Ten feet back from the septic tank, under the eaves
of the house, a lantana had grown for thirty years. Friend
of sulphur butterflies, it bloomed miniature bouquets of
orange, yellow, and pink, which I'd loved to pick when I
was a child. I was digging beside the lantana, worrying
that its roots were clogging the drain, when a dated white
truck turned into the yard.

"Hey," Mama called to a woman getting out. "You
don't have to unholster for us."

The woman was wearing blue jeans and cowboy boots.
She had long red hair and tattoos stenciled up and down
her arms, intricate designs that started at her wrists and
disappeared into her T-shirt.

"Time to take it off," she said, unstrapping a pistol
from her belt. "I've been squirrel hunting with Daddy
down in Shug's pecan trees."

I had found, as I suspected, that the lantana's roots were
woven around the pipe and entering it at a loose joint, and
I was attacking the roots with fury. Only a few hours of
daylight were left. Between shovel blows, I watched the
woman approach, Mama and Daddy smiling wide.

"You know your cousin Sue?" Daddy asked.

"Not officially." I stopped slicing at dirt and roots
for a few minutes, long enough to apologize for the

circumstances. My overalls, a gift from Uncle Percy (his old ones), were muddy and dirty; my hair went every which way. An embarrassing stench filled the air, relieved only somewhat by the odor of fallen and dried pecan leaves crushed against the ground.

"I'd shake your hand if I could," I said.

"Don't worry about a thing."

"We're kin somehow, I know," I said.

Sue smiled. "Your grandmother was my daddy's aunt," she said, slowly. Sue's daddy being Grandmama's nephew made us second cousins.

"Close enough for me," I said, leaning on the mattock.

"Keep working," Sue said. "I've been wanting to stop and say hello. I saw you all out in the yard."

"Glad you stopped." In between chopping and digging and pulling, I listened. Daddy was asking after Uncle Mike and what they would do with the squirrels. The lantana was too deeply rooted for a shovel, the pipe embedded in its tan roots. Excusing myself, I went for an axe. With a few blows, I twisted the pipe out of the root-grip and it broke open under the house, spilling raw sewage across the dry dirt. A Cracker house is built two or three feet off the ground for ventilation, so I climbed under and started shoveling fast, dumping the sludge into a five-gallon bucket. It was sure stinking under there, and I was embarrassed. It was an awkward time to have company, since I couldn't very well quit. At least fixing the pipe was easy now—simply fit it back together. But Lord, the stench.

I'd heard Sue raised rabbits, that she knew how to fish and how to tan hides. I'd heard she liked to get out in the woods, that she liked heart-pine houses and worn knives and good stories. She knew things I wanted to learn. I

finished under the house and crawled out, filthy, hair cha-
otic, and not exactly smelling like a rose.

"You gotta come to the syrup-boiling," she said. "The
day after Thanksgiving. It's at Tommy Davis's place."

"Where's that?"

"Not far. On the other side of the church."

"I hope you mean it. I might show up."

"You'd be welcome."

Houses Mourn, Too

The family farm is seventy acres that Great-grandfather Walt deeded to Grandfather Arthur, in a settlement in upper Appling County peopled by the descendants of pioneers. My ancestors have lived here since white settlers forced their way into south Georgia, in 1818, displacing the Creeks from their prime hunting grounds. I own none of the farm. When my grandmother died, she divided it among her seven children. They have children and grand-children of their own, who live in cities not so far away. My mother has a section of field and a strip of the branch past the water hole. The piece with the farmhouse, built by my grandparents in the 1920s out of heart pine, belongs to the eldest boy, my uncle Percy.

We call the place a farm because it still grows soy-beans, corn, rye, and cattle for Uncle Bill Branch, really my mother's first cousin. Southerners often use the word "uncle" as a term of respect for elder kin. Uncle Bill leases land from my aunts and uncles, although many parts of the farm are long forsaken.

The town of Baxley is located at the crossroads of two recently four-laned highways, U.S. 1, which runs from Maine to Miami, and U.S. 341, the principal artery from inland Georgia to the coast. Baxley is a place people pass through going somewhere else. At the center of town, on Main Street, is a courthouse built of marble in 1907.

Four clocks, one facing each of the directions, are inset in its cupola; the four clocks do not keep the same time, and sometimes they stop altogether. The courthouse is painted every decade or so, and is now yellow and gray. On its lawn a conifer gets decorated at Christmas with blinking lights. Here on Saturday afternoons, when I was a girl, street-corner preachers would park their old trucks, equipped atop with powerful loudspeakers, and blast passionate sermons—warning against sin and predicting Armageddon—at passersby.

One block south of the courthouse, parallel to Highway 341, are railroad tracks, upon which trains run too fast to the coast with loads of pine chips, and too fast back with loads of shiny new cars. The town has a few beautiful old churches downtown, but most of the historical buildings were bulldozed in a 1970s flurry to be "progressive," or to raze the past; during that era, both 341 and Main Street were four-laned, destroying the small-town feel, the angle parking, even the front lawns of some townspeople. A department store at the main stoplight has a mural of the town's history on its side, from the Creeks through timber rafting down the Altamaha, through tobacco farming and turpentining. History ends at the far right of the brick wall with an image of the nuclear plant built on the river in the 1970s, not anything we are proud of, but rather a fact to be documented.

Until I was grown, Baxley had one stoplight. Now there are three, with more on the way. In my town, people still drive slow and they wave even at strangers by raising one finger off the steering wheel. If a funeral procession is encountered, they pull their vehicles off the roadway until the last mourner passes.

The farm is north of Baxley, toward the river, miles
best taken in the rusty green 1972 pickup, sitting high,
with the dog in the back, pecans on the dashboard next
to a bird's nest, and empty soda cans rattling back and
forth in the doors (the lower panels are gone). The road
from the highway is dirt, shaded by trees until it makes a
ninety-degree turn around the corner of a field. Along the
fencerow, Chickasaw plums and wild cherries grow among
a hodgepodge of oak and sweet gum, their origin ascribed
to the seed-eating birds that land on the fence.

At the house, the road narrows and turns sharply down
to the branch, and you have to slow here; the road cuts
on one side through a steep clay bank covered with short
vegetation, vines, and fallen leaves. A third of a mile past
the farm, the road splits and both paths run to paved
country roads within a mile, and to more roads and to
highways and to interstates.

I will warn you that if you were to see the farm, you
would not see the same one I see, the place where I spent
happy days as a child. Turning in, you'd see a working farm
fallen into disrepair: a farmhouse half obscured by six-foot
azaleas; Uncle Percy's mildewed doublewide trailer; a huge
water oak between the two domiciles; other tall, ancient
trees in the yard. You'd see the outbuildings gray and weathered, rotten here and there, and the tin that covers them
rusty and buckling, flapping in windstorms. You'd see a car
shelter, connected to what we call the packhouse; a boiler
shelter, where they used to make syrup, with a decaying
washroom; a big barn where Granddaddy fixed cars; a
garden-tool shed; a corn crib (the prettiest building); and
a log chicken coop where I store wood. These original
outbuildings are leaning, missing boards, or sinking into

the ground. Others, like the privy, are gone, rotted and fallen back to earth, never to be replaced.

The house, though dear to me, is timeworn and tacked together, sided these last thirty years by sheets of brown asphalt shingles of a design resembling brickwork. What wood lies beneath we do not yet know. Poor and dilapidated it may be, but it is a falling-down place that I have known all of my life and that I love. The house is a sixty-by thirty-foot rectangle with eight rooms, two by two: living room and dining room, living room and kitchen, bathroom and bedroom, second bedroom and third bedroom, which has become a study. Each room has at least three doorways and sometimes four. Because it is very open inside—the traditional Cracker style of architecture designed for air flow—you can see straight from the front door to the back. From one front corner, you can see diagonally to the back corner. It's a plain, unpretentious house, built quickly, with eight-foot ceilings that allow room for summer heat to lift above head level.

This is the second house that was erected on this spot of ground. My great-grandparents lived in a pine house over on the highway, what is now U.S. 1, although it was only a dirt trail when Uncle Percy was a boy, with a ford at the creek marked now by concrete culverts. Walt Branch divided his land between his sons, and Granddaddy got this piece. He was thirty-one when he married Grandmama but had no house for her, so after they married she returned to her own parents' house until he could build one. Their first home was not many years old when it burned, its pine shakes set afire by a spark from the fireplace. Walt was a renowned carpenter, so the house had been lovely. The replacement was cobbled

together in a hurry to get a roof over the family's head.
That was in the early 1930s.

When I was a young girl, cramped with a sister and
two brothers in a tiny frame house my father built on the
junkyard, this was the house where we came to spend
Saturdays with Grandmama. I remember, then, her house
being endless, room after room of quiet refuge. Here we
were most free, having escaped for a day the endless work
Daddy demanded of us at the junkyard—long hours of
hauling, toting, stripping, stacking, pulling nails, chipping
bricks, digging, picking up, painting, washing, cleaning,
cooking.

To earn our keep at Grandmama's, and to ensure an
invitation to return, we worked for her as well, but it was
clean, easy work. My sister washed Grandmama's short,
permed hair over the bathroom sink and rolled it on pink,
prickly curlers. I polished silverware with a rag and a little
jar of polish, making the forks and spoons gleam. We
swept the walk. Mostly, however, when we got dropped
off at Grandmama's we were at liberty to pursue frivolous
interests: paper folding and recipe copying and woods
looking. Nor did she have the same rules as my father,
so her house was a place of freedom of thought. We could
watch television and read the newspaper there. And did.
We wandered and played, exploring the pasture, the water
hole, the creek, the wooden bridge, the cow trails through
the woods. We dared not enter the woods beyond the
water hole, for there lay a bottomless head, where springs
seeped to the surface through quicksand. Daddy had once
plunged a cane pole twenty feet down, without hitting
bottom.

Grandmama's house was the horn of plenty. She had

food that my own parents could not afford and time that
Mama didn't have to bake. A chocolate or pound cake
waited under the bell-glass at Grandmama's, or in the
freezer to be thawed. Always. Grandmama's candy jars
were full. At Christmas, which was not a celebration at
our house, she cut a two-foot limb of many-branching
haw and stuck sugared gumdrops onto the ends of its
twigs; we would gape at the candy tree, mouths watering.
We yearned toward the cookie jar Grandmama kept full
despite the humidity and the sugar ants. We knew better
than to ask for food, so we prayed that Grandmama would
offer a sweet to us. We would sit politely, as we had been
taught to do, hoping beyond hope that she would ask, Did
we want a lemon drop? When she was in the back of the
house, or in the bathroom, one of us would check out the
cookie jar in the corner cupboard and report back.

"Are there cookies in it?"

"Yeah." At a whisper.

"What kind?"

"Kind of big and flat, with curved edges."

"Store-bought?"

"Yeah."

At our house at the edge of town, nothing lasted. We
were forever running out of something. I know we were
well fed, but we felt eternally hungry, ravenous; Mama
was always trying to fill us. There was never enough food
to sate us. I remember staring into Grandmama's freezer
and refrigerator, and standing before the pantry shelves,
gawking.

"What are you looking for, honey?" she would ask, and
I would turn away, embarrassed. "Just looking," I would
say. I could not believe such plenty.

Sometimes, unable to help ourselves, we would snitch a cookie or a piece of candy if the jar was close to full and the loss wouldn't be apparent. If one of us took, we all did—at least we three younger, hungrier children did. Sometimes we agreed beforehand that one of us would pocket enough for all three. My sister, who was four years my elder, showed more restraint.

Grandmama was shorter than most women, so I was not yet ten when I grew taller than she and had to bend to hug her. She lived in her rich, sugary house with a younger, dapper Uncle Percy, who worked the counter at an auto parts store in town and rode a '47 Harley. By then, Granddaddy Arthur was dead of cancer. He died when I was five. I remember him as benevolent, bringing gum and candy, the same treat for each of us. I never remember an unkind word spoken by or about him. Except for his pipe stand and gun rack, by the time I was old enough to pay attention to the depths of things, no sign of him remained in the house.

Most any week in summer or fall, Grandmama had fruit on the trees in the yard or in the lane. Tormented by visions of peppermints and candy corn, we foraged outside like bear cubs, eating dewberries, blackberries, huckleberries, plums, crab apples, apples, pears, grapes, pomegranates, peaches, pecans. Nobody cared what we ate from the vines and trees. The fruit was often small and worm ridden, but a wasp sting on a green apple was the least of our concerns.

We loved this place that was not our life. We loved its normalcy and the flowers that bloomed all over the place. We loved the fact that our grandmother looked and acted like other grandmothers. She did not mean to withhold that which we craved—she had no way of knowing how much we longed for her treats, and for her grandmother-liness. At midmorning she would commence to preparing dinner, the midday meal—creamed corn, fried ham, biscuits, boiled okra, green beans, stewed squash, rice, and tomatoes. The vegetables came from the garden, which she plundered before breakfast, before we arrived. We ate until we could hold no more, but not piggishly. We were on even better behavior at Grandmama's than at our own iron-ruled house.

The ancient longleaf pine outside the concrete steps of the back door dropped piles of needles, making a rug around itself, and it was often our job on Saturdays to rake the straw up. Grandmama kept her tools in good working order, so when called to rake we might choose from many instruments—bamboo and flimsy, iron and heavy, tin and light. A heap of leaves and straw is irresistible to a child, who will run and leap into it, over and over, and sometimes burrow to the ground, emerging covered with pine debris, looking like a porcupine. Especially when cousins were visiting, we made ourselves houses from the pine straw. We outlined rooms like an architect's plan—kitchen, living room, bedrooms—constructing the walls of pine straw, leaving gaps for doors between the rooms and for doors to the outside. We piled the walls as high as they'd go.

When our house of straw was built, we played charades through the rooms, cooking in the kitchen, making beds, sweeping with our rakes. We sat in the rooms and talked about what we would become one day, teachers and nurses and engineers and truck drivers. In our imaginary house under the blue sky, we lived out not our dreams, for we were too young to know dreams beyond those inherited from our parents, but a continuation of the lives we had already entered.

As an adult, I walk the same yard where I pretended to sleep on a straw bed, and I walk through walls I would not have dared ignore when I erected them of nothing, and now I do not live in the imaginary house but in the real house the imaginary one was modeled on. It is a dream I never dreamed, and if someone, an aunt or my grandmother, had told me that it would come to pass, I would not have believed them. As a child I never would have believed it would be my great fortune to live in the real house, the one made to last lifetimes, not an afternoon, the one full of chocolate pie and gingerbread, and endless peace.

What is it in us that wants to return to the dream of childhood, to reenact it or fix it? What is it in us that keeps coming back to that potent place? Sometimes I am afraid the house will burn to the ground, the way the original house burned, the way we were finally forced by oncoming dark to destroy our imaginary houses and haul the straw in Uncle Percy's wheelbarrow to the burn pile.

The outhouse fell. The smokehouse fell. Three of the pines in the yard blew over in a storm, like towers of cards. An apple tree fell. The chicken coop fell. The sassafras in the field fell. My grandmother fell. I don't think the house is a dwelling anyone ever thought would last. Yet it stands, and because it represents what lasts, or what so far has lasted, I was happy to live in it. Something from long ago was yet alive, both inside and outside of me. Finally, the two were one.

Living on the family farm, I was surrounded by all

the ghosts of my ancestors, with their undying desires, although all I knew about most of them was the stories that were told, long after their deaths. How all my mother remembers of my birdlike great-grandmother, Mary, was one glimpse she got standing on tiptoes, peering into her casket. Mary's husband, Walt, was a tall man who loved to work with wood. By day and by night I could feel the presence of those who had also known and loved this land, who had brought my life into being, whose names were written in stone in the graveyards or lost forever. I lived much closer to the dead than the half mile to the cemetery would indicate.

I had a dream once in which my grandmother, who was as small as a child, was lying in a sickroom, close to death. My grandfather and Uncle Percy were in the room as well, but as ghosts, Granddaddy hovering tall over the foot of the bed, and Uncle Percy on his knees beside it. Uncle Percy was holding his forearms open in front of his chest, imploringly. "Come on, Mama," he was saying. "Come with us." Granddaddy, too, was begging her to join them.

I had walked into the room to check on her and saw at a glance what was happening. "No, Grandmama, no." My voice rose. "Don't listen to them." I began to beg her to ignore her husband and son.

"Honey, go sit in the other room," she told me, "so I can hear what they're saying."

After a few minutes I rushed back into her room. The ghosts of the men were gone, and Grandmama was lying still. I ran to her, panicked, calling her name, and gathered her up in my arms.

"I'm taking you to the hospital now," I said, knowing

I needed help. Something in me was trying to keep my grandmother alive.

Now it was my duty and my honor to be the keeper of my grandmother's house, to uphold, rebuild, and sustain it, and to decide what parts of it to replace when they deteriorated. In the house I found myself bending—to wash dishes at the low sink, to slice summer squash on the counter, to add a column of figures on the pine table Granddaddy built. I bent to enter the screen door of the front porch, to duck under the drooping branches of the pine, to water small plants. It was as if, still, I was bending to greet my grandmother, to embrace her, to keep her. In that bending I was becoming her.

The corn crib, shaded by chinaberry.

Finding Wiregrass

Out walking on the farm I found a few clumps of grass that made my heart lurch. Unsure at first, I ducked under the electric fence that keeps the cows in and put my knees into the hot dirt.

Wiregrass.

Funny how a few clumps of grass could make me want to do a jig out there in the cow pasture.

When Cracker settlers first crossed the Altamaha River into what had been Creek hunting grounds, they found a forest we can now only imagine. The entire Southeastern uplands grew longleaf pine, 93 million acres of it from southern Virginia to east Texas. Now you can find little pieces; but out of 93 million, only 3 million acres of natural forest (meaning forest that regenerated naturally, consisting of trees of all ages) remain.

The longleaf pine can't be talked about as a tree, really, but as an intricate and intriguing ecosystem. The original forests held a legion of animals that had evolved to live in them: red-cockaded woodpeckers that bored out cavities in old-growth heart-pine trees; fox squirrels; and stunningly docile indigo snakes. Gopher tortoises, a long-lived species of land turtle, dug long burrows in the ground that became home to more than 300 other species, especially when the woods burned. Diamondback rattlers found refuge in the holes, along with gopher frogs, gopher snakes, scarab beetles.

You can't talk longleaf without talking gopher tortoise, nor tortoise without indigo snake, nor the snake without gopher frog, nor the frog without flatwoods salamander, nor salamander without Bachman's sparrow. You can't talk mole cricket without talking indigo snake. The list goes on and on.

Although a pine flatwoods usually grows only a single species of tree, an incredible diversity of flora can be found in the ground cover. But one kind of grass grows most commonly beneath longleaf pines, and that is wiregrass—tough, wiry, flammable. Mixed in with the wiregrass, a panoply of grasses and wildflowers prospers: toothache grass, meadow beauty, pine lily, orange fringed orchid, Kentucky bluegrass. Per square meter, this ecosystem is as diverse as it gets. You have to crawl around on your hands and knees to see everything.

Periodic wildfires thwart the encroachment of hardwoods such as oak and sweet gum into the pinelands, so the trees have evolved not only to survive fire but to depend on it. Wiregrass has evolved toward flammability to help push fire quickly through the forest, and it needs burning in order to reproduce well. Some of the forbs that grow with wiregrass won't even seed unless they have been scored by fire. Afterward, new ground cover springs lush and green from the ashen ground.

Just as longleaf pine is lashed to fire, a marvel of species is tied to longleaf pine, and the pine is laced to the highly diverse understory—the grasses and forbs, such as curtis dropseed and summer-farewell and blazing star—that is also bound to fire. The animal inhabitants are tied to the understory. Amazing the way everything is woven together.

Because most of the ancient forests have been cut, you don't see red-cockaded woodpeckers or gopher tortoises or indigo snakes or fox squirrels or even diamondback rattlers much anymore. You don't see wiregrass. But in a ribbon of woods that borders the cotton field, I found a little patch. Imagine my joy, because where a few clumps of wiregrass linger, there's no telling what else remains.

Uncle Percy

U ncle Percy was sixty-nine when I returned to live
next door. He was not a man to take risks, although
it was not fear that kept him on the farm, I think, but a
blindness to alternatives, having lived so well and been so
loved in his birthplace. Here Percy was master of circum-
stance. He had imprinted on the life of a farm and was
never able to ponder another life. He graduated high
school at sixteen and joined the Air Force, a four-year
stint that was to mark him as much as farming had. Its
stories would occupy him all his life and form the lens
through which he saw everything. When he was dis-
charged, he went to the city, as all rural folks were being
encouraged to do, to help rebuild the country. After six
months at a factory in Jacksonville, Percy returned to the
farm. I found his valise in the attic, the only relic up there—
never to be used again. In that postwar atmosphere, which
lured rural people to industrial centers to "be productive,"
many would have considered Percy a failure. But not his
parents.

Percy became the boy-child, so common in Southern
families, who stayed. He moved back into his childhood
room at the farm and lived there as a member of his parents'
household for most of his life. He married once, briefly.
Uncle Percy was over fifty when he took up with a young
divorcee new to town. He moved a doublewide trailer

next door to Grandmama and married. During their
brief matrimony his wife bore him a son, who after the
divorce came on occasional Saturdays to visit. After the
divorce, Uncle Percy moved back into the farmhouse with
Grandmama; Grandmama's sister, Aunt Linnie, made the
trailer her home for a few years. Neither before nor after
his ill-fated marriage had we known Uncle Percy to date,
or to socialize in any way independent of church.

Short and slight, he was at all times well shaven and
trim, never slovenly. He would have to announce that he'd
gotten a haircut because I could not discern any change.
He smoked like a winter chimney, constantly. When I first
moved into the house, where Uncle Percy had not lived in
almost a decade, I washed a yellowish film of nicotine off
the ceilings, walls, and furniture. Entering his trailer was
like crawling into the attic of a bar. Smoke had permeated
and jaundiced the carpet, the curtains, the rugs, the pillows. Although I never liked it, he would light cigarettes
in my house when he was visiting, and because he was its
owner I couldn't protest too loudly.

Uncle Percy's day went like this: when he woke, he
opened the doors if it wasn't winter. He fed the horde
of feral cats outside the back door. There were twelve or
thirteen of them, skittish, bone skinny, and often with ears
or eyes infected. They suffered only Uncle Percy to approach or pet them. "Say you like the cats?" I heard him
joke to someone once. "You can take you home a sackful."
Unspayed and untreated, they bred fervently among themselves, introducing a few sickly kittens to the pride every
season. Uncle Percy's only obligation was to feed them.

Next he made himself a breakfast of sorts—usually a
slice of toast and a cup of thick, black, instant coffee. He

was never a big eater. Then he came out to his front steps, under the water oaks beside the trailer, and sat smoking. When I returned from ferrying Silas to school, he would be there, and I would spend a few minutes with him.

"Anything that grows here, they's a pest waiting for it," he would say, and talk about the worms in the peaches. Or cutworms at the pepper starts. Because he sat so much, watching, and because he loved birds, Uncle Percy saw things I never saw. He would tell about a barred owl that had flown last evening onto that very limb there and watched him. Or the fox that had crossed the yard at a run. Mockingbirds fighting. Nighthawks. Blue grosbeaks returned.

What drove me most crazy was how fast my life was—even in the country—and how slow his was. I would pack a day full, top to bottom. Maybe it's a disease, the great desire I have for this world to be better. I know that faith is the evidence of things hoped for, and that faith without works is dead. Every day had an impossible list, and every item on the list was backed by a dream, a scheme. Uncle Percy would frustrate me with his refusal to lift a hand to make life better. Around him things disintegrated. But every morning, unless I was too busy to feel guilty, I crossed the unraked sand yard that separated our dwellings, sat on the wrought-iron bench outside his door, and talked of the world-changing events that had occurred in twenty-four hours.

"Did you hear about a wreck last night over at the school crossroads?" he asked.

"No. But come to think of it, I heard a siren."

"'Bout nine o'clock?"

"'Bout then, yes."

"That was probably it. I haven't heard who was involved, they said a car and a truck."

"That makes two accidents over there in the last month. We're gonna have to get a caution light up." That was me saying that. Then there was a long silence while we listened to nuthatches pecking in the water oak and watched a male cardinal flaming on the power line. I was thinking about the caution light.

"I read in the paper the Gardners have put up Christmas lights all over the place. They say thousands. They let people drive right through the yard."

"Let's ride over there one night. That would be fun. We can ride around a little and look at Christmas lights. I've seen some pretty ones other places. I have to remember where."

"JoNell from church said to me she puts up a lot. She invited me to come by and see them."

"Okay."

Uncle Bill, seeing us, stopped to chat. The men talked about the fuss over at the church. Baptists don't ordain women preachers. The Sunday school superintendent was a woman, and the men wondered if that was too immoderate, too impious, to allow. Some of the church said nothing was wrong with a woman being Sunday school superintendent, but the old-timers didn't like the idea one bit.

Sometimes my uncles would tell me stories. "People used to think Ten Mile Church was haunted," Uncle Percy said. "Remember that, Bill?"

"You mean when they kept seeing the ghost there during bad weather?"

"That's right."

"I remember hearing that one." Uncle Bill chuckled.

As Uncle Percy told it, one night one of the Tillman boys was riding his mule home when a bad storm came up. He decided to take refuge in the church, but as he climbed the steps a white form appeared at the window casement, bearing horns and a long white beard, illuminated eerily in a flash of lightning. The young man's heart almost stopped beating, and he bolted from the porch, back into the rain, and rode his mule home at full gallop. The next morning, a group of his neighbors went to the church to try to decipher what he'd seen.

"Turns out there was a white billy goat up in the church." Uncle Percy laughed.

"It was scared of lightning and thunder," Uncle Bill said.

"I heard Mr. Henry Eason say one time, with the advent of paved roads and electric lights, there ain't near as many ghosts as there used to be," I said.

"That's the pure truth," Uncle Percy replied.

I loved their stories, the fabric of their lives, which was the cloth from which my own was sewn, and reluctantly I excused myself to get to edits, phone calls, assignments, research, and press releases. I had only the hours until school was dismissed to do my work. I would do three or four things at once. I never talked on the phone without occupying my hands with a mending basket or a bowl of cracked pecans. When a friend bought us a cordless phone, I would take notes or search for papers or address envelopes while I talked. Sometimes I washed dishes and hung laundry and cleaned, holding the phone with my shoulder, getting the housekeeping done. I would get so thoroughly out of breath from the work I could barely converse. So much needed to be done. The phone seemed to ring constantly.

Uncle Percy's phone almost never rang, and when it did it was either a wrong number or our neighbor Roger down the road, who liked to keep up with goings-on. Uncle Percy never made calls. He was not a man to reach out, nor did he demand much from life. He did not travel. He did not read. Each day was a tintype of the last. He was as extreme in his quiescence as Hemingway had been in his ardor to eat life's marrow. Percy nibbled at the crust.

Two tasks Uncle Percy accomplished with great joy and dedication. He mowed grass and he attended church. Nobody could match his faithfulness at either.

He worked at the mowing like a job, and he cut on the same schedule as the barber cut his hair. We have an immense yard, maybe an acre when you subtract the houses and outbuildings, studded with peach trees and pomegranate bushes and bird feeders and a gas tank for each house and two mailboxes beside the road, his and mine side by side, and the sum of antiquated sheds and buildings.

To mow the entire yard took four or five days. Uncle Percy would mow in the morning, have dinner, then mow some in the afternoon, every day until the yard was done, and then he got a few days' rest before he decided it was time to start over. Many days I have written with the blare of the lawn mower outside, closing windows to block the noise. Often Percy circled round and round the office window where I worked, and sometimes he came to the window and called to me to say he was going to town for a certain part, or to tell me something he had seen. On off days, he performed chores attendant on grass mowing (sharpening the blades, buying the gasoline). Keeping the lawn mower in working order took hours and hours.

Often on Sunday mornings I passed Uncle Percy on the back way to church at Spring Branch, through the dirt lane of Dub Baxley Road, I jogging my two miles while Silas yet slept, he with the car windows rolled tight, pulling on a cigarette with a fury; he would be unable to smoke during the two hours of service.

After church he heated a TV dinner and in the afternoon he napped. The times I felt most free, unwatched, were the times he slept or while he was away at church, as if I could live life unscrutinized by this uncle who loved and accepted me but did not understand me. Why didn't I eat meat or go to church or have a husband? Why did I drive a truck and let Silas run wild and have long hair? Why didn't I have a normal job? Yet those first two years back, Uncle Percy was significant in my life. Although most of the territory available to us he could not enter, or consider, he took care of me. He guarded me. He was what I had, and our relationship was simple and inelegant.

On Sunday night church convened again, and on Wednesday night prayer meeting, and on Tuesday evenings he surprised me by participating in visitations, going with the preacher to visit the sick or elderly. "He was as faithful as I've ever seen," the pastor said to me. "Curious" was the adjective I heard used most often to describe him, not meaning inquisitive but queer, quaint.

He hated to spend money. Though he could have easily afforded a new riding lawn mower when the old one coughed its final shake, he pieced together a frame from neighbor Danny, Uncle Bill's son, and an engine Daddy found.

Once the water pump tore up and Uncle Bill came
to help him fix it. Uncle Bill was like a brother to Percy.
Neighbors all their lives, they had grown up together, gone
to church together. Uncle Bill farmed Uncle Percy's land,
and they saw each other every day. It was nice watching
the two of them work. Uncle Bill was vigorous, with a
dogged will to see a thing done. Uncle Percy was almost
frail. They talked of the Sunday night service as they
worked; a visiting minister had spoken.

"I thought he'd never hush," Uncle Percy said.

"I'll be honest," Uncle Bill said in innocence. "It wasn't
the *length* of the service. His talk was over my head."

First cousins, these two men had known each other a
lifetime. Their existences centered on the comings and go-
ings of the community; events like a water pump breaking
or a hard rain that dropped three inches or Sadie being
sick marked significant moments in their lives.

Intrigued, I observed their friendship as closely as I
could. I could see how utterly they respected and loved
each other, although they would have never used those
words. The words they used were "toadstrangler," "hay-
bailer," "stud," "pigweed," but they meant so much more.
With each other, Uncle Percy and Uncle Bill were unerr-
ingly polite and flexible, so that a casual observer would
not understand how very much they meant to each other,
and each to the entire community.

I realized then that the two men, like our other quiet
and unassuming neighbors, possessed a great dignity.
Since birth they had been vital and esteemed members
of this small society. Here, they had never been anonymous and never would be; they were not only accepted

but were highly regarded. They had gained the authority that comes with a lifetime in a place.

ဆ

I know, too, the danger of silence, as well as of leaving things unnamed and unrecognized. By understanding what you feel as love, by naming love, you claim it. By claiming a thing, you give it life. Then when something happens to yank it away from you, you are prepared for the sorrow that befalls. You are prepared to create anew that which is beloved. Then you will do whatever you can to keep it alive.

Keeping the Old School Open

On a Sunday afternoon, my son, Silas, and I were putting up our last sign eight miles north of town, on the edge of U.S. Highway 1 where the road to the school crosses. Across the road lay cotton field.

"Where would the most people see the sign? There at the corner or along the highway?"

"I think here," Silas said. "It stands out better."

Silas, nine, struggled with his end of a four-by-eight sheet of plywood. We dropped the wood and Silas took up the posthole diggers, which were a good foot longer than he, and started grubbing a hole beyond the right-of-way in Dave Sellers's clearcut.

I looked out at what was left of a forest. A year ago, this had been fifty acres of mature longleaf pine, with evidence even of red-cockaded woodpeckers, the endangered bird that nests in old-growth pines, especially longleaf. Now another precious piece of that diminished ecosystem was gone. Four or five of the trees with woodpecker nest cavities were saved. They were ugly and gnarled, stark against the sky. Around them the land was freshly disked, plowed into wide beds and replanted in rows of slash, a quick-growing "improved" pine.

Across the clearcut, a third of a mile away, I could see our rural, red-brick school that would soon no longer be a school if our county school board had its way. This time it was not forest we were trying to save.

"Don't Waste Taxpayer Money," our sign, the one my son was helping erect, said. "Vote No to School Closings." It was two weeks before the county referendum.

∞

What we learned soon after arriving home was that in order to fund a brand-new elementary school in the county seat, a school board almost a decade before had agreed to close two rural schools, one, Altamaha Elementary, eight miles north, the other, Fourth District Elementary, fifteen miles south. Those facilities were obsolete and hadn't been maintained. Altamaha's roof leaked and the windows needed replacing. Entrance ramps had deteriorated and classroom walls were faded and smudged. For years the threat of the closure loomed. Now the time had come to let go of them.

Altamaha is a rural school of about 250 children, named after the wide, chocolate-milk river a few miles away. We have enough students for about two classrooms per grade, up to fifth; Silas is in third.

Altamaha has special meaning to my family. My mother went to school there, as did most of our neighbors in Spring Branch Community. Uncle Percy was a fourth grader the year the school was built, 1936.

It's a pretty little school. The main buildings are deep-red brick, flanked by white-painted additions: a cafeteria, an art room, a gymnasium, kindergarten mobile units, two playgrounds. The older children's playground has a track and a baseball diamond, a set of swings and a long slide. The little ones have a playhouse and a merry-go-round.

The school has a particular deep-pine smell, the smell of local history, that overwhelms me every time I enter its wide dim hall. This is the same smell my mother studied in, a fragrance that transported her back to a wide-eyed, drag-footed little girl when she came to eat with Silas on Grandparents Day.

"It hasn't changed a bit," she said.

Of course it has, but what hasn't altered is that the school defines the community. The teachers know students by name; they know their parents and grandparents. After school the front lot is Grand Central Station—clay instead of asphalt—with farmers in pickup trucks fetching grandchildren and mamas milling around their vans, talking, and the uncle who's out of work retrieving his nephew and the nephew proud to be seen in his uncle's lipstick-red Camaro. Not to mention children yelling out the windows of the three yellow buses that are loading.

Down the road at the corner, there's a gas station and convenience store. The storekeeper, Terry, used to own a mastiff named Rocky, who loved to visit the school. When the dog showed up, the principal, Ms. Smith, would put him out and close the front door, then call Terry.

"He wants an education," Terry would say.

The principal ousted Rocky again one day, but the pre-kindergarten class was on the playground, so the dog lingered with them, craving their delight. He discovered, by following some tickled third-graders to class, that even if the front doors were closed, the back ones might not be. The principal heard the ruckus, hauled Rocky out again, and called Terry. Before the owner arrived, Ms. Smith lettered a certificate of graduation for the dog, which she presented to Terry, who laughed until he cried.

On certain days, Johnny Jordan would come by the school peddling cabbages, cucumbers, onions, collards.

Off-duty teachers would slip out to buy vegetables from the back of his truck, because Johnny piled them high, a heavy sack of carrots for a dollar. Johnny battled cancer a few years ago. He had no insurance, but teachers took up collections for him. Once he was well, he wrote each person who contributed a thank-you.

The school is not all good. Our state is one of the last bastions of corporal punishment, and early on I had to visit the principal over the matter. "I haven't raised my son using physical punishment," I told Ms. Smith. "Likely he will never be sent to your office. Should he be, however, he may not be hit."

She nodded. She and I had a lot in common; she gardened and liked the outdoors. "We would never spank a child against a parent's wishes. But most parents want their children spanked if they get in trouble. Sometimes the child gets another spanking at home."

"They don't understand there are better ways to parent," I said tersely.

There are other matters of educational philosophy and practice that I disagree with. Field trips aren't allowed, for reasons of safety. Class treats are mostly full of sugar and artificial colors. Sometimes bullying goes unnoticed or unchecked by adults; disputes are not so much resolved as the probable offenders punished. The curriculum lacks art and music. But the school is serious about education, and it is small, close-knit, and nearby. I don't have to worry about my child there.

One day I read aloud to my nephew Carlin's pre-kindergarten class a story about a king. I paused to explain that in our country we have a president instead of a king. "Does anybody know who the president is?" I asked.

An elfin boy raised his hand. "Ms. Smith?" he asked.

Then Carlin spoke up. "I know who the president is," he said. "God."

I want a school like Altamaha for Silas.

සා

For the past century, rural places have steadily bled people, mostly to big cities, where they migrate to find work. The falling apart of rural communities intensified during World War II. To rebuild our war-broken country, an advertising campaign was launched to entice rural people away from the farms to the cities. Industrial capitalism needed a workforce, and what it promised in return was certain prosperity. Jobs were plentiful in the city, and factory labor was much easier than the hardscrabble life of a farm. To leave the farm was as much an act of patriotism as a service to self.

The ad campaign worked. There ensued a mass exodus of rural people to the cities, looking for a better life, and this movement has not stopped. Now, four-fifths of the people in the United States live in urban areas.

Across the country, you see evidence of this "hollowing out" of rural America—abandoned small farms, ghost towns, country stores with dark windows. Rural places have lost their intellectuals, thinkers, organizers, leaders, and artists, along with the children of these people. In the wake of this loss, rural locales have suffered a loss of imagination that has led to a cultural poverty.

Recent decades have witnessed a new agrarianism, defined by Eric T. Freyfogle in his anthology, *The New Agrarianism: Land, Culture, and the Community of Life,* as a reinvigoration of ties to the land. Evidence of this is found not only in the trickling resettlement of rural farmlands, but also in watershed restoration groups, native plant societies, and community-supported agriculture.

We do not want to confuse rural reinhabitation with urban sprawl. Being in a country place while remaining connected to a city for work and entertainment, and demanding urban amenities in the country, is not a rural life. This simply increases urban areas.

Even now, knowing that we must rebuild rural landscapes and communities, not by destroying more wild places to build homes but by moving into the abandoned places, I hear many people say, "I would die if I had to go back there. I couldn't wait to leave. Nothing's there."

Appling is a large county, as much as sixty miles from top to bottom. Of the more than sixty rural schools that have existed in this county over the years, all are shut down now except two. A few of the wooden schoolhouses still stand. Although 40 percent of our county's populace hasn't finished high school, education is important to us. Closing the last outlying schools doesn't sit well with us country people, who don't want our children hauled to town to sit packed in overcrowded classrooms with a teacher who might or might not know them. We don't want our small children riding school buses for more than three hours a day.

When we look at test scores, we find that children in country schools consistently score higher than in-town children. Students at smaller schools can visit the school library daily instead of weekly, and classroom teaching aids, such as computers, are more accessible. Altamaha's parent organization raised over $10,000 one year to fund school events and awards.

What amazes me—really amazes me, because I am from this locality, where many of us are too polite to fight or too scared of ostracism to speak out—is that a group of people said no. They decided to fight the school closings and started to meet together to strategize what might be done to keep the schools open. One parent called the state Department of Education. Another called our state representative. Someone was present at every school board meeting, lobbying.

The school board refused to cooperate. Its hands were tied, the superintendent said: it had signed an agreement with the state that couldn't be reversed. The board simply needed to carry out a duty—close the last rural schools.

Then someone learned that Statesboro, Georgia, had faced the same dilemma and had organized a referendum to oppose the forced closing of their school. Friends of Altamaha Elementary and Fourth District could do the same. What was needed were the signatures of 25 percent of the registered voters supporting a referendum on the issue.

The county had ten thousand voters, so that meant collecting twenty-five hundred signatures. Petitions passed from hand to hand, neighbor to neighbor. Parents stood outside the grocery store or left petitions at convenience stores and other businesses in town. In two months they had the signatures.

ಬಬ

In May, three months before I had returned, at about the time the school board announced the closing date of Altamaha Elementary, I was sitting on a chilly metal folding chair in the big barn at the Land Institute near Salina, Kansas, along with about four hundred other people who were interested in sustainable agriculture and rural community. Early morning of the first day of the annual Prairie Festival, Jim Lentz was speaking.

Jim was superintendent of schools in Howard, South Dakota. That morning he talked about educational food for a starving rural America and began by quoting Paul Gruchow, who wrote in his book, *Grass Roots: The Universe of Home,* "We raise our most capable rural children from the beginning to expect that as soon as possible they will leave and that if they are at all successful, they will never return. We impose upon them, in effect, a kind of homelessness. The work of reviving rural communities will begin when we can imagine a rural future that makes a place for at least some of our best and brightest children, when they are welcome to be at home among us."

Jim started there. "A school and community cannot be separate," he said. "One survives in direct proportion to the other." He said that we need to reverse the trend of loss in small towns and work to rebuild them, and he told how his schools were doing that. While Jim talked, nesting barn swallows flew among the rafters of the barn. The sun rose higher in the sky, dried the prairie dew on the bundleflower and wild rye, and warmed the listeners.

Jim told us that Howard, South Dakota, has a simple plan with two basic tenets:

1. Our community must meet the basic needs of the people who live here. (A community is only as well-off as its most destitute citizen.)
2. Our community must grow and develop only within its ecological limits, meaning the people must inhabit it in ways that sustain it for future generations.

I was spellbound. What Jim was saying made sense. To live in friendly association—with real neighbors—was possible. By the end of the talk, Jim's voice was breaking—he's that

passionate about his work—and tears were flowing down
my cheeks. I could go home and try for that kind of tribe.

A couple of months later, driving cross-country from
Montana and Georgia bound, I purposely veered through
Howard. Jim was away, so I'd been unable to reach him
by telephone. I parked in front of the bakery, bought milk
and a homemade eclair, and sat on the curb in the sunshine. Silas had flown to Vermont, where his dad lives and
where I would pick him up.

Howard was neither big—I could see from one end
to the other—nor bustling. A pair of girls ranged by on
bicycles and said hello; people strayed in and out of the
bank. After awhile I asked the baker for directions and
found the high school. It was summer break and no one
was likely to be about, but I wanted to witness Jim's work,
to see if there might be a visible difference between this
small town and those that were disappearing.

The school looked normal enough: long and brick,
somnolent except for the football team practicing on the
side lawn. The front door was unlocked and I entered the
quiet hall. The light was dim and my footsteps made no
sound. A sign directed me to the Rural Resource Room
Jim had mentioned in his talk, a kind of local museum in
which volunteers put together exhibits on the grain harvest or history of the town. Local groups meet at the long
board table.

"Visitors must walk through the school to get to the
Resource Room," Jim had said, "which is as it should be."
I entered an unlit, deeply quiet room. The current exhibit
featured rural schools in the county that had long since
closed. Students had collected old primers, chalk holders,
teachers' grade books, antique desks, and black-and-white

photographs of the buildings. Near the door were two guest books to sign, one for retired teachers, one for the rest of us.

Here, I thought, is the point where Howard, South Dakota, is turning around. Here's where the new begins. It begins by honoring the past, armed with new information about how we can live better, more sustainable lives. We can reinhabit our rural farmlands.

At the rear of the school grounds I found the market garden and school orchard, rows of apples and pears, planted so that students, who paid themselves for their work and then deposited the profits into a scholarship fund, could sell produce to the local grocer. The strawberries needed picking.

ॐ

By the time Silas and I arrived home, the signatures for the referendum had been assembled. I don't like to remember the next couple of months—how busy they were and how scared I was that we would lose. I volunteered at the school on Fridays, teaching art to third graders. The children drew posters that said, "Keep Our Schools Open. Please Vote Nov. 4." We hung them in businesses downtown. Sometimes we would return to stores where we had obtained permission to post signs and find the merchants had removed them. The owner of the tractor company wouldn't let us erect a sign at the edge of his land, saying the issue was too controversial, that he had customers on both sides. People here are seldom vocal about their leanings, and it was hard to tell which direction political winds were blowing.

A group calling themselves Concerned Taxpayers

organized to fight for school closure. Their arguments—
that consolidation meant progress, that country schoolchildren were getting special treatment not afforded town
children, and that keeping the schools open would cost
taxpayers more money, especially for facility repairs—appeared in the weekly newspaper. The owner of the radio
station was one of the concerned taxpayers, and he frequently aired his editorial views, couched as unbiased
facts: "What You Should Know," he called his editorials,
then proceeded to list reasons to close the rural schools.

To make matters worse, the wording that would appear
on the ballot had purposely been made confusing. The
ballot read: "Do you agree to the school board's decision
to close the two rural schools?" People would have to vote
"no" to keep the schools open, opposing the school board's
decision to close them.

We used Parent-Teacher Organization money to print
bumper stickers. We bought full-page ads in the paper, and
radio ads. We set up a save-our-schools booth at school
carnivals. One night I manned the booth at the county
fair. I stood in the flow of people wearing a VOTE NO
button, clutching a sign that asked people to favor rural
schools: VOTE NO TO ABANDONED FACILITIES. VOTE NO TO
TEACHER LAYOFFS. VOTE NO TO CROWDED CLASSROOMS.

I had come back home to be part of a community, and
I didn't want, at this crucial time, to lose a vital element
of it. Sending Silas to town school was contrary to every
reason I had for being in that place at all.

We divvied up voter registration rolls and began calling
people to ask them to keep the schools open. As many
people seemed to be for as against. We had a chance, but
it was only because—and this is the glory of it—a group of

us were meeting and working together, having fun. One evening a week we met in Neil Eunice's crop insurance office, small groups of seven or eight, hashing things over, planning. We decided to throw a party on election night whether we won or lost.

Election day found me stuffing fliers under windshield wipers in parking lots. About noon, I spoke to an elderly woman walking to her car.

"Did you vote today?" I asked her. She leaned tiredly against the car and said she was sick, that she wanted to vote but that she'd been to the doctor and was going home.

"I'm trying to keep the schools open," I said.

"That's the way I planned on voting," she said. "If we close those schools we'll have to build a new one in town."

"We need your vote badly," I said to her. We had seven hours to go until the polling doors closed. "I'll drive you to the polls."

"I just don't feel like it," she said. I pointed out my truck and said I'd bring her back to her car if she would vote.

"OK," she said, and I ran to bring the truck around.

The voting precinct was located in the rear of the chamber of commerce, and it was empty except for five polltakers, who sat inside the small room gossiping, one crocheting a white afghan. They helped Mrs. Dixon through the protocol and into the booth, where she vanished behind a gray curtain. "There's only one thing to vote on?" she called.

"That's right," one of the women said.

"I'm eighty-seven years old," Mrs. Dixon told me on the drive back. Her mind was excellent, no part of it flaccid; only her body was failing. "I hope to be able to stay out of a nursing home."

I was posted at one of the town precincts, in the Jaycee Building, at seven that evening, when the door was locked. Ten minutes later I had the precinct's results in hand: yes beat no nearly two to one: 247 to 141. Close the schools.

When I came out the door, bad news in hand, it was dark, the sun an orange stain in the sky above the shadowy fairgrounds. I'd never been able to go to the fair as a child, and not two months before, Silas and I had gone for the first time. By now the carnival had packed up and departed for another town, but I remembered its excitement—lights, candy apples, rides, music you could hear at the courthouse. People carried big stuffed tigers and a woman in battered heels guessed weights and ages. I was a girl again that night, screaming at the top of the ferris wheel, eating cotton candy. We took Silas's friend Caleb with us, and he ran ahead and got on the roller coaster alone. When we caught up, we stood at the picket fence watching him ride, a frightened wonder on his face as he held on, a look that left Silas and me doubled over the waist-high fence laughing.

That evening flashed through my mind as I stepped outside the Jaycee Building. I craved a candy apple. Double against. How could we win, even if this was only one precinct? I stood by the car and took a deep breath, looking up at a newborn moon in the sky, the stars following Venus out. Suddenly I was weary.

If Silas has to go to town school, we'll make it work, I thought. *I'll volunteer a lot. We'll make it work.*

I folded into the truck and headed back to Eunice Crop Insurance. We'd tacked a huge chart on the wall for recording precinct reports, and I made the first mark on it: 247 to 141. Another parent, Rod, had the other town precinct, and he rushed in. "Double against," he said. Surely we'd lost.

When results from the outlying precincts began to arrive, the number of noes began to creep toward the number of yeses, then to equal it, and then to pass it, and by the time our reporters in all voting districts had called in, the figures had reversed, unbelievably double in favor of keeping the schools open.

We had won!

People began to arrive at the insurance company, hugging and slapping each other on the back. We brought out homemade cookies, chips and dip, sausages, punch. Teachers drove up. Children ran around gobbling chocolate chip cookies. The two principals whose jobs had been in question walked in. I called the Savannah paper and the television station.

Because we live in a community that is, with few exceptions, Christian and highly devout, Neil, whose wife teaches at Fourth District, asked everyone to squeeze close and form a circle. The ring was two or three people thick. "We have fought hard to keep our schools open, and we have won," he said. "It is time to thank God for hearing our prayers."

The next day we paid the owner of the radio station to air our gratitude. "Yesterday was a great day for Appling County. Together we decided that our children and their education are important to us and that we will do the best thing possible to preserve the quality of education throughout the county. Today, Friends of Altamaha and Fourth District Schools want to thank you sincerely for your support and your vote. Without the attention and

concern voters across the county gave this matter, a bad
decision might have quietly been made, and our children
would have been the ones to suffer. With that in mind, we
have, for a minute, to appreciate the democratic process in
this country—that it still works, that we still have a voice,
a say, a vote. . . ."

When our school turned sixty, we collected recipes for an
anniversary cookbook and planned a celebration. The fight
to save our school had not made us complacent but more
aware than ever of how lucky we and our children are.
On a Saturday morning, in ninety-five-degree heat, about
fifty parents and teachers showed up to build an outdoor
classroom, complete with a split-rail fence. None of us had
ever built a fence the traditional way before, but together,
with a lot of joking and redoing, we figured it out.

My mother attended rural Altamaha School.

Syrup-Boiling

Strangely, I felt as if I descended into the syrup-boiling, although I parked in the pasture like everybody else and walked up. It was the day after Thanksgiving, and I was there at the invitation of my cousin Sue. This was the scene if you could have looked down on it: steam leaked out of a long building that was open on one end, the light from inside it casting an isosceles triangle onto the ground. Outside the building, in a circle inscribed by a yard light, a fire blazed in a metal drum and a couple of sawhorse tables sagged with food. People milled in and out of the light. At the periphery children chased in the dark, harvested field.

Near the drum fire a knot of people, maybe nine or ten, had drawn together, their hair and shoulders silvery as moth-glitter in the night light. They faced inward, intent.

They were singing! I could barely keep from running.

Once among the singers, I found my brother, and Sue, singing harmony with a strong, clear voice. Other faces were familiar, and some turned toward me, smiling, holding notes and singing hard, *When morning breaks eternal, bright and fair.* They edged together to make space in the circle. *The saved of earth shall gather, over on the other shore.*

When the song ended, Sue grinned, said, "We're glad you made it," and introduced Uncle Mike, her daddy, and

Uncle Tump and Walter and Linda. Minnilee, to my right, wouldn't stop hugging me, and I didn't mind. She knew me less than whom I came from—my grandmother—and it was a long, trusting history.

More arms got thrown around me and I didn't know whose they were—people who were kin or not kin or neighbor to kin or neighbor. Their names puddled up in my mind, and I didn't even try to figure out the big tangle this community appeared to be, having landed so abruptly in the middle of it.

Then we were singing again, a traditional hymn, singing seriously, for the joy: *When the trumpet of the Lord shall sound and time shall be no more.* A lot of people have been away from a place and gone home to rediscover what's there and have been welcomed by the ones who never left, or who have already returned.

I have been told it is the sweetness of mother's milk that causes our sugar craving, and that we humans evolved as fruit eaters in the trees. It is a sorry place that cannot produce a sweetness for its animals—maple, molasses, sorghum, honey. In south Georgia our sweetener is cane syrup, boiled from the pressed juice of sugarcane. The syrup has a curious taste that a lot of people can't stomach. But those of us raised on it, who never had Aunt Jemima, who didn't know anything else, we sop it up with hot biscuits and pour it over griddle cakes and wet our cornbread with it. We boil it up and pour it over popcorn.

The making of syrup is laborious. The cane has to be grown and cut, its juice squeezed out through what's called a grinder, although nothing is ground up. The machine is really a roller. The juice is boiled down meticulously, the syrup bottled. It's easier to store-buy. With the loss of small farms, we were lucky to see a syrup-boiling at all. The farm's syrup boiler hadn't been fired in thirty years, and the grinder was gone.

ഇൻ

Tommy Davis, whose farm this was, knew how to make syrup. He was a sweet-faced man of sixty, wearing overalls. He had worked hard for syrup making—planting the cane and harrowing it and fertilizing it. He chopped it (best done the day it's to be pressed), hauled it to the shelter, and fed the stalks through a grinder. Years ago, a mule harnessed to a lever would have walked around and around, spinning the gear that pressed the cane. Tommy had hooked an electric motor to his.

For a long time, he didn't make syrup, but a few years ago he decided to take it back up. He was standing by the boiling syrup when I tore away from the singing and went inside.

"Glad you came," he said, sticking out his hand. "Sue said you might."

"I haven't been to a cane grinding since I was a girl," I said. "There aren't many of them anymore." He told me it takes three hours to boil off a making, and this one had been going two and a half. The juice was cooked in an iron kettle about four feet in diameter, mortared into a chimney. In the old days, you had to build a good fire under the kettle, build it of fat lighterd, the resinous heartwood of old-growth longleaf pine, and keep it roaring, but

Tommy had welded a propane stove under his. He used twelve gallons of propane in a cooking.

"Have you had any juice yet?" he asked.

"No."

He lifted a flap of blue tarp at the back of the long-house and led me outside. There was the big grinder, and in the shadows outside the reach of light, a trailer loaded with sugarcane. Tommy flipped a switch and fed two or three six-foot stalks through the metal rollers, holding a paper cup under the outlet. Cane juice ran down, cloudy as fresh lemonade, and thin.

He handed it to me and I drank deeply.

"Years," I said. "It's been years." To tell the truth, I always thought sugarcane juice too sweet. It's like drinking sugar water. But it's one of those tastes that's becoming endangered, like the taste of blackberry cobbler, and when you get a chance to drink it, you drink it. Some of us talk about past times and rattle on about what holds a community together. The Tommy Davises of the world don't say a word but set to work. They make a cane grinding happen, year after year. They harrow and plow and plant and fertilize and weed and water and harvest and grind and cook. Tommy returned to syrup making because it was dying out, the way our small towns are dying out and our farming communities and our longleaf pine forests. The way family time is dying out. Events like this keep us connected. Tommy's not standing by, watching what's important vanish.

Back inside, a couple of people leaned over the hot vat with wet cloths, skimming dregs—black specks of cane— off the foamy top. Rhythmically they rinsed the cloths in a metal bucket and skimmed again, carefully dabbing at the foam, filtering impurities. There was no hurry; they were slow and steady. Parents kept small children back.

I observed awhile, then tried my hand at skimming dregs, swabbing and rinsing, careful not to scald myself. The bucket filled with skimmings. "That's the part that'll make you drunk," they said, laughing. "It'll make dogs drunk."

Now Tommy was eyeing the kettle, not leaving it. It was about time to dish up and there's one moment when the syrup's ready, when the yell comes to shut off the gas. He couldn't miss that moment, he couldn't be too early or too late, and he couldn't be unprepared for it. He clothespinned a clean piece of white cotton over the top of a steel vat with a valve at the bottom—the cloth would catch the dregs that the skimming didn't.

The syrup was bubbling madly and reddening now. Tommy lifted a dipperful and let it run back into the vat. It wasn't quite ready. Too thin. But much more heat and it would burn and ruin the entire cooking. Nobody was talking. Everybody was watching, waiting for the perfect moment. Tommy's wife, Jeanette, grabbed a long-handled dipper made from a bucket and a slat and set to dipping and pouring the syrup back into itself to dissipate heat. Young neighbor Kenyon seized another dipper. Tommy concentrated.

Finally he unhooked from the wall a hand-sized instrument that tests viscosity. The syrup was thin yet. In a few minutes, he tested again and it was ready. In a flash the syrup was ladled into the cloth-lined vat, Tommy working on one side and Kenyon on the other. I had learned that this batch was Kenyon's syrup. He grew the cane and Tommy boiled it down for him.

When they were done, a scum of white taffy stuck to the rim of the boiler. People edged up to eat it. "Dog candy," they explained.

Kenyon handed me a length of cane stripping about as long as a fork. He motioned for the man beside me, his father, to show me how to use the stripping to spoon up the candy. It was delicious, warm, without the bitterness of molasses. If our history had a taste, this would be the good part. I could have eaten mountains. I ate more than anybody else. I made sure the entire rim was clean of dog candy before the men started washing the kettle.

Meanwhile, another relative was draining the vat into quart jars. Someone else stuck on labels, "Pure Cane Syrup Made by Tommy Davis." Toward the end, Kenyon handed the valve operator a tall, pretty bottle and the man filled it. Kenyon screwed the lid on and handed it to me.

The bottle was hot in my hands, filled with dark syrup that by night appeared almost black but that would lighten to the exact amber of a tannic creek when held up to the morning sun. The thick syrup ran slowly toward the neck of the bottle when I upended it. A golden bubble traveled down the bottle's length and disappeared.

"It's beautiful," I said to Kenyon, and handed the bottle back.

He kept his arms by his side, a bashful and happy look on his face. He shook his head.

"I can't take your syrup," I said. "You've worked too hard for it." I again held the bottle toward him.

He shifted sideways. "You're not taking it," he said. "I'm giving it to you."

"Let me pay for it. I'll gladly buy it."

"Your money's no good here," he said.

"Thank you," I said, pleased with the gift. "I'll remember where it came from."

৵৹

I've talked about the syrup and not enough about the people. Once I passed Sue and she led me to rabbit, roasting on a grill, from animals she'd raised and butchered. The piece she gave me was delicious. Jeanette brought in a baker of hot biscuits that we proceeded to drown in syrup and eat. Later I went out and shucked oysters with Walter and Uncle Mike. Everybody wanted to talk, to catch up. Linda asked me to send family information and photographs for her genealogy project. She and Walter live in Orlando now.

Everywhere I turned, people were asking how long I'd been back and where I was staying and how the folks were, and remembering my grandmother, and telling me stories of their own lives, how their son was killed and they were raising their granddaughter, or how they loved the homeplace but their life was too tied to Atlanta or Dallas to leave. Every time I turned around, somebody was hugging me and telling me to come see them *when the roll is called up yonder*.

It's sweetness keeps people together. Sweetness. The sweetness of our tongues, of kind words, of praise, of invitations extended and invitations accepted, and the sweetness, too, of acts of imagination and love. Forgiveness, tolerance, and the courage to reach out. Every morning I pour the syrup on thick. *I'll be there.*

Calico Scraps

Everything that seems empty is full of the angels of
God.

           —St. Hilary

In winter of 1998, Mama and I began to piece together a
quilt from cloth scraps she had gathered from the cotton gods. Some were bright yellow and red and blue, and
shades in between, and shades of those in-between colors,
and others were printed with flowers, stripes, polka dots.
She and I were butterflies among the cloth scraps spread
about us, and we raised one piece next to another, asking
how it matched, as if trying on a roomful of gowns and
shoes for a ballroom dance. We opened and closed pieces,
butterflies fanning their brilliant sparkling wings, to see if
there was enough yardage to cut a few squares.

After awhile, I looked around. The tide of weaves
had come in while we were occupied, and we were up to
our fannies in stacks of cloth. Often we dipped into the
current to find a piece we remembered seeing that should
have matched some newly discovered piece.

Piles of browns, piles of blues. Two pieces that needed
a third. Nylon and polyester cast off in a heap. Denim too
thick. Silk too thin.

My mother has what seems to me the oddest tastes
in colors, but when she finishes a quilt, it is a work of art.
Her quilts are stunning. They don't look like anything
you'll ever see in *Southern Living*, or in the quilt books.

They look like somebody real made them, somebody who has boiled grits thousands of mornings in a row, somebody who worries about her children's lives, somebody who has never had more than two nickels to rub together. Mama comes from women who quilted from necessity, using rags and torn clothes. The need for usefulness, I think, produces objects of the greatest beauty.

Mama put a red bandanna next to a lime green floral pattern with irises, and it worked. When she asked how two colors looked, I never said, "Terrible"—even if I wouldn't have recommended them to my worst enemy—because in the end, magic happens, and she, with her unhampered eye, can create something bigger than I can, with my steel color wheel and catalog-influenced rules of design.

"Let's try it," I said. But Mama wanted me pleased, wanted my approval, because this was my quilt we were making, maybe the one quilt of my life.

"Absolutely no flowers," I said. "No pink."

I knew what my mother was thinking. For generations, women in her family have made pink flowery quilts—little pink forget-me-nots with flecks of green leaves, little pink tulips with happy green leaves, little pink morning glories connected to each other by threads of light green vines, little pink flowers of every kind.

I hid the pink yardage in the bottom of the packing box. I wanted a turquoise quilt. Not that I wanted every piece of cloth to be turquoise but for that color to tie disparity together the way ivy binds architecture on cobblestone streets. I wanted the quilt to be the color of unentered woods on a foggy winter morning. I wanted to make it the wings of a glorious, somewhat turquoise bird, a quilt fit for indigo buntings and boat-tailed grackles and purple martins. I wanted something you could lie beneath and dream you were sauntering a dirt road barefoot, swinging a bucket filled with blue plums, so when you woke, you tasted the wild fruit, the fruit rendered to jelly.

What we were doing was trying to create a beautiful thing, step by step, together, mother and daughter, in spite of our differences. Making a quilt is about being able to talk.

When I became a teenager, I entered the realm of my mother's disapproval. I was on a busy, one-way street out, unable to stop, unable to turn around. Mornings, at the last minute, I rushed downstairs to meet the school bus and my mother's evaluation: Was I wearing make-up? Was my shirt buttoned high enough? Why did my skirt seem short? Who was the man who kept calling long-distance? Was that a romance novel I was reading?

Here the schism began. I could not be the person my parents wished me to be. If they couldn't accept who I was, then I would hide that person. And I did.

I began to question my father's doctrine; I began to not believe. It wasn't simply that I left the church but that I quit the belief system that guided their lives. I'm an atheist now, I'd tell them. They would look at me and not know who I was, this daughter who had so recently belonged only to them. I betrayed them. They thwarted me.

In my early twenties—their mid-forties—one particular silence began between us that lasted for three years and ended with the birth of my child. During those years, I was forbidden to call them, to write, to visit. They could not accept the outrageousness of my spiritual beliefs, nor the lifestyle I had chosen: hippie, communal, back to the land, wild. I was living with a divorced man who was gardening in the nude one day when my father drove four hours to see the state of my depravity for himself.

Disowning me was my father's idea, I am sure, but I could not forgive my mother for agreeing to such nonsense, for allowing him to break off communications instead of waiting, as totalitarians eventually must, to come to terms with the opposition, to let the heart hammer out a design for acceptance.

But my parents could not deny an infant grandchild their love, and after Silas's birth my parents and I began painfully to iron out a functional relationship, a careful construction of tolerance, avoidance, and empathy. Because Mama understands that love governs everything—that God is love, that dogma melts like butter in the face of love—she and I have looked for common ground.

Over the years, Mama and I have metamorphosed. We think more nearly alike than we once realized. We know what subjects are not worth the pain they possess, and between us, slowly, even the taboos have disappeared. Our mothers' lives are enriched, my friend Myra tells me, if they can learn to talk to us about things like sex, like men they don't know, like cults, like despair. What price, our willingness to be dishonest, to lie for the sake of pretense? What gain, the truth? "When a woman tells the truth she is creating the possibility for more truth around her," wrote Adrienne Rich. We looked for a safe place to talk. One place we found it was in a quilt.

Handiwork leaves the mind free to think and the tongue to converse, which is why it is fun to sit around shelling peas or peeling peaches together. No one wants to make plum pudding alone.

Mama and I talked of where a certain piece of cloth came from and what had been made from the bigger part of it, and what it reminded us of. She told me stories of my nephew, then-four-year-old Carlin, my youngest brother Stephen's boy. She told me stories, if I asked, from childhood, and from the time before I was born. We talked about the homeplace and what would become of it. I told about what had happened to me most recently, what I'd heard, and sometimes we talked about the price of bananas, or the benefits of green tea, or how she didn't cook with salt or fatback anymore. We didn't often talk about concepts—art, socialism, feminism, or intellectual theories. We didn't talk about physician-assisted suicide or global warming. I am reminded of Kathleen Norris's line in her book *Dakota*, about going to live in a small town. "When we gossip we are also praying, not only for them but for ourselves." We gossiped.

Smiling, my mother silently watched me angle intemperate colors next to each other, a piece of batik I bought for ten dollars a yard beside a scrap of canary yellow from a gift sack of yard goods, the way a bird's nest might be threaded with strips of snakeskin. The colors matched in a way that was alien to my mother, but she is not narrow-minded and picks up whatever strikes her fancy at the moment.

Anything big is a lot of little pieces stitched together, a page a day, a day at a time. A quilt is made of pieces of cloth sewn into squares, each about one foot by one foot. Every quilt is a pattern repeated over and over, so that when finished the quilt looks intricate and impressive: log cabin, Dutch girl, monkey wrench.

Finding the pattern was the hardest part. I wanted one

with historical significance, but it had to be simple: no inch-wide triangles, no circles. Sewing circles to octagons seemed to me like sewing raccoons to squirrels. I'd sooner get a tattoo.

We found a yellowed pattern of my great-grandmother's, four paper pieces folded into a cigar box among lace at the back of a chest in the sewing room. Mama remembered a quilt made of that pattern, three triangles of different sizes and a long rectangle. For a week we fit the pieces together many ways, like trying to solve a geometry puzzle, but never could make a square. Something was missing. Neither could we find the quilt; probably it had fallen apart in the mouths of moths.

From a book in the library, I copied a pattern called shoo-fly, based on nine five-inch squares, with each of the four corner squares divided into two triangles. If you use three colors—one for the outer triangles, another for the middle square and the inner triangles, and the third for the remaining middle squares—and if you squint when you look at it, and if you tilt your head at a certain angle while you squint, the pattern looks three dimensional, like a pinwheel. It looks nothing like a fly, or a pie, or a flyswatter.

We tried to set aside an evening a week to quilt, often on Sundays after supper. On any particular night, we either cut pieces or we sewed them together. It was easier that way, with the strewn cloth, to spend one evening cutting.

"Mama, are these stitches too far apart?"

She looked. "Maybe a little."

My father came in and sat down, idle. We smiled at him and kept pinning, snipping, stitching.

"You know, if somebody goes to hell," he said out of

the blue, addressing me, "a person in heaven would be able to look down and see them." That fast, he was talking religion.

"You know I don't believe in hell," I said. I tried to be patient, although we'd had many variations on this conversation.

"Well, there is one, whether you believe it or not. And let's say your mother goes to heaven and you to hell. She'll be able to look down and see you suffering. But she won't cry. She won't shed a tear of remorse, for there'll be no crying in heaven."

I tried to imagine it. "I can't feature it," I said obliquely. It was a conversation I hated. Here my father and I have no common language. For him, the Bible is a holy book, and for me, it is a glorious, poetic, historical account of a people searching for the meaning of life. In the middle of making a quilt, he was attempting to convert me to his rigid certainty. Perhaps he, too, is looking for common threads to bind things together. But his tools draw more blood than our pins and needles.

I no longer say I am atheist. The universe is too marvelous and magical, and I have seen too much of providence and the inexplicable not to believe in spirit. Something more than heartbeat left my grandmother's body when she died. The idea that spirit exists, that some things are not what they appear, pleases me. Some things lie beyond the realm of human knowledge. Even that concession is not enough for my father, who has been visited by the Lord above.

"When Jesus appears to you," he said, "you'll know the truth. He hasn't appeared to you yet."

I remembered a story that a friend, John Lane, told me

about a young man teaching in Japan, in a small village where he was the only American. The teacher wrote the words "Jesus Christ" on the chalkboard and not one person knew who that was. Imagine having to explain what those two words mean. (The teacher called it one of the best moments of his life.) In the middle of the discussion, one of the students interrupted and said he really wanted to know who this guy Santa Claus was.

⚭

For years I could not kick the feeling that I had to be good. Everything I had been taught led me to purity. Above all. I wanted to be a saint, a poet, a goddess. Even after I had forsaken Christianity, I could not shake the watchful eyes of God, who counted the beers I drank, the men I slept with, my sacrilegious, shameful friends. He tallied the sins. Backslider. Infidel. Heathen.

I tried to define "good." I knew my father's definition was different from my own. For me, it had less and less to do with edifice, affiliation, and separation; goodness came to be synonymous with kindness, justice, peace, tolerance, and service. Goodness was in the heart. God, then, was around us.

I certainly have no proof for my argument for spirit. Spirit is walking to the crossroads east of the swamp, to the very middle of the dark sandy road, beneath the stars, to pray. Not knowing to what or to whom the prayer is directed, but praying anyway, turning to four directions, one by one. Of the south I ask, "Take care of my people." Of the east I ask for light, of the west for changes—for help accepting them and weathering storms. When I turn toward the north, something happens in my body and I only pray to be shown the path I am supposed to be walking. Even in stinging rain, I go prone before this great force that owns us, sink to my knees, fall on my face. *Keeper of the North, I am yours. Do with me what you will.* Saying to the earth, *I'm yours, do with me what you will.* The wind begins to blow hard from the north. I stumble home better somehow, humble and grateful and connected to something.

გია

"Do you believe in angels?" my sister asked me at the end of one midnight conversation.

"I'm not sure," I said. "I think so. Why?"

"I was wondering," she said.

"Do you believe in them?" I prodded.

"Yes," she said.

"Do you have one?" I pressed, trying to be open-minded. What was she getting at?

She hesitated. "I think I am one," she said.

An awkward silence erected itself around us. Was my sister losing her mind?

No, I suddenly realized, she had returned to the possibility of spirit.

"Then you are," I told her.

გია

My father was again at the kitchen table. "Over and over," he said, not resigned, "I hear about atheists on their death beds turning back to Christ."

I looked at him, thinking sincerely about what he implied. "Don't count on it."

"Happens all the time," he said. "I heard somebody talking about it the other night."

"On a talk show?" When he can't sleep, he listens to night radio.

"It was about people believing in God or not."

"I can't ever see myself turning back," I said. "When we die, we return to the earth." I paused. "Listen. I don't want you to worry about my soul."

"Worry?" he snorted. "I don't worry."

"I'm comfortable with my beliefs. I'm not afraid. Not of eternity or anything else."

"You know what I think?" he asked.

"No, what?"

"That we get what we ask for."

"What I ask for is a good life," I said. "If there's a heaven, this may be it." Exasperated and ready to leave, I got up and ran hot water to wash dishes, and Daddy departed the room. He removed himself, I knew, because he was happy I was there with Mama.

When the quilt is done, I will look at it and think that I can never be the daughter my parents desire, and that I can be more than they ever imagined possible. And that art is somebody loving creation, however it happened, whoever made it. But mostly I will look at it and remember how my mother and I found a place to talk.

Finding a Man

The first question my new neighbor asked me: was
I married? I'd been back only a few days when he
waited for me one morning in his overgrown front yard. I
jog a couple of miles early each day, passing his house, east-
ward, crossing Little Ten Mile Creek where the wooden
bridge used to be when I was a girl, before culverts.

I was almost past when he yelled, "Hey."

Glancing back, I waved and kept jogging. I remembered him.

"You merit?" he yelled. You merit: you married.

"Yes," I yelled over my shoulder, lying.

"No you're not," he called down the road. By now I was
approaching the head, the spring branch, that separated
his property from ours, and I let him have the last word.

I was very unmarried, even concerned as to how I
might find companionship here, in a world very different
from those I'd found for myself afield. By chance, I hoped,
there would be a man about my age who had returned to
Georgia from afar, who was educated, tolerant, just.

I would probably have abandoned the possibilility of
such a man after the first few months had it not been for a
woman I met soon after returning. One morning, delivering Silas to school, I noticed a tall, strong woman dropping off a child. She wore boots that climbed her tan legs
almost to the calf. We passed near each other and when I
said hello she smiled, big and white.

Not a week later I saw her in the grocery store. She was behind me in the checkout line, and I secretly investigated her groceries as mine passed the scanner: yogurt, fresh beans, sugar-free cereal, cantaloupe, plums, cheese. I turned. "I saw you at Altamaha School the other day," I said.

"Yes." She smiled. "My son goes there."

"What grade?"

"Kindergarten."

While she paid, I played with her daughter, who was three, she told me, and whose name was Alexandria. Then we stood and talked. Her name was Carly, a single parent new to Baxley. Before long we were friends.

Most of our comradeship in the beginning centered around the need for intimacy in our lives. Carly was dogged in her willingness to go out with men, driven by the hope of finding someone compatible.

That first winter I was home, we hit all the nightspots, including a dance hall in Vidalia where bouncers frisked us on the way in. After working and taking care of our children all week, we had to have a social life. One trailer salesman ten years my junior asked me to dance four times.

"Are you married?" he asked on the first dance.

"No," I said, watching the couples jump-jiving around me. The rhythm was strong and easy, ideal for swinging.

During the next dance the same man asked the same question. "You sure you're not married?"

"Why don't you believe I'm single?" I asked. "I've been single eight years. I was married for a year and I have a boy who's nine."

"You wouldn't believe how many women tell me they're single, but they're not," he said. "It happens all the time."

"Well, I'm single but that doesn't mean much."

"What?" he says.

"I just want to dance."

One Saturday night we decided to try a different club, a very famous watering hole. I got to Carly's house early, in time to play with her makeup. She had everything—colored pencils for lips and eyes and eyebrows, lipstick in slim cylinders, a hundred different colors of eye shadow, nose powder, blush, gloss. She had perfume and fingernail polish and a hair dryer. We made ourselves look like magazine women.

The club was almost out in the country. Loggers had been cutting between the club and the highway, leaving the land raw and ugly. The clay road had been stirred to mush by the log trucks and by weeks of relentless rain. I drove carefully, sloshing through the mud, following car lights ahead. One slip of the wheel and we'd be in the ditch.

The dirt lot of the club was filled with cars and trucks—mostly trucks—and we squeezed into a space and sat talking. The rain streaked down the windshield, ghost runnels in the distorted light of the floodlamp. Cars circled the building, looking to park.

"Ready?" I said finally.

"Here goes," Carly said. We dashed through the rain, not failing to notice a couple of men also picking their way though mud.

Two white-haired women took our money at the door, four dollars each. They stamped the backs of our hands. The room was about the size of a school cafeteria, and resembled one, low ceilinged, with metal folding chairs dragged around rectangular brown tables.

The band was not yet playing but the club was filling with rough-looking men. I quickly counted the women to make sure of plenty. A lot of women usually means there'll be a lot of men. Singles outnumbered couples, another good sign. Men stood around the back, along the walls.

Carly and I took one end of a long table. The band cranked up—Fred & Evelyn Hand was the billing, but Evelyn was a mannequin. Fred played guitar, sang, and adjusted knobs on his backup machines. Drums, brass. Evelyn stood there with her shiny black plastic hair, a guitar strapped into her rigid arms. Carly told me that the previous time she'd come here Evelyn's hand had been wired to move back and forth, as if she were strumming.

Fred sounded all right for one man. Nobody asked us to dance, although men were cutting eyes toward us while we sat through a couple of songs. A few couples scuffled across the concrete dance floor.

Fred cinched up his guitar and bawled out a fast beat. Carly and I looked at each other, nodded, and rose. If nobody asked us to dance, we danced anyway. No sense sitting around waiting. The floor half filled with mostly mature couples.

After a few fast dances Fred strummed the first chords to a slow tune. We walked to the bathroom.

"This is pathetic," I said. "We won't find a date here."

"I don't care about finding a man," Carly said. "I want somebody to dance with."

Not me. I was waiting for someone to ask me the greatest pickup line I ever heard: *So, are you on city water or do you have your own well?*

We went back out and sat. "There," I said. "I'm going to ask that man to dance." He was well-kempt, with short graying hair, forty-fivish, slender. He turned out to be a contractor from Hazlehurst, and he danced easily.

A mechanic asked Carly to dance, then a grizzled logger asked me for a waltz. The man's beard was gray and shaggy, and he was wearing work boots. He kept pulling me too close, bending me toward him at the waist. He spat on me like light rain when he talked.

The second time I danced with him, he said, "You ever want to be a queen, look me up."

"Thank you," I said.

Carly got asked to dance for the next one, a slow. When we got back to our table, two women were sitting at the other end. We'd noticed them already, staring at us, whispering. I leaned toward Carly.

"Do they think we're lesbian?" I muttered. "Or too threatening?"

The women were younger, in their mid-twenties, and one of them, a blond, stared at us.

"She'd better think twice," Carly said out of the corner of her mouth, and we laughed good-naturedly. Carly is stronger than an oak limb from training horses.

"Hey," I said, spotting a young man standing along the wall. "There's an interesting man." I got up and went over. He said yes and put down his beer. He was about twenty-five, dark haired, with a handsome face and a very round belly.

The dance was slow enough so that I found out he was a dairy farmer from Jesup before someone knocked me on the shoulder.

"I'm cutting in," said the blond and stepped into my place. Around me couples swirled beerily together.

I followed the dairy farmer and tapped the blond.

"No you're not," I said.

She drew her hand back, then lowered it.

"I don't want none of you," she said with a hateful look, and edged off the floor.

∞

One time a young man Carly met at a party took us both to Frank's CC Club, a country honky-tonk in the woods near Cedar Crossing. The establishment was tacked together of plywood with a Coke machine lit red outside the front door. It had two pool tables and a big Confederate flag on one wall. On a tiny dance floor beneath an elevated platform for the disc jockey, young people were dancing.

Carly's date was supercilious and macho, and insisted on being in control. We were in my truck, but he demanded to drive. I asked him once to slow down.

"Like this?" he said, and swerved into the left lane. He couldn't have been over twenty-three.

He was too drunk to drive home but not inebriated enough to outwit for the truck keys he'd kept. Within a mile, at a dark T in the road, he almost didn't make the turn and a mouse's breath kept us from jumping the fence and landing in a field. I screamed.

That scared him, and he let Carly drive. The fuel gauge was below empty, but the first gas station we came to was closed. Carly drove to town to gas up. When she got out to pump, he turned toward me.

"How about a kiss?"

"You're out of your mind."

"Let me see your legs. Come on," he said.

I got out. "We're taking him home," I said to Carly.

He wanted us to drop off Carly first, but I'm not that stupid, so we turned down Buckhorn Road and up to his one-bedroom trailer, pulled into a pine plantation. Carly got out with him, and I watched them saying goodnight in the rearview mirror. He turned from her and approached the truck from behind. It was February and I had the window up, but he rapped and I lowered it. He bent and stuck his mouth to my ear.

"She's going home," he said. "You're coming back here."

"I'm not coming back here," I said, emphasizing the personal pronoun. Where had he learned imperiousness?

"Yes, you are. If you don't, I'll follow you."

"Do what you like, but count me out."

"We'll see," he said, and swaggered away. It was two in the morning. Although Silas was spending the night with a friend and I was free, Carly had to get back to her children. She climbed into the truck. When we got to Carly's house I waited for her to get inside. At the bottom of Carly's drive, on the highway, I saw slow truck lights. He had followed us.

The truck sped off. I was sure he would top the next rise—Carly lived at the bottom of a sand hill—and turn around, but I hoped that would give me time to elude him. I drove out and turned right, away from town.

Good thing I knew the roads. Within seconds I was speeding away, heart crashing against rib cage, watching the rearview for lights. In fifteen minutes, I pulled into the farmyard, shaken, cutting the headlights, in hopes Uncle Percy wouldn't notice the time. Inside, I locked the doors and, when the phone rang, as I knew it would, I did not answer it.

Many times, as a single woman living alone in the country, I felt vulnerable and occasionally afraid. After a year Carly moved away to teach at an elementary school near Savannah. Without Carly, I kept looking, but in better venues. I never gave up hope that I'd find the right man. I wanted a kind Southerner who liked to read, who liked wilderness, maybe one who played music. Someone who wanted to share a life close to the land. But most of my time I spent with Silas and his friends, or alone. Alone can be a bleak way to live.

The Picture-Taker

E.D. McCool has lived in a school bus in Baxley since I was a girl, forty years ago, and beyond that, people say. When I was young, he drove his 1946 Chevrolet bus here and yon, clicking sepia-tone photographs of people for a dime, then a quarter each.

He would park in the Piggly Wiggly parking lot most any day, but surely on Saturday and Sunday afternoons, and open up for business, hanging out his carefully lettered shingle that advertised a photo for a quarter. People would stop to have their picture taken. A customer could stand around and wait for the picture or come back for it. E.D. took a heap of pictures over the years, a share of them belonging to us. If a customer never returned, E.D. kept the photos—boxes and boxes of strangers' faces.

He used a camera that entailed his sticking his hand up a dark sock, made from a pants leg, and fumbling with a light meter and other gauges far in the body of the camera, and sometimes even sticking his head under a dark curtain before he ordered you to prop your hand this way or lean that way and look this way. If he didn't feel like photographing or didn't like a certain customer, he would announce that he was closed. "Too hot," he'd say. He might stay closed until a carload of young girls came by. Then he'd jump up and get official, start fiddling with his light meters, unfolding the black canvas backdrop. He loved to photograph women, although he was certainly too shy to talk to them, and would not have considered marrying one.

As dark began to overtake the land, E.D. would say, "Too dark for picture-taking. . . . Time for me to go home."

"This is your home," my brother might say.

"I'm sort of like a turtle," E.D. would say, nervously. "Even a turtle has a place he likes to spend the night."

Every evening he would lid up his chemicals, pack away his three-legged camera, and drive to the spot where he parked for the night. He parked at different sites over the years. All he needed was a water spigot.

Every little place has people who make a town special, and E.D. is one of those in Baxley. He has been a friend of my father for years, and of my grandfather before that. He is crazy about animals, and E.D. puts out pans of food scavenged from dumpsters for the homeless animals of the town. He feeds cats, dogs, mice, birds; he won't kill rats or let anyone else kill roaches in his bus.

When I was little, he'd drive the mile out to the junk-yard, park his bus by the road, and come feed some animal or other. We had a collection at the junkyard—sheep, a pony, dogs, cats. He drove out almost daily to bring special food to our aging horse.

"He likes peanut butter and jelly sandwiches," he would say.

"Who are you talking about?" Daddy would ask.

"Him," E.D. would say, mysteriously.

"You mean the horse?"

"Yes. He likes sandwiches. Especially peanut butter and jelly. You got to put a little salt on them."

"E.D., that horse will eat anything. He likes grass. Anything that likes to eat grass won't be particular about whether you give him a sandwich or a piece of cornbread."

"That's his animal fare. This is a substantial meal. You give him a sandwich first, then an apple." Then E.D. would pour a two-liter bottle of soda into the horse's trough.

Once E.D. didn't come out for about a week. Daddy ran into him one day in town.

"You ain't been out to feed in a while," Daddy said. "The rabbits done died. They died with their jaws locked on the cage, they were so hungry."

E.D. shut his eyes. "Uhh," was all he said.

"They perished to death," Daddy said. "With their ribs sticking out."

"Uhh," said E.D.

"Naw," Daddy laughed. "We been feeding them." But that very evening E.D. pulled his brown bus up alongside the highway and disembarked with his hands full of lettuce and carrots.

E.D. held curious convictions and odd notions. He lived his life by crazy rules he concocted: what and when to eat, what day to visit the bank, what color clothes to wear. He did not live by the customary traditions of the town. Years before he had become a follower of a nutritionist named McFadden, who advocated eating only one meal a day, at evening.

"Can he afford food?" I asked Daddy.

"Sure, he can afford it. Whether he decides to spend his money on food is another matter."

"What does he eat?"

"I have no idea. He is very peculiar. You won't ever see

him eat. The only person I ever heard of him eating with was my daddy. Daddy said he ate enough for three meals in one meal.

"He's the kind of man could live on a dollar a week if he hit hard times," Daddy continued. "Even by today's prices. He'd buy him a ten-pound sack of potatoes. He don't have rent or utilities. He don't buy clothes. He's the kind of man, if he owes you, he pays you. He doesn't make unnecessary debt. He watches his pennies.

"And he don't let you in on his personal business," Daddy added.

Because of his eating habits and his penury, E.D. was gaunt, a feature his height accentuated. His hair was shockingly white. His clothes never fit, as if they had belonged to other, fleshier people; he kept his pants up with a belt that I would bet money he still wears.

After I was old enough to cook, I'd wrap up food for E.D., slices of cake or pieces of fried chicken, and drop it off at his bus if he didn't come out, or if he did, hand it to him. He never in my presence examined the food, made further mention of it, or thanked me. I suspected that he ate it, but I never knew.

After his old bus quit on him, E.D. parked it permanently over by the railroad track, near the pecan warehouse, and acquired a riding lawn mower to drive around town. He drove the mower down the sidewalk, as if it were a car in its own special lane, and townspeople watched for the yellow flag flapping high above his head. Crossing the streets, he stopped and looked both ways many times. He was on the lawn mower when I saw him after I returned home. He'd been an old man when I was a girl and now I did

not know the right adjective to describe his age. He was
ancient. He no longer could find a supplier for the film
and chemicals his outdated sepia-tone camera used, and
he had closed his picture-taking business. When Silas and
I saw him, we often stopped to talk. He remembered well
who I was—Daddy and he were still good friends—but I
don't think he could ever accept that I was the same girl
who had dressed up as a pioneer for a picture with her
musket-toting brothers, the one who had left brownies
on the hood of his bus. He stood and stared. He'd never
been good at talking.

"Are you Frank's older girl or younger girl?" he'd say.

"Younger," I'd reply.

"How's yore sister?"

"Fine, fine. She's married with a little boy."

"She was a pretty girl," he'd say.

One day a couple of years after we moved back home,
Silas and I found ourselves having to give away a litter
of kittens. Our cat had gotten pregnant before we had a
chance to spay her, and she had five healthy kittens, gray
striped and giddy with kittenhood.

One Saturday morning when the kittens were two
months old, we carried them in a wire cage to the grocery
store. "You better tape ten dollar bills on them," a friend
laughed.

The kittens did not like the cage and were hollering. The
mama cat was in there with them, although we were keeping
her, and she was less happy than the kittens. I saw E.D. driving up on his lawn mower with the yellow flag waving.

"Uh oh," I said. "Here comes E.D. He'll be feeling
sorry for the cats."

E.D. hobbled over to where we were. He stood and watched the kittens awhile, not saying much. Finally he began to speak.

"Look at the mama," he said, "how sad she is. It ain't right to take a mama's babies away from her. She may never get over it. They don't look big enough to give away. They need their mama's milk right on until she weans them."

"E.D., we can't keep all these kittens. They're eight weeks old. They're grown enough to be weaned. If we wait too much longer, they won't be kittens." I didn't admit that the kitten giveaway was sad for us too.

"You could give them another month or two with their mother."

"You can't give cats away."

Shoppers, some we knew, would stop and talk, and finally someone took a kitten. Before long E.D. was gone. "He couldn't stand it," I said to Silas. E.D. came back fifteen minutes later with scrambled egg and toast.

"They looked like they needed egg," he said. Empathy had blossomed in his heart and the one sure way he knew to give to the creatures was to feed them. He deposited his offering, stood a few minutes, then left again, and before long we'd given away all the kittens except one, which we kept.

One day E.D. asked Daddy to take his body out to the woods when he died.

"What woods?" Daddy said. "You can't just go haul a dead body to the woods."

"I got it all figured out," E.D. said. "Take me way out Ten Mile Road. I want you to put me facing north, under an oak tree out there. I want my body to nourish an oak tree."

"I bet that's against the law, E.D., " Daddy said.

"Take me way out in the woods," E.D. said. "Where nobody won't see me." He gets his mind set on a thing.

"What are you gonna do when those dogs out there start dragging your head around on the highway?" Daddy asked him. "They'll scatter your bones everywhere." E.D. stopped talking, said he'd get back with Daddy later.

The next time Daddy saw him, E.D. said he'd made arrangements with the undertaker.

"I reckon he got to thinking about those dogs," Daddy said.

Not long ago I came upon E.D. shuffling through the supermarket, dragging his feet one at a time with effort and appearing very fragile. He had one item in his basket, a bag of shoestring potatoes ready to cook. His old-man's pants were cinched around his shrunken hips. I approached close to him and said hello. He gave me a second glance.

"Hey," he said. "I ain't seen you lately. I thought maybe you'd left town."

"No," I said. "Still here. How you doing?"

"Not good," he said. "I've got seven disorders. Seven ailments." He said it like this, ay-l-mints, distinctly three syllables. When he grasped a candy bar display to hold on, his arms were trembling. I was sincerely worried about him.

"What are they?" I asked.

"I've had a stroke in my right leg," he said. "That's one. Then there's this Parker's disease, got me shaking. I've got the old-timer's ailment, just the start of it. It makes you forget things." He stood quiet a few seconds, shaking and thinking. "My hearing's going bad—that's just starting too. How many does that make?"

"That's enough," I said. "I'm sorry."

"I've got more ailments. I just can't recall them at the moment."

"If you don't mind my asking, how old are you now?"

A quick, weak smile flashed across his thin, pale face. "I'm in my nineties," he said. "I'll soon be a hundred."

"That's great. When will you be a hundred?"

E.D. ignored me. "I'm one of the oldest people alive," he said.

I learned a long time ago, to keep people talking, you don't say much. "Congratulations!"

"The oldest person I ever knew was Frank Walker," E.D. continued. "Lee Walker's dad. He lived to be 107. I've got a picture I took of him when he was 107."

"I'd like to see that."

Abruptly E.D. turned with a few jerky nods of his head and, scuffling his weak legs, set his basket on the cashier's conveyor belt. I asked would he let me buy his potatoes for him, but he wouldn't even acknowledge my offer. He took his purchase and limped from the store.

When I reached my truck I sat and watched him hobble to his lawn mower. He stashed his package on the back and took a long time to seat himself atop the conveyance. An angel squirmed inside my heavy heart, the same angel that quarrels with me to give hitchhikers rides and rescue animals wounded on the road.

E.D. had lived for decades at the margin of our town, documenting its history, obeying a similar angel camped in his own heart. When he had a stroke, he had to live in a nursing home for a few months. He hated it. He tried to stash the food the nurses brought for breakfast and dinner, so he could eat it at his one supper meal. As soon as he regained mobility, E.D. moved back to his old bus. He wanted to take care of himself.

The least someone could do would be to take the picture-taker's picture.

E.D., the picture-taker, beside his home.

Heroic Vegetables

Frank Thueatt of Riverdale, Ga., grew watermelons which weighed 130 and 115 pounds in his backyard garden. . . . Ann Bullock holds a head of broccoli grown in her family garden near La Fayette, Ga. The broccoli measured 13 inches in diameter. . . . Ruth Evans, 89, of Cedartown, Ga., grew this tomato that measured 15 inches in circumference and weighed over three pounds.

—PHOTO CAPTIONS FROM THE *Market Bulletin*

૪૭

My brother Dell is a pipefitter who sporadically works jobs where he has to live in a motel somewhere for a few weeks at a time. Then he comes home, motivated mostly by his desire to get into the *Guinness Book of World Records* by growing tomatoes.

Our family members are pretty competitive, I guess, eager to lord over each other. Last year we had a bet to see who could produce the first ripe tomato, and each of us thought we'd win. I was watering mine extra, and Daddy was pouring on the fertilizer, but it was Dell who plopped the first salmon-pink tomato on Mama's table. Dell had tomatoes almost year-round, until way about February, when frost killed his plants, including one in its third season. On the coldest nights, he had covered it with two quilts. Dell was picking tomatoes long after the rest of us had pulled up our vines and started to buy the cardboard kind. By March he was planting starts. This year, although I had tomatoes in the ground before he did, his bore first again.

He had the biggest tomato, too, he said, especially this one. Every time I saw him he'd tell me I needed to go around and see his big tomato. "It's still green, and growing," he said. "And already bigger than anything I've ever grown."

"Don't count your chickens before they hatch."

"I don't think it'll break the world record, but I'm hoping," he said. "It'll be close."

"What's the record?"

"Seven pounds."

"I've seen big tomatoes before," I said, shrugging him off. "I remember a German Pink I bought at a fruit stand in North Carolina this big. Big as a slice of bread."

"Mine is big as a mixing bowl," he said. "It's a Beefsteak."

When Dell's not pipefitting, he leads an orderly, scheduled existence. He sleeps late, and when he gets up he drives directly to the library, where he reads the paper, looks at new books, and wanders around on the Internet. He eats noon dinner at Mama's house. In the afternoon he helps our friend Lewis, who does yard work for a living. After supper he visits me, or his friend Dewayne, or our other brother to bring bubble gum and suckers to the children.

Every night between 8:45 and 9:00, he meets Mr. Frank, who is Daddy's age and retired, at the Flash Foods on 341 West. Mr. Frank comes down for a cup of instant cappuccino before he retires for the night, and he and Dell swap stories, joke, and opinionate about current events.

I don't know at what hour he checks on his tomatoes, which grow in Aunt Jean's yard.

"You got to come see my big tomato," he often said to me. "It's monstrous."

Finally I rode over and, sure enough, it was the biggest tomato I'd ever seen. It was bigger than a big grapefruit.

"It's not full grown yet," Dell said. "It's starting to turn, which means it's still growing."

"It's still growing," Aunt Jean said. She's the wife of my uncle, Daddy's brother, who's dead. She is in her seventies, wears fashionable shoes, and has an elegant flair to her, even in the way she holds her cigarettes. She loves to wear hats and is not stingy with bright makeup. Dell carries her around town the first of every month, when her check comes, to pay the bills and buy groceries. She was happy to have him growing vegetables in her yard.

"When I pick it, I'm gonna leave a few inches of stem," Dell said. "For the weight. I'm gonna take it down to the newspaper office and get a picture taken. After it's in the paper, I'll send it to the *Market Bulletin*."

Every time I saw Dell, he'd have an update. "I've raised it up on straw," he said. "To keep it off the ground. I need to rig a sling for it. A cradle. You got a pair of torn pantyhose?"

"Why a sling?"

"To keep it from detaching. And to keep it off the ground so it won't rot or get a bug."

"Bugs fly."

"Worms crawl."

"Come on. I have pantyhose I never wear. This will put a pair to good use."

A few days later, he said, "It's not a world-record tomato, but it's close. Ain't nobody around here seen one any bigger. I measured it and it's thirteen inches circumference. I tried to weigh it on the vine in case of accident."

"What did it weigh?"

"I never got it weighed."

"Why not?"

"I thought it might unplug if I used a fish scale."

He measured the tomato's diameter at six inches across the top (not at the widest part) and the depth at another six inches. "Yep, it'll take y'all a long time to raise one that big," he gloated to me and Daddy. "You'll spend the next twenty years trying to top that."

He never did get to have his picture in the newspaper with his big tomato. Somehow he missed the worm that bored in from the underside, and he missed the start of rot, and when he finally decided to pick the tomato, which appeared perfect from the top, it was spoiled beyond use. Most of its weight had drained right out the bottom. He tried to eat the blossom end, but rot had permeated the entire fruit.

The following season, still lusting after glory, he tried the same variety of tomato in the same spot in Aunt Jean's yard. It barely produced.

Dell still talks about his lost champion, lovingly and humorously.

"It'd fill up this bowl here," he said once, nodding toward a lathe-turned bowl holding wooden fruit on Mama's table. The bowl is maybe ten inches across.

I hooted. "You wish."

Dell grinned. "Humor me."

"What were you putting on it?"

"Whatever I could find. Miracle-Gro, sheep manure, 10-10-10."

"No wonder it got so big. It had thyroid problems from all the chemicals," I said.

"It was a fluke," he said. "A tomato like that comes once in a lifetime."

"Was that tomato symbolic in your life?" I teased him.

He's quick for a joke. "It was my one hope of leaving this place!" he said.

"All that glitters isn't gold," I returned.

The tomato, however, had served its purpose. Anybody who saw it was impressed, and it made my brother a hero among us, the people who matter, even if Guinness never heard about it.

∽

Dennis McCann of Lavonia, Ga., proudly displays the 8-pound sweet potato he grew despite drought conditions in his area.... Wilton Baker of Adairsville, Ga., is shown with the 32-pound cantaloupe he grew on his farm.... Thomas Waddell of Canton, Ga., grew these turnips in his garden. They weighed 13 and 15 pounds.... Mrs. Willie B. Mathis grew this German Queen tomato in her washtub garden. It weighed 2 pounds.

—PHOTO CAPTIONS FROM THE *Market Bulletin*

Local Economics

O ne day the truck ran hot on the way to town and I
called my brother to bring me home from the repair
shop. I tried to give him five dollars.

"No way," he said adamantly.

"OK, how about ten dollars?" I asked, knowing his
problem wasn't with the amount.

"Never."

"I would've paid twice that for a taxi."

"I'm not taking your money."

"Why not? We used your gasoline."

"You may have to come pick me up one day," he said.
"And I may not have five dollars to give you." He laughed,
delighted to have found the truthful answer.

"Then you'll stay where you are," I joked and put the
money away.

It's a shame, I suppose, to distill a graceful and affec-
tionate way of life into financial terms, but a household
economy benefits from a functional community. The most
costly life of all is one devoid of friendship.

I do not subscribe to a tow service because if my truck
breaks down anywhere in south Georgia, I can call any number of acquaintances until I find one to rescue me. I trade
childcare with the mothers of my son's friends. Rita Faye not
only lends me her rototiller, she comes and helps with the
tilling. She lends me her canoe because I do not own one.

When the washer that had been Grandmama's stopped

washing, I called Daddy to ask him what might be wrong. He has spent a lifetime fixing machines so as not to replace them. He dropped by one afternoon to look at it and pronounced himself baffled. He promised to be on the lookout for a used one for sale. Two days later, when the *Shopper* with the free ads came out, Daddy bought one for seventy-five dollars. He and my brother picked it up, delivered it to the farmhouse, and switched it with the broken one. A new machine would have cost a fortune, which I could not have afforded.

A community system of giving and sharing establishes a local economy. For it to succeed, this system requires of its participants:

- *Trust.* If a person breaks what she borrows, she will repair or replace it.
- *Availability.* If a person depends on his community for help, he must be willing to return favors when another person is stranded or in crisis. This is why I found myself one afternoon squeezed behind Uncle Bill's toilet—it leaked water and annoyed him with its wastefulness—grinding off a wing nut that had corroded onto the bolt that kept the tank on the seat. Wing nut off, he could lift the toilet and replace a leaking seal.
- *Balance.* One person cannot habitually take and the other give. Not that an accounting method is necessary or sensible, but in the long run, favors must balance out.

Two nights in a row I dreamed of a sign. "Community Makes Sense," it said. When I woke, I remembered distinctly looking at the dream sign and reading it aloud. *That's what I'll tell people,* I thought.

I have lived on my grandparents' farm, in a net of family and a growing circle of friends, on $14,000 a year. What amount would I require to live elsewhere, disconnected? Maybe $30,000, or $50,000.

This economic system, called reciprocity, seems to
be most suited to poverty, especially in rural areas, where
motivation and hard work and even genius do not always
translate into commensurate monetary gain. Why else
the barn raisings and quilting bees and hay makings? One
member of the ward is willing to help another, knowing
the number of her own need will be called.

One morning after Uncle Bill had fixed his combine
and harvested the rye, Silas and I came upon him burning the stubble. Almost his entire family was there to help
him, gathered in the road as we passed. I paused to speak.
"It takes a whole family to burn a field," I said.

Uncle Bill laughed. "It's Field Day!" he said.

For years I tried to be self-sufficient, meaning not
being dependent on an electric company with its nuclear
plants and its dams, on a transportation system to bring
food to the grocery store, or on a doctor to treat the flu.
For me, self-sufficiency also meant a certain independence
from currency. I homesteaded twelve acres of land west
of Tallahassee, Florida, growing fruit trees and a big garden, living without electricity or running water. ("Walking
water," I heard that called.) Because I had little spare cash
and plenty of time, I was interested in what I and my
neighbors might produce or provide.

Years later, I realize the term "self-sufficiency" is a
misnomer. "Self-sufficiency" implies that we can singly
provide for our needs, that we need no one. It seems to me
that the more we are hurt, starting in infancy, the further
we retreat into independence. We are smart creatures who
learn quickly to protect our vulnerable selves by hiding
them. Yet the truth is that we are all deeply dependent
on each other, and on the earth, in a complex system of

mutual beneficence. To share and to cooperate means to take great risks, with high returns for our bravery. Better, then, that we strive for co-sufficiency than self-sufficiency.

What I am talking about is not barter—an even swap of this thing for that, this many hours of my time for that many hours of yours—although barter is in economic terms a viable, functional system. This is more than barter. It is the belief in the decency and interdependency of human beings, and the willingness to help others because you have seen your own helplessness and understand that it will come again.

Money is a way of keeping count of reciprocity. Although reciprocity can utilize money, it is not dependent on it. Capitalism, on the other hand, the economic system in which methods of production and distribution are privately owned and operated for profit, requires money. The power company has no accounting system other than the one based on dollars, nor does the telephone company, nor does the gas company. What I am saying is that coexistence beyond money forms a very delicate structure made of something like rubber bands, which stretch one way and then another but hold. Or hold for a long time. No matter what the economists say, a countryside lies beyond money, even beyond barter. Its accounting system is love, honor, respect, decency. The only thing we have to show for it are stories we tell.

I pull you out of a bog and you help me build a dog pen. You till my garden and I bring you a load of firewood. You give me squash seeds and I give someone else tomato starts.

The more the focus is on money, the more of it we want; the more of it we earn, the less we seek this community life where we rely on each other. Money gives us a kind of power and freedom, to be sure, but so does friendship. Ask money to play guitar with you. Ask it to come over when you are sick and hold your hand. Ask money to shoulder your load. Ask it to love you.

Often we falter in our attempts to rely on each other and to be reliable. We drill our own well, sink our own swimming pool, buy our own truck. We do not ask for help; we hire it. The way of the work party, the barn raising, and the hay gathering dies. We live alone and see few others. The more isolated we become, the less sympathy we have for the common human condition.

Is there a need for community? I think so. Biologically, humans depend upon each other for many of the reasons wading birds that nest in colonies depend upon each other—to get the benefits of a group: shared knowledge of foodstuff, help in raising the young, protection from predators. For these reasons, we are social animals, evolved to live together, geared to cooperate. We are not, at heart, solitary creatures. A society is more highly evolved, more intelligent, and more capable than any individual.

The work of living in consonance is difficult. It is so much easier to secure ourselves behind fenced yards, so we do not have to examine our neglect of each other. In our neglect of the communal, we neglect our humanity.

I will hurriedly admit that many people are more involved in community than I. I like long stretches of silence and solitude. Yet, when my solitary work is completed for the day, I like to mingle with friends and family, to be an easy part of a whole. I need people. Most of us do. We humans are a communal, tribal, interdependent species.

If we are not engaged with our communities, if we are not in relationship with others besides ourselves, we are missing a necessary part of living, of learning, of being human.

ཉཉ

Miccosukee Land Cooperative is a land co-op in north Florida, ten miles out of Tallahassee on a canopy road overarched with live oaks. It has been functional since the '70s. About 125 families own pieces of land that are joined by winding dirt roads; ninety acres of common land hold a community center, a fire station, mailboxes, a community garden, a swimming pool, and a playground. In a way, the people of the co-op are a tribe, living in large wooden houses, driving back and forth to town jobs: latter-day natives. I have attended many of their events—christenings, weddings, dances, solstice rituals, wakes, lectures, anniversaries, reunions, birthday parties, benefits. The land cooperative is a successful model of how people can live together. Getting along is not always easy, as any of the residents will tell you, but for twenty-five years they have been living in community, tolerating, testing, hoping, working together, compromising, sharing. It's a rich life they have.

One need not relocate to a commune to enjoy the benefits of a community life, but can start anywhere, with the smallest of things. I have an easy example. When we lived in Montana, Silas had the same teacher two years in a row. At the beginning of the school year Becky Sorensen distributed a sheet to all parents with each family's address and phone number so that parents could communicate with each other. A directory is a simple thing, but it links people, and if people are linked, then they can offer each other assistance and ask each other for help.

Even when money is involved, I try to think in terms of community. I support local businesses because I've seen how malls and chain stores, especially Wal-Mart, disrupt the economics of community, which is, ideally, based on *local* resources and enterprise. The arrival of corporate megastores and chain restaurants can kill a town. When traveling I am not comforted by the presence of a cookie-cutter restaurant in every town, because what fascinates me is the particular, the local, the uncommon.

When a chain video store set up shop in Baxley, although the town already had three locally owned video shops, I watched closely. In a spate of high-energy advertising, the brand-new, shiny store offered inexpensive movie rentals, the latest releases, and free membership. It sounded great, and many people began to rent movies there. Within a month, the smallest of the local video establishments had gone out of business, and before another few months passed the second folded. The third hung on. After a few more months the fantastic deals that the new store first offered ended. Rental fees tripled, back to their normal level. The managers had almost accomplished their mission: to eliminate competition. Once customers were dependent on their merchandise, they could raise their rates.

We never once set foot in the new chain. When our favorite video store folded we took our business to another, and when it did not last we went to the third, where we still rent our occasional movie.

I enjoy knowing who my money is upholding. I like calling the person behind the counter by name. When

I buy a bundle of greens or a watermelon from a farmer selling from his pickup at a corner, the experience is far richer than a dash into a chain grocery. Likewise, when we eat at local cafes (where you speak to the owner, recognize the artist who designed the menu, and maybe know who grew the salad mix) the act is deeper and more fulfilling than consuming a generic meal on a strip that looks—and is—simultaneously like anyplace and like none. Virginia's Diner is a microcosm of our town. In patronizing it I support my place. Becoming a part, even financially, of our own community makes us more connected, more human, more responsible, richer.

We are great believers in our capitalist economic system. Even as climate rearranges globally and polar ice caps melt and seas inch higher along coastlines worldwide, we remain lost in our belief that capitalism will bring prosperity to all the world, starting with ourselves. Comfortable in this prosperity, wooed by its trinkets and entertainments, we fail to see that the industrial capitalism we have managed to spread globally does not mean prosperity for all but for few; that it cannot go on forever producing more and more; that global industrialism succeeds at the expense of local communities, local economies, and local ecosystems; that it causes problems—like cancer or ozone thinning—that technology has not been able to fix.

The only solution I know about is to become involved in local economics, to furnish for yourself and your community what you can, to join in providing services to each other, and beyond that, to know where the products you buy are made or to make them yourself.

Isolate people and we struggle in silence. Join us

together and we reach out. Isolation from every aspect is a kind of poverty, and community a certain wealth. Another night I dreamed of digging a splinter out of my foot. It turned into a huge metal placard with something written on it. The sign said, "Community Makes Sense."

Tupelo honey is one of our regional products.

Martin Luther King Parade

W hy you want to go march in that parade?" Mama asked when I called to say I'd be in the town parade for Martin Luther King Jr. Day. She worries about my being outspoken.

"We have to start somewhere," I said.

The parade began at the old junior high school, now a community center in a mostly black part of town, and looped downtown and back, probably four miles. That's a lot of marching. If the route were shorter, more people would walk, I think, but the parade has become a cavalcade of trucks, tractors hauling flatbed trailers, floats, four-wheelers, golf carts, motorcycles, and horses.

At the school I parked and found some walkers, a few young women. I asked could I walk with them and they said sure. The high school marching band struck up a tune and I noticed that some of the students in the band were white. The paramedic driving the ambulance was white, too.

Our straggling parade worked its way up Sursson Street, past a section of ramshackle housing and the squat, red brick juke joint, the Vixen Club. People came out on their porches to watch us, a long, scattered movement of people keeping the traffic stopped. We turned left onto U.S. 1, where an officer had four lanes of traffic halted, and I felt the drivers looking at me. I kept smiling, looking around nonchalantly. A few people were watching the parade from car hoods near the Dairy Queen, including Stan and Sandy, returnees like me, and they waved and grinned broadly.

The statement I was making was simply one of solidarity. Martin Luther King had been a visionary, and I celebrated his memory. I, too, had a dream that people of all races could live together, peaceful and fulfilled. What we as people lacked wasn't tolerance, but plain old love— this in a town where I've seen shoppers avoid a grocery aisle where a biracial couple shopped. The people shopping told me so. They'd rather not be that close, they said.

We marched slowly toward town, a mile away. Before we got to the stoplight in front of the courthouse, a couple of the women—there were five or six of us—dropped out, picked up by a vehicle behind. Because we were the only walkers, besides the band, we had to trot to keep up. We turned east at the stoplight. Another few walkers fell behind to ride in a truck bed. Somewhere near the grocery store, the motorcycles overtook us. We weren't yet halfway through the route. I looked at the one woman left beside me and swiped my forehead.

"We can't keep up at this pace," I said.

"Ain't that the truth," she replied.

"I'm going to catch a ride if I can."

"Me too," she agreed, and flagged down a truck behind.

A man on a motorcycle passed in first gear. He wore a white T-shirt under a leather vest, with a red bandanna knotted around his head.

"Can I ride with you?" I called above his motor.

He pressed the brakes. "Hop on." He grinned.

His name was Vegas, I found out. He was from

Douglas and worked in manufacturing. He rode with bikers from Baxley.

On the backstreets, the parade stalled, and after awhile the man and I quit small talk and sat waiting for the queue to inch ahead. On Allen Street, close to the junior high, as we sat idling he turned his head slightly.

"What's the worst thing ever happened to you?" he asked.

I contemplated the question, my cowboy boots hooked on the pegs, fingers light against his ribs, which I could feel through the cool leather. Surely, as a young black man, he had suffered discrimination, had been misunderstood, misjudged, stereotyped, maybe addicted or imprisoned or shot.

"I've been pretty lucky," I said. "Not a lot of bad has come to me. Maybe the worst is a friend killing himself." I paused. "Why do you ask?"

"I think about the bad sometimes," he said.

"What's the worst thing happened to you?"

"My best friend drowned."

"How?"

"I was twelve years old. My friend and I wanted to go to this borrow pit to swim but my mama wouldn't let me go. She said I might drown in there. It was about a mile from the house and my friend went anyway. It wasn't long before I got scared and decided I better go check on him. I ran all the way. When I got there he was floating face-down in the pond."

"I'm sorry," I said.

"That was the worst thing," he said. "I'll never forget it."

We were silent after that. He wanted to ride me home, but Uncle Percy didn't cotton to mixing the races. Uncle Percy watched every move I made, and if a black man brought me home on a motorcycle he would not have spoken to me for weeks, maybe not ever again.

Borderland

I headed for longleaf pine forest, driving south from the farm, crossing the state line into Florida at Jennings. From any direction the landscape, agricultural and silvicultural, wouldn't be much different. Was there no rest for land anywhere?

Cotton field. Pine plantation. House.

House. Cotton field. Clearcut. Pine plantation. Trailer. House.

Hardly any forest was left. It flew past me. Field. Plantation. Field. Clearcut. Church. Trailer. Field. I saw this everywhere I went.

Across the state line, I pulled over for a roadkill raccoon. I wanted to make Silas a coonskin cap, and I needed the tail; where the coon had been killed, a hawk was dead, too, hit on the road, and I moved both of them to the grassy ditch and sawed off the coon's tail. I felt odd, taking the tail like that, dumping the young coon cheerlessly by the road, but the tail was large and bushy, striped, pretty, and Silas would value it.

Where I-75 crosses the county road, I stopped at a convenience store. The store was full of cigarette smoke, and against my better judgment I bought a box of crackers, brushing away a coat of dust to read the price.

More fields, more young pines. A few houses. Then,

when I got to Blue Springs State Forest, where County Road 143 meets State Road 6, there was forest.

Longleaf forest.

It stood out like a kingdom of heaven, suddenly tall and very green, praising the sky. It triggered something in the back of my mind—some prehistoric, mossy, creaky memory of what the forest that used to be here, that once covered this land, looked like. It came edged out, this old memory, as if I had been suffering from ancestral amnesia and had just been hit on the head.

You'd have to drive a hundred, two hundred miles to see anything like this. I was glad I had.

We have so little left that we're forgetting what it looks like. In books at home and in files and in my mind I have pictures of longleaf pine forest. I've seen two virgin tracts, and some handsome, mature ones. Still, I forget. What about people who don't know how it was—young people and newcomers?

They may not like it at first. The forest takes some getting used to, because there's only one kind of tree. Some people want more tree diversity than that—they want to be able to stroll through a forest and say, "Magnolia. Maple. Hornbeam. Cherry laurel." I'd send those people about a mile west to the Withlacoochee River and have them meander in the floodplain.

But here, in the uplands, that was the way it was supposed to look. One kind of tree—longleaf pine—everywhere I turned. Sometimes I want diversity—I don't want to wear blue every day—but with these pines, I want stability. I want them relentless in their monotony, their monarchy. Only a powerful tree can claim a whole landscape for itself, a piece of a continent, from Virginia through the Southern coastal plains, clear out to east Texas, 93 million acres. It has to be a noble, indomitable tree.

ဢ

Growing up, I witnessed a fragmented landscape, with only pieces of true forest left here and there. The landscape, I thought, mirrors our lives. For obvious reasons, then, and for reasons not so obvious, I began early to associate homeland with loss.

Somehow, as the landscape fell apart, so did what bound humans to it. Perhaps what got increasingly lost were the stories we told each other—about the hornet's nest we found in the woods while walking, or ghostly flutterings through a dark wood that turned out to be phosphorescent moths. Perhaps we needed each other less to weather the vagaries of a life dependent on the world, on rain and trees and sulphur springs, or to help interpret the mysteries of the world as they were destroyed.

Decade upon decade, a sassafras stood in the middle of the upper field at the farm, a record-size sassafras. Carefully, year after year, my grandfather and my uncle plowed far around it, and when the tractor chopped its roots into pieces, they gathered them and brought them home for my grandmother to make tea, a spring tonic. After my grandfather died and the fields were leased, perhaps the farmer plowed too close to the tree, and whether this was the reason for its death or whether it died of some other, natural cause, I do not know. But die it did, leaving a hole in the middle of the field where it had stood. Some of us had used the tree as one might use a particular mountain, to orient by, as a landmark. In its dark limbs, the sassafras held the stories of my family and my people.

How fragmentedly we live, in broken families, crippled communities, landscapes chopped into pieces; we become disconnected from the sources of our survival, the land and each other, alienated from the earth and from things that hold meaning. I had come back to live in the stories of my people, to live a life that made sense. Somehow it wasn't working. Too much had been lost. Instead of wholeness I was finding scraps. Day after day I stared my life in the face, examining what I was missing. I was desperately lonely in the fragmentation, which was as much grief as anything, hanging on to remnants of beauty, spirit, art, touch, truth. For months I had felt cut off from the landscape of poetry. What else to call magic and spirit and truth? I had found only glimpses. Bitterly now I admitted that I had been torn apart in my homeland, these coastal plains, separated from intimacy, cut off from much of what I knew myself to be, waiting for the chance to flourish, to grow again. Waiting for what might not happen—for the logging to stop and the land to heal, and simultaneously for the communities that depended on the land to function again.

The last summer I was in Montana I noticed on the ground by an interstate exit a sign that had belonged to a homeless person, ballpoint letters on a scrap of cardboard, and I stopped for it. "Anything Will Help," it said, and I hung it on my apartment door, seeing it as found art, and a good reminder to myself to be helpful. Now I felt something of what that signmaker must have felt.

∞

I went to Blue Springs to write a story. I parked and walked out into the forest, eating cheese and crackers (they *were* stale). I sat on a pine log, eyeing an empty gopher tortoise shell. Soot from a recent burn soon streaked my pants black. The forester arrived. He worked with the state Division of Forestry, the lead management agency for this tract, which was almost two thousand acres, purchased in 1994. Previously it was owned by Champion International and managed as a quail-hunting preserve for the timber company's executive guests.

"This was their playground," Doug, the forester, said. He looked like Dustin Hoffman, clean shaven, with chocolate eyes and dark eyebrows; his black hair threw gray sparkles in new sunshine. It had been raining for two days and I was camping that night, so I welcomed the sun.

Dustin Hoffman drove me around the hunting roads. He answered questions, but he wasn't verbose. The trees were fifty to ninety-five years old, most around seventy-five. Foresters burned about 600 acres a year. Longleaf restoration was under way in the few fields on the property. The red-cockaded woodpecker cavities might have been abandoned—the birds hadn't been seen since 1994—although one cavity appeared active. He saw a bobcat there once.

He told me that gopher tortoises in the forest had been dying. Last year, after a prescribed burn that torched the waist-high grasses, between thirty and forty shells were found, glaring bone white against the scorched ground. "They were in different stages of decomposition," he said. "They didn't die in one year's time." In the forest across the highway, the loss was worse. "You could quickly count fifty shells."

Joan Diemer Berish, renowned tortoise researcher, tested live animals on the sites for the respiratory virus they can carry. The tests came back negative. Why, then, were the tortoises dying? Was it fragmentation of a landscape they depended on?

It wasn't until the forester showed me where to camp and told me the gate combination, just before he left, that I learned what lay inside him. He confided how much he loved his job, caring for the state forests. "You're excited about camping out here," he said. "It's kind of like that every day for me. Work is something I look forward to."

"You're a lucky man."

"I know," he said. "On every wood desk that's made, a skull and crossbones should be carved."

∞

At Blue Springs, I hiked for hours, miles in the forest, and was never bored. I spotted almost every species of woodpecker possible. A juvenile raccoon scrambled up a sapling and peered around at me. Deer tracks sprinkled the ground. In this one piece—almost two thousand acres—the longleaf forest could be what it was supposed to be. It could function, could have what it needed, even while it was surrounded by clearcuts and pine plantations and fields.

∽

That night, as a young owl made her harrowing cry in the dark, I was cradled in poetry. The next morning I rose early and walked again. Before I dismantled the tent, I again lay awake in it, loving the warmth, the quiet, the stillness, my drowsiness, two thousand lovely acres completely to myself, wondering again why it had been so long since I felt whole.

Most of the longleaf trees in the Blue Springs forest weren't old growth—their crowns hadn't begun to flatten, nor had they gone to heart pine. But they were close, closer than anything for hundreds of miles, a forest springing from the fields, plantations, and clearcuts. I wanted the forest left alone to be as whole as it could be. I wanted it to be what it had always been, what it wanted to be. I wanted it for all the years of my life, and beyond.

Family Reunion

After nineteen years of silence between her and my father, my sister, Kay, took up her pen and wrote a note addressed to both our parents. She signed it "love." My heart seemed to skip a beat when Mama showed me. We had waited years for one of them to make the first move at reconciliation.

I imagined Kay writing her letter surrounded by a bed of roses she planted herself; she is a small, lovely woman, whose fragility belies her strength, both inner and physical. The short note told of small news: sinus infections and summer soccer for Ian, her son. "The ordinary can be like medicine," Sherman Alexie says.

After nineteen years of silence, two people become strangers to each other, and it is better not to say much at first, but to start slowly, as Muslims might end a day of fast with a single bread date, then a segment of orange. Maybe after so long one should say nothing at all, but send a basket of dried figs and let them speak instead. We humans have proven that kinship is not inviolable, that it can be broken and broken again, and that to build it back we must set to mending.

My sister's note came in August. Kay's birthday falls in late June, and Mama had picked out a card from the flea market that said, "No obligations. No commitments. You don't even have to write back. I wanted you to know that I love you." After she bought it, she asked me what I thought of sending it to Kay. "It's wonderful," I said, and watched Mama sign it, then hand it to Daddy. He wrote "Papa" at the bottom. None of us ever called him Papa. He was Daddy, a man of tough love.

He was not asking his lost daughter, then, to love the father she knew, but the man he had become, with Social Security about to start and a hernia that needed fixing and a grandson he would not recognize on the street. This new father was more whole, less proud, more sane, more humble. One who regretted.

෮෮

The rift began over grits. My sister was fresh out of college and not long married, her Marine husband shipped off to Beirut, when she invited us to visit her in her new, lovely home outside Camp Lejeune. Mama, Daddy, and I drove up. Eager to please, my sister woke early the first morning of our visit to bake blueberry muffins. Ninety-five percent of the mornings of his life, our father had breakfasted on grits, eggs, and toast. Where had this daughter learned to eat blueberry muffins?

"What's this?" he asked, cranky from a bad night's sleep on the pullout couch. "Don't you have grits?"

Kay got mad. "This is my house and I made muffins. If you don't like it, you can leave."

Leave he did.

We had been raised in a fundamentalist, isolationist world—no drinking, no dancing, no pants, no makeup, no competition, no dating, no Halloween, no Easter, no

Christmas, no jewelry, no television. Daddy's was an iron hand. When my sister went away, she fell in love with the world—the grand, glorious, imaginative world. The wound between her and my father, deep down, was about a long history of dogmatism and inflexibility. Kay was establishing her independence, as we all must, and the separation was painful, as it often is.

There was a young man who left town sixty years ago, after a fight with his father that I do not want to recreate. I am told their angry words slashed like mule whips through the fields, bearing the pain and poverty of their lives. The words could not be unsaid. The boy shouted to his father, "You'll never lay eyes on my face again," and from that moment he was dead to the family. Where he was, no one knew, so when the old man died, years later, no one could call the son with the news, nor could they when his mother died. The parents left nothing to inherit, nothing to remember them by. Not long ago the boy, his own life lived, returned to be buried in this broken ground.

It has taken me years to understand that we have to trust, even when we're vulnerable, even when we have been hurt and may be hurt again. Family is more rewarding than pride, love and cooperation more honorable than fear. The soul is a jar, with each act of love and bravery earning us a thimbleful of wisdom. There are two ways of being in the world: you can choose fear, or you can choose love. Everything that is not love is fear. *What are you serving?* I ask myself constantly.

I think we must take risks to unite and reunite with our families. The hardest work of world change is what happens between two people, to open the deepest recesses of the heart.

Are you taking risks? I ask myself.

ɷ

For nineteen years my sister's place at the table had been empty. Sometimes a visitor sat there, but in general my father's table had shrunk. When I talked to Daddy, he would ask if I'd heard from Kay, and how she was. He realized how short life is—or how long—and how much he needed his daughter. He wanted her back but didn't know how to ask. "You have to apologize," I told him, "even if you feel you have nothing to apologize for." He practiced writing letters to my sister, and also to her little boy, and he read them to me, asking for an opinion that I freely gave: "You have to apologize." The letters didn't get mailed.

ɷ

A few years ago, when I was in graduate school in Montana, I was invited to spend Christmas with a friend's family in tiny McCall, Idaho, population 2,000. I was far from home and my son had flown back East to be with his father. My friend, Tom, kept telling me how wonderful Christmas would be. He came from a family of actors who ran the community theater and for years had performed an elaborate home circus, a real production, with clowns and bears and trapeze arts. "I was the lion," Tom laughed.

On Christmas Eve two of the uncles built a piñata,

an outlandish chicken with a blue head and tail and pink wings. Snow fell all day. That night there was a big party. Before dark the first friend arrived through the snow with a gingerbread house of beautiful, odd-colored candies. Someone else came with a braided challah, someone else with venison and wine, until the house was filled with people and food and music and light. When it was time for the Swedish Saint Lucia ceremony, the children came slowly down the stairs dressed in white, candles on their heads, reading parts that welcomed the return of the light. Tom had hung the piñata, and we closed around it, taking turns from the youngest (who was two) to the oldest (who was sixty-five) to be blindfolded and swing thrice. The piñata was wired and duct taped shut so well that by the time everyone had a turn it still hadn't burst, although the Christmas tree, cut from the family's woods and decorated with homemade ornaments, had been knocked over in the hilarity and resurrected. Finally we had to slit the piñata with a knife and dump out its treats.

People laughed and told stories. Some gathered around the blender, mixing brandy flips. We put on polkas and danced until late at night, until the neighbors left slowly through snow that had not stopped falling.

On Christmas morning, I was not forgotten but had a stocking over the fireplace like everybody else, and in it were dried fruits, candies, and nuts. When presents were distributed, they were simple things—a laundry basket, new socks, bubble bath—opened one by one and exclaimed over. I got a book to read to my son. I sat back from the hubbub, in a corner, watching wistfully the loving ways in which a family could interact. I have missed that joy.

What we all seek is intimacy, I have come to realize,

the deep canyon filled with the sound of rushing water
far below, where we find each other's spirits. Our differences force us to acknowledge the complexity of the human
psyche. In learning how to tell the truth about our compli-
cated lives, and in learning to accept the truth, we deepen
our relationships. We inhabit that beautiful canyon.

The closest our family came to this intimacy was the
Thanksgiving before Grandmama died in 1995.

The usual fear about being together surfaced
Thanksgiving morning; family events often included
someone saying something ill-tempered, or a tease being
ill-taken, and someone leaving with hurt feelings. Creating
a loving family felt hopeless, considering how our attempts
at family congeniality had failed in the past. One aunt was
jealous of her mother's favoritism toward a sister. Some
disliked an uncle, who was known for meanness. When
I called Mama, she said, "Why don't we have dinner
at home?"

"Is Uncle James still coming?" I asked.

"I guess so," she said.

"What about Uncle Percy?"

"He's talking about staying home too," she said.

When Silas and I arrived at my parents' house at
midmorning, I was surprised to find Mama's table bare;
instead, the potato salad, creamed corn, turkey, and dress-
ing were packaged to go. Mama said that she and Daddy
had resigned themselves to being with the whole family.

To return function to a family requires effort on the
behalf of the most fearful to move past fear. Or it takes a
few members who are determined to love each other, and
who will not allow discord to become divisive.

Uncle James blessed the food and the hands that had

prepared it, and all of us, our gathering together. He blessed family members not present, that they might be with us in spirit. He asked that we be guided by love. Amen.

We unbowed our heads and happily began to pass bowls of food. When I asked Silas if he wanted creamed corn, someone at the table said, "Here, eat some of this down here. This is very good. We made this."

"Okay," I said cheerfully, knowing that my own mother had made the corn at my end of the table.

"This is better," my relative insisted. "They do it differently than we do. They cut off the whole kernel."

Nobody said a word in reply, and the meal continued in good faith and spirit. One uncle ate in the kitchen, supposedly for lack of chairs around the big table, and vanished after dinner to a football game on TV in the back room, a room so full of smoke that no one ventured there except the other two male, smoking, football fans.

After dinner Aunt Joan turned to me and asked me to read aloud from a children's easy book she had brought. It was *Love You Forever* by Robert Munsch, about motherhood. As I read the story, voice breaking, Aunt Joan sang the repeated chorus, a lullaby, with me. Grandmama listened as if she understood, although her mind was failing her. She would not be with us much longer. We *would* love her forever.

When the book was done my aunt scooted to the kitchen, but not before everybody saw her eyes brimming. Mama sat where she was and wiped her eyes. Daddy bent down to tie his shoes until he had composed himself. We sat silent until the stories began: ghost stories, snake stories, war stories. Cameras appeared, flashed. Grandmama listened awhile, sometimes nonsensically joining in, then hobbled feebly to the sofa and fell asleep amid the party.

The conversation turned to deeper things: how Aunt Joan was plagued with nightmares. Always she was being chased. Her son, our cousin Doug, had them, too, she said. For the first time since Doug died a few years earlier, we heard his mother speak his name freely and we were relieved.

∞

I do not want to write anything that will cause hurt or shame. All I can say is that the hardest things I've ever done or will ever do involve repairing relationships, especially in my family, where the hurt and distress got laid in early. Sometimes it has meant slinking back to a person on hands and knees, asking forgiveness. Sometimes it has meant letting someone know that his or her conduct or words were unacceptable. I've acted in poor judgment, ignored honor, and failed at sagacity, but I also know that I long for kinship. I long for the refuge a family can offer. I long for love. To live with mistrust, isolation, and anger is to let our hurt speak for us, and nothing is more inexcusable. To do the work of opening the heart, of being vulnerable and full of love, of attempting to be what the Buddha called "a light," is so difficult that it sometimes feels easier to die; yet this work saves our lives.

Once, in the worst argument I ever had with my father, he asked me to leave his house and not come back. I stood gently but firmly in front of him and chanted, over and over: "You are my father and I love you and I'm not going anywhere. You are my father and I love you . . ."

Time and again I return to Adrienne Rich's wisdom, in her book *On Lies, Secrets, and Silence:*

> An honorable human relationship—that is, one in which two people have the right to use the word "love"— is a process, delicate, violent, often terrifying to both persons involved, a process of refining the truths they can tell each other.
>
> It is important to do this because it breaks down human self-delusion and isolation.
>
> It is important to do this because in so doing we do justice to our own complexity.
>
> It is important to do this because we can count on so few people to go that hard way with us.

A year after returning to Georgia, I decided to organize a family reunion. Grandmama had been the family's glue, and in losing her three years before, we had lost each other. I sent invitations. I asked people to bring a quilt that was special to them, maybe one Grandmama made, and to bring food.

Part of my agenda was to give my father the gift of his lost daughter. Not long before, he had said to me, "We should be able to get together one day a year, shouldn't we? Is that too much to ask?" The day before the reunion Kay called to say she wasn't coming. Disappointment turned my mouth metallic. I offered to drive the eight hours to get her, to meet her halfway, to pay for airline tickets. She was sending a small quilt she had made, she said. It should arrive on time. She wanted us to put names in a bowl and draw for it.

Uncle James arrived first, about 9 A.M. He would be back later with Aunt Joan, he said, just wanted to know if we needed anything. Before long, aunts and cousins started pouring in, until a small crowd of us sat around

Grandmama's house laughing and talking. The person who came the farthest drove ten hours, from Tennessee. Not everybody came, but enough did.

It was a magnificent day with not a hint of cloud. The yard flowers were holding their own festival, every azalea bud wide open, the irises in bloom, the wisteria wild with purple. The dining table held all the bowls and platters it could manage, and before we ate we gathered in a lopsided circle to hear Uncle James pray for a greater grace for our family. In the afternoon, we hid Easter eggs for the children, then rode down to the graveyard to pay homage to our ancestors. Most everybody stayed for supper.

The letter carrier slid a package from Kay into the mailbox midafternoon, and inside was a purple-toned table runner she had quilted. About three feet long, it was of the rail-and-square pattern, ending in a point at either end. Aunt Joan exclaimed over it the minute we pulled it from the box. It was obvious that having it would mean a lot to her.

We put names in a cup and I drew. The first one said "Uncle Percy," but when I called out his name, there followed a good-spirited uproar that Uncle Percy, being outside, didn't hear. "Draw again!" someone exclaimed. "Uncle Percy doesn't need it!" The cousins took up the cry. "Redraw!" I drew again and only pretended to read the name: Aunt Joan. "Hurrah!" everyone cheered. Aunt Joan squealed and cheered too.

A few days later, a neighbor stopped me in the post office. "I hear you had a family reunion on the weekend." She smiled.

"Yes, ma'am," I said.

"Keep having them," she said. "And they'll all come back."

Moody Swamp

W hen I was a girl, I heard of a mythic piece of
land along the Altamaha River in north Appling
County called Moody Swamp. Alligators marbled the
duckweed of the shadowy sloughs and in the bottoms
panther tracks slowly filled with dark water. People got
lost back in there; disoriented hunters spent nights in
hollow tupelos.

The land was owned by the Moody family, namely Jake
Moody, a spare man drawn by arthritis at a young age,
whose fiery eyes bored out from whitened photographs.
Jake was a pioneer conservationist whose epic love for the
tall pines is a story we still tell.

Jake never married. When he died, he willed Moody
Swamp to the three unmarried children of his brother's
second marriage. He specified that they were not to cut a
stick of timber unless absolutely necessary, a promise he
had given his own father before him. Through the lives of
the two nephews and the niece, Jake's plan worked. None
of them married, and they lived simply in their heart-pine
cabins, eking out money for taxes.

Word about Moody Swamp circulated among conserva-
tionists. Stretching along two miles of the wild Altamaha,
the 3,500-acre property contained some of the best river-
bottom left in the South. The uplands included one of
the last pieces of virgin longleaf pine forest left anywhere,
replete with fox squirrels and gopher tortoises. A tree-ring

scientist came and bored the trees and found longleafs over 200 years old, and massive bald cypress 200 to 600 years old. Archeologist Frankie Snow found 11,000-year-old scrapers and projectiles in archaeological sites along the Altamaha River near Moody property.

Yet the Moody siblings refused to consider for a moment selling the property, even for preservation. They had a promise to keep.

The first time I saw Moody Swamp with my own eyes was in late 1992, long before I moved back. Ornithologist Todd Engstrom, a scholar of red-cockaded woodpeckers, having heard stories about the virgin longleaf pine, suggested we go see the place for ourselves.

On a brisk winter day Todd and I pulled in front of the shotgun cabin where the Moody heirs lived. A thin, graceful woman in her eighties came out onto the porch, into the nipping cold, and invited us in before she even had an idea of who we were. Her long, brindle-colored braids, thin as ring-necked snakes, wrapped and joined at the top of her head. That was Miss Elizabeth Moody.

Inside, a small fire licked at a couple of oak logs in the fireplace. Beside the hearth, a heavy, pink-faced man dressed in a pair of faded overalls hunched in a rocker.

"Get up here to the fire and warm your faces and hands," Miss Elizabeth said. The fireplace, completely blackened with soot, had been hand laid out of thick bricks, its hearth set even with the scuffed linoleum floor.

"Miss Elizabeth, I'm Beulah Branch's granddaughter," I said.

"Yes, yes. You're Lee Ada's daughter," Elizabeth said. "This is my brother, Wade."

"How is Miss Beulah?" Wade asked. His family had

Jake Moody's heart-pine cabin at the Moody Forest.

been friends of my grandparents—Grandpa Arthur was mechanic for their father, Joe, and their uncle Jake. Our two families had settled the land together, farmed together, traded labor and goods. I'd been told we were kin, but we were not—not by blood. It is a common history, including the unique struggle with the limitations and possibility of place, that joins the yeomen of a region; in a clan, chance knows no one by name. Of course Wade and Elizabeth would welcome me like family.

At that time Grandmama was living, but she had Alzheimer's, and someone had to stay with her almost constantly. My mother and aunts were afraid for her to cook anymore: she left burners on and scorched food. She caught potholders afire. Sometimes she talked about the cows being out when they weren't and about purty little ducks she'd seen in the yard when there had been none.

"Sit down if you will," Miss Elizabeth said. "The old chairs ain't much." Four chairs were clustered around the fire, three of them rockers, in a room that held no television or radio that I saw. An outdated naugahyde couch, smoky-brown with dust, took up the back wall, and along it framed photographs of schoolchildren leaned.

They wanted to know how my mother and father were, how Uncle Percy fared. Neither of them inquired after our business. Long moments in our visit were filled with the whispers of flames. The cabin was about twenty by twenty-four feet, fashioned of hand-hewn heart-pine logs, squared off, fit flawlessly together without nails by dovetail joints at the four corners. Its walls inside were a deep amber, dusty from years next to a red clay road. In some places, where wall met chimney, for example, the wood didn't fit perfectly and sky shone through the walls. Where one window frame met the wall, cracks were big enough to slide silver dollars through.

"What a wonderful house," Todd said. "When was it built?"

"This house is over a hundred years old," Wade said. The kitchen, he told us, was separate, joined by a wooden uncovered walk called a breezeway. In pioneer times cabins were completely constructed of highly flammable heart pine, from the foundation to the wood shingles. Houses burned frequently, so people began to build kitchens separate from the main structures, since cookstoves were apt to set walls afire.

Wade and Elizabeth were happy to have company, confined to home as they seemed to be by loss of agility, and by winter to the environs of the fireplace, with no other heat in

the house. Above the mantel hung a picture of Joe Moody—
her daddy, Elizabeth explained. He died in 1952, the same
year as Jake. A huge iron bed crowded one corner of the
room, near a table covered with a worn quilt made with
gathered circles of cloth. A chest with odds and ends on top,
including a kerosene lantern, stood against the back wall,
next to more pictures. One was a plaque I could read from
where I sat. "To the Moodys. For taking care of the forest."

When we finally asked Wade about the woods, he
glowed. "So you've heard about the big timber," he said,
and he began to tell stories. After awhile we asked could
we walk out through the woods and Wade said, "Be glad
for you to. Wish I could come along."

From the county road, the tract of longleaf appeared
overgrown and messy, in need of a good hot burn. The
two-path road leading in was full of bogholes. In sections,
the fence was down. But that is not what I saw.

The trees: they were tall longleaf, crowns flattened in
the habit of old growth of that species. Here was virgin
pine, timber that had never been logged, that the Creek
Indians had stood beneath, that had been standing when
Oglethorpe landed his debtor's prisoners in the new colony named after King George. Most trees of this caliber
had been laid low at the turn of the century by sawmen;
this wood was a miracle, a monument. Todd and I walked
into the forest, he jotting names of birds. A ruby-crowned
kinglet cheeped in agitation, no more than four feet away.

Then Todd spotted a candle tree. It was a cavity tree!
We were in the middle of a red-cockaded woodpecker
colony, the trees here and there marked with resinous
patches, called candles, where the birds had pecked at resin
wells around their nesting cavities. The sticky resin deters

predatory snakes. Despite the underbrush and catface scars, we were in a real forest that could be returned to complete function. All the elements, except fire, were present. In that moment, I saw how I belonged. Across our Cracker history flows the signature of longleaf pine, the endless forests that greeted the first inhabitants. If a landscape could be returned to function, so could a family, and a community. I could be returned to a life rooted in the fullness of place.

By the time I visited the Moody Forest again, a year later, Wade had died. It was raining and the clay road was slicker than a ballroom floor. I crept down it, slipping from ditch to ditch. The farm looked the same. The 1950 Ford the Moodys still used was parked under the shed. I cut my engine in front of the yard gate and peered through the rain, swiping at fog on the windshield. The house was unlit. Where was Miss Elizabeth? Then I noticed what appeared to be a head in the doorway. Sure enough, she crossed the porch to the half sheet of frayed plywood that kept the dog from coming up the steps and knocking over her flowers. I dashed toward the house, skipping puddles along the line of curled boards that served as a walkway. Miss Elizabeth grabbed me.

"I'm so proud you came to visit," she said, then grabbed me again. Her hair, still tinted golden at eighty-five, was in the same matching braids that wrapped around her head, meeting on top.

I wasn't sure she remembered me. "I'm Lee Ada and Frank's daughter," I reminded her. "Beulah's my grandma. I came by about a year ago." She hugged me again.

"Course I remember you," she said.

In the house, she turned on the light. The house looked different—one of her nephews had refinished the

inside walls with pressboard. It was bright, new looking.
I could see outside only through one small crack. A new
air-conditioning unit stuck out of the wall.

Miss Elizabeth was ambivalent about the changes,
even saddened. She told me that Wade had been failing, becoming increasingly bedridden. The doctor said
he needed an easier life, amenities like running water. He
needed air-conditioning for his health.

Wade took to having crying spells, she said, would
break down often, saying how much he hated to leave her.
He knew death was near. "I couldn't hardly take that," she
said. "Even after the stroke he would sometimes boo-hoo."

The family decided to fix up the house for Wade's sake,
even put in a bathroom. The day the workers arrived in
June, Wade had a stroke. She said she thought that fixing
up the house hurt Wade. Elizabeth hand-fed him during
those next months, until he died on January 3, 1994.

"We buried him in overalls," Elizabeth said. "That's
the way he would have wanted it. They was new ones, of
course." She spat a thin jet of snuff juice toward the fireplace, which wasn't lit, a black oven of rocks, two simple
firedogs.

"I heard they might move a trailer in for you," I said.

"I was born in this house," Miss Elizabeth replied, "and
I tell them I'd like to stay here as long as I can."

A month later, on the phone long-distance, Mama told
me she'd heard that some of Wade's woods were being cut
to pay estate taxes. Suddenly I was faced with the loss of
what was left, a forest that marked the continuation, the respect, the tradition, the home that I longed for. I contacted
the Nature Conservancy of Georgia, because I'd learned
that organization was interested in buying the piece. Their

land-acquisitions director, Andrew Schock, wanted me to find out what was going on. It was late October of 1994, still three years before I would return to live in south Georgia, when I made a special trip to see Miss Elizabeth.

The fall had been one of the wettest on record. We were up near seventy inches for the year, someone said. Although it had rained sledgehammers the night before, East River Road appeared passable, thick with orange mud.

The farm was on top of the muddiest hill of all. Gripping the wheel, I motored the truck up the clay hill and pulled under the familiar live oak, again admiring the house, sided with raw pine that had aged into a warm, amber loveliness. Its patchwork porch sloped toward a pebbled groove cut into the front yard by rain dripping off the eaves. A huge four-o'clock, out of bloom, thrived half under the overhang.

Miss Elizabeth was already on the porch, peering out.

I identified myself, remembering she had recently undergone cataract surgery. The doctors operated first on her best eye, so her vision was at this moment more impaired than ever. Blindness didn't interfere with Elizabeth's trust. She was already swinging back the plywood scrap.

"Come in. Come in. Thank you for coming," she said.

She hugged my neck. She was dressed this time in sweatpants of a frothy green, her light-blue overshirt fastened by a safety pin, white sneakers on her feet. She poked the fire up. Why, yes, her eye felt fine, she said. Her voice lilted, her sentences ending in vocal curlicues.

"Did you remember the time change tomorrow?" she asked. "Have to set back your clocks."

"Yes, ma'am." I'd noticed the last visit that she didn't follow the time changing. During daylight savings time,

the clock on the mantel and the one on the back wall ran
an hour off.

Before we could say more, the phone rang. It was an
old-fashioned rotary phone with a full-bodied peal, not
the whine of the new touch-tones. Elizabeth sprang to her
feet, nimble and spritely, and dashed unsteadily the few
feet to the phone.

"Hello," she yelled into the receiver. Someone was asking about her eye.

"Good, good." To the caller's inquiries, Elizabeth yelled
answers, as if her voice needed to carry the actual miles to
the person's house. After the conversation wound down,
Elizabeth delivered her final soliloquy.

"I shore appreciate you calling and checking on me." A
quick breath. "I'm doing fine, I'd be proud for you to visit,
thank you for calling." Down went the receiver.

Elizabeth returned to the quietness of our rocking. The
fire crackled, licking the bottoms of the oak logs. I got
up and fetched a log from the back porch. Out through
the cold ran the walkway to the kitchen, and now off the
porch a new door opened into a modern bathroom. I'd
never been to the kitchen, only as far as the back porch.

I came back in, poked up the fire, and asked her about
the timbering. She hadn't seen it—just one load of trees
parked at Sam Beasley's store. Then she said the same
things she'd said the visit before, how she thought it was
easier to have nothing, how Wade and Causs (the third
sibling, dead a number of years) had hated to cut even one
stick of timber, how the government was about to take
everything they had.

As I sat there, surrounded by the simplicity and
outdatedness of her life, a recurring hopelessness overcame

me. Miss Elizabeth had not been trained to make business decisions. The way we were both raised, girl-children were to be seen and not heard. Women were not to express opinions but to serve as their husbands' helpmeets. Since woman came from the rib of man, equality was impossible.

For years I'd struggled to overcome those limitations. I'd determined to be adventuresome, courageous, outspoken, daring, demanding, even rude. Deciding to act against injustice, on all kinds of levels, took a summoning of nerves and collecting of wits on my part; it took both arming and steeling myself. Sometimes my boldness met with success, but more often than not it left me defeated, wings clipped, full of tears.

Even as I had driven away from my parents' house that morning, my father had warned me to mind my own business. "Don't push this too far," was what he said. What I wanted my father to say was, "Many daughters have done courageously, but thou excellest them all." I couldn't accept hopelessness. A rare virgin forest full of endangered species *could* be saved for good.

We heard a truck, then footsteps on the porch, and Edsel, Elizabeth's nephew, pushed open the door. He was dressed in a baseball cap, blue jeans, good work boots and a flannel shirt. He was shy, wouldn't look at me, so I didn't introduce myself right off. He asked Elizabeth how she was. His voice had a slight impediment.

Elizabeth asked if he knew who I was, and then she told him. We said hello and chatted. "What do you do?" I asked.

"Drive a timber truck," he replied. "I work for J.D.'s Timber." For a minute my breath suspended. That was the company timbering the land. I released a breath and asked him a question. Been at it four weeks, he said. Hauled over 300 loads so far. Few weeks to go. May have to quit awhile because of the rain. Yeah, he'd take me to look at it.

"Miss Elizabeth, do you want to go?"

"No, honey." I'd heard that even when her brothers were alive she wouldn't go back with the men to look at the timber. She thought it was her obligation to stay at the house. Wouldn't even get her picture taken.

Edsel and I headed west, then north toward the river, through farm pastures and timberland. We passed underneath the big power lines that strung electricity from Hatch Nuclear Plant to run far-off people's televisions, air conditioners, and streetlights. Although we were deep in the woods, the road was busy, truck after truck of cruising hunters dressed in gray or green camouflage, so close the sides of our vehicles almost scraped. The Moodys had allowed access for hunting and fishing, Edsel told me, as long as folks kept the cows in.

"One of the last places around here like that," he said. We kept pulling off the one-lane road to let the hunters pass.

"Do you know all these men?" I asked.

"They're from the neighborhood," he said.

"Are they good people?"

"What you see is what you get," he replied.

I locked the passenger door.

He heard the lock go down. "I always carry a little back-up with me," he said.

The road narrowed further, and soon I could see signs of logging ahead—the dull orange of heavy machinery parked among the trees, this being a Saturday. Then we were in the middle of it.

Loggers had decimated a forest. You could see that the trees had been huge, because the sawyers had left catfaces,

the bottom six or so feet of trees that had been turpen-
tined, their slashed side potentially hazardous to sawmill
blades, and some of those stumps were as big around as
phone booths.

"They're cutting everything," I moaned.

"Not everything," Edsel replied. "They're leaving six
trees to the acre. Those are the seed trees."

It didn't take a college professor to see that the trees
left for reseeding weren't more than six inches in diameter,
and not longleaf. They looked like slash. The ground was
littered with young trees and with limbs from trees that
had been overrun in order to get to the bigger trees. The
heavy machinery had torn the ground until it looked like
a field fresh plowed by a crazy fool on a runaway tractor.
In spots the ground resembled a forest floor, with pine
needles and remnant wiregrass.

"I hate it," Edsel was saying. "I wish they could've
come in and selective cut."

"They could've," I said. I was angry. "Why didn't they?"
He was the one who worked for the company.

"I don't know," he said. The executor of Wade's estate
had made the decision to do this. "I think this'll be the last
of the cutting," he said, "until Aunt Elizabeth dies."

"What then?" I asked.

"Elizabeth says it'll be divided among the in-laws." By
that he meant extended kin.

"Will they cut it?"

"I tell you the truth," he stammered. "When Aunt
Elizabeth dies, all this may look like a cemetery."

Many of my people are squirrely, suspicious of government and of each other, clannish, used to being poor, to
not having much. I'd been raised with this attitude—accept
what you can't change and assume that there's not much

that you can. My people would sit back, silenced by a society of manners, and by will-lessness and low self-esteem,
and let a magnificent old-growth forest get destroyed.

This is how our history fails: loss of forest, of farms,
of elders. That the past slips away does not preoccupy me,
but how it passes does. Important, irreplaceable things are
being lost.

Edsel and I eased through the devastating clearcut until
we reached a line of pink tape in the trees. "Here's where
the cutting ends," he said. "That's all Aunt Elizabeth's land,
all the way down to the river, but we won't cut any farther
back for now."

I told him about the Nature Conservancy, people who
buy land to preserve it. He listened. "Pass the word," I
said. "Even after Miss Elizabeth dies, it'd be better to sell
the land than to timber it. There's no need for this forest
to come down."

Elizabeth waited with chilled Cokes when we got
back to the cabin. The day had warmed until it was colder
inside than outside, but still a weak fire labored to warm
the house. Elizabeth invited me to use the bathroom if I
needed it, said even though she had a real bathroom now,
sometimes she forgot to offer it.

After that, every time I was in Baxley I visited with Miss
Elizabeth. I sat with her because she hoed my history like
a garden. Since she was both a child and an elder of this
place, and with my own grandmother dying, Elizabeth kept
the past alive for me. Perhaps from her, I thought, I could
learn how to be an elder, how to hang onto the things that
mattered, how to be a true daughter of the pine flatwoods.

Three Deadbolts and a Female Socket

Jimmy Johnson courted me a little toward the end of high school. He sent flowers a few times, and frequented the public library where I worked after school, supposedly to check out books. He had not long before graduated college with a journalism degree, although when he returned to Baxley it was to run his daddy's hardware store and lumber supply.

I was rather high-handed with him. When he sent red carnations I said, "Thank you, but I prefer wildflowers," and before I knew it a florist's courier delivered a huge bouquet of outlandish lilies and purple orchids to our door. I was interested in leaving, then, when he was returning, and we were young. Nothing ever came of the gestures toward romance.

So when I returned to live in Baxley, it was with a thumping heart that I took my first hardware business to Hunter Johnson Lumber, hoping to renew a friendship. Jimmy had married the beautiful high school physics teacher, my friend, and they had a bright-eyed daughter.

Jimmy was behind the counter. He looked exactly the same. He stared at me a few seconds longer than anyone would casually, then said, "Well, hey!"

"Hey, Jimmy," I said, as if I still checked out his books at the library. But you can't undo the fact you've been away eighteen years.

"What can I do for you?" he asked, somewhat coolly, I thought. I explained what I needed, a piece of two-inch plastic pipe and some glue. He led me toward the rear of the store.

"Are you visiting or home for good?" he asked.

"For now," I said. "Maybe for good."

"Where you living?"

"In my grandmother's house, out in Spring Branch Community."

"Well, it's good to see you."

"You, too."

After that, if I needed a fitting or a gallon of paint I bought it from Jimmy. One day he asked if I was writing. "I've seen a few of your pieces in the paper."

I told him I was attempting to do so. I had recently authored a miniscule grant that brought six writers to our library for public readings, one a month, and Jimmy had been coming, with Miriam. I had noticed during the question and answer sessions that he asked questions about writing.

"What about you?" I asked. "Are you a writer?"

"Working on a novel," he said. "It may not get published, but I'm writing it."

"You interested in a writers group if we got a couple other people? To read each other's work and critique it?"

"Probably," he said.

At the next reading at the library, I announced that anybody interested in forming a writer's group should let me or Jimmy know. A man appropriately named Wright, who looked like John Denver, said, "Count me in." Jimmy knew of another guy writing a novel who worked at the nuclear plant, and he called him.

"I'll try it," the guy said. His name was Steve.

Our first meeting convened in a low-ceilinged room in the back of the hardware store. Around us were shelves with catalogs detailing tools and rope and hardware, big notebooks of paint samples, and boards illustrating different kinds of tile and molding. The business computer clicked away in a corner, doing the accounting.

I liked Jimmy, and I liked Wright, and when the last writer walked in, I thought I'd bust from so much liking. He had bright mischievous eyes and a thick cowboy mustache down around his chin.

From the start, we had a lot of fun, although we were nervous sometimes, when our own pieces were on the table. We didn't slam each other too badly, and we tried to include praise, even if we said a lot of disagreeable things.

Nobody ever wanted to go first, and from our initial meeting we started a meticulous system of order, sometimes drawing straws—shortest straw starting—or Jimmy writing four numbers on scraps of paper and us picking. I had to be strict about time. I left Silas with his grandparents, and if the group started at seven and finished at nine, that still put him late getting to bed. With two hours, we had thirty minutes each, fifteen to read aloud, fifteen to hear comments. I was timekeeper. I'd ruthlessly call, "Time's up," when thirty minutes had elapsed.

About eight the first night a mockingbird began singing loudly from somewhere in the building.

"Is that a mockingbird in the store?" I asked.

"To kill a mockingbird," Steve joked. "Why would you want to do that, Jimmy?"

"It's in the clock," Jimmy said.

"The clock? How did it get in the clock?" They laughed.

"One of those bird clocks people are tipsy over."

"Oh."

Jimmy was writing evenings after work, trying hard for serious fiction. Wright wrote nautical adventure, mystery on the high seas. He had at least one novel finished that he had not been able to sell. Steve had a couple of novels completed; they were dark fantasy. I wrote nonfiction essays about nature. Sometimes Jimmy brought in a poem, or Steve an essay.

I looked forward to our meetings. Being around other writers was fantastic, especially since they were from my town. Jimmy would read something from his novel about a young guitar picker who fell in love with a girl in a blue dress.

"You've got her staying at the Patterson house, don't you? You made it into a boardinghouse. And that's Virginia's Diner she's working at, isn't it?"

In a story, the bank sign would tell the temperature, and we could imagine that sign. We had all seen it read 100 degrees. When someone wrote about driving through the no-stoplight town of Surrency, which was famous for a ghost, we could see the place. Our town became real in a whole new unreal way for us.

∽

Writers are desperate for any kind of advice. Mostly we try to learn rules that will make us good writers. It's like any trade; you want axioms: Sand with the grain of the wood. If you're nailing near the edge, drill nail holes first.

Rules make a process easier. If we follow the rules, we think, maybe we'll get better. Maybe we'll get published.

We talked about everything. How to make dialogue interesting. How to show not tell. How to use action verbs. How to avoid unnecessary words, how to write sparingly. Anything we heard or read that might make us better writers, if it came from a published writer, we attempted.

"I'm trying not to use adjectives," Steve proclaimed one session. This was an odd announcement, for had adjectives been cows Steve would be lead cowpoke. One character had an inescapable grip of strength, another a melancholic despair. An ivory cheek glowed with fiery pain.

Relentlessly and heartlessly we pointed out redundant, bloodless adjectives, merciless in our scouring. Steve listened, his eyes occasionally narrowing. "You've got to have a thick skin and you gotta want to write," he said. "Because this is a study in humiliation."

I quit using the word "just." "It's filler," I insisted.

"Good thing there's a search button on the computer," Wright said.

"I heard a bunch of sentences beginning with 'there is' and 'there are,'" Jimmy said. "You'd best search for those."

Of course we realized that magic in writing springs not from a Book of Laws but from a territory of lawlessness. But we tried the shortcuts. We experimented. We practiced. We searched and deleted.

Jimmy got on a kick about not using the passive voice. So adamant was he that he quit using the word "was."

"The words 'just' and 'was' do not appear in this section," he told us as he began his fifteen minutes of reading one evening. The next month he told us, "I now have seventy pages that don't contain the words 'just' or 'was.'"

After that, sometimes someone would ask, "What's the 'was' count in that piece?"

"Seven," Jimmy would say. Or three. Or none. Once after reading a piece of mine, Jimmy stared. "How many times can you use the w-word in one paragraph?" he asked.

"What can you do about 'was clinking'?"

"I don't know. 'Clinked,' or 'clunk'? 'The ice clunk in his crystal goblet'?"

"Where's the dictionary?"

"Hardware stores don't need dictionaries."

"You better go home and look that up. I think it's 'clunk.'"

"'Clunk'?"

For some time we lazily tried to invent a name for our writers group, bandying titles about. "All writers groups have names," Jimmy said. "What if we start a movement? Like the New Agrarians." Because we lived in the pine flatwoods, Jimmy suggested Longleaf Pine Writers and then South Georgia Writers and others, but nothing rang true.

"We could be the Not Was Writers Group," Jimmy quipped one evening.

"The Wasn't Writers," Steve said. We laughed so hard we pounded the table.

Steve returned the next month with another suggestion. "I've thought of a name for us," he said.

"Oh yeah?"

"I was trying to think of hardware, since we meet here."

"Spit it out."

"Three Deadbolts and a Female Socket."

We guffawed. Three deadbolts and a female socket. Although the men never really liked it, I thought it the best name of all.

ɷɔ

We met for a long time like this, in the back of the hardware store, where we tentatively but bravely read our fragile, raw stories, hoping to make them sing. While we counted words behind a CLOSED sign, life went on in our town. Grass got mowed, babies were born, the football team went to state. Another fast-food restaurant got built. One night we emerged to sirens and flashing blue lights. The small-engine repair across the highway had caught fire and was awash, floor to roof, in flames. Firefighters dashed to and fro in yellow coveralls, from shadow to leaping light, like actors on a burning stage. We could hear their urgent calls above the hissing and popping of the fire. Thick, black smoke roiled, spreading its pall over the east side of town.

"You miss a lot being a writer," Jimmy said.

After a year Wright dropped out to remodel his house on the river, and Randy joined us. He wrote mysteries, too, technical intrigue set in southern Georgia. Jimmy published a story in the *Atlanta Journal-Constitution*. Steve won a writing prize at a conference. The first book I wrote came out. With the obligatory readings and signings, finding a date to meet that accommodated everybody's schedule became harder. I missed some meetings.

The next thing we knew, Jimmy unexpectedly sold the hardware store. "I want to do something else," he said. "Another life. Write more."

"There goes our name," Steve said.

We kept meeting—at Jimmy's brother's law office, at the Mexican restaurant, at my house, at Steve's. Jimmy got an editorial published in the *Orlando Sentinel* and a rave review on a novel he submitted to a contest. He started a second novel. Steve's book *Gothica: Romance of the Immortals* was accepted and published, and he started doing signings. He was a voluminous writer, now working on his third or fourth book-length manuscript. Randy wrote every day and got a rejection letter that made him hopeful. We kept meeting.

I've lived in places where so much happened that you had to choose, evening to evening, to stay home or go out, and if you chose out, you had to decide which event to attend. In our rural place, sometimes the writers group would be the only event that happened all month for me. It was community within community, it was succor, it was friendship, it combated the gigantic isolation. Our group clicked, it swung on its hinges, it got nailed down. Maybe we didn't create a literary movement with Baxley, Georgia, at its vortex. And maybe we did.

Wild Card Quilt

On winter days Mama took to cutting and sewing when I was not there, during weeks when I couldn't find a free evening. She wanted to sew a square a day.

"Look what I've done," she said when Silas and I appeared for supper. She brought a shank of squares to the kitchen table. At first our work fit a shoebox. Now it needed a wicker basket.

"This one," I said. "Nice."

Then, "Wow. This is beautiful."

Flowers frequented Mama's feminine and complex squares. Laid next to them, mine were elementary, reckless. Even a child would be able to divide hers from mine.

"I don't know if you'll like them," Mama said. "You can have the ones you like for your quilt, and I'll start another quilt with the rest."

Every square was fascinating in its own way. Her quilt squares told of meekness, gentleness, long-suffering, wisdom. They saluted a strength to keep going, to put food on the table when you didn't know where it was coming from, to love even when things had fallen apart. The flower-spangled squares told that my mother had been through fire and was not charred. Some worked better than others, but repetition of pattern would overwhelm any one failed square. Plus I banked on the wild card my mother throws that turns out quilts with character. With my mother's hands in a quilt, it would be well wrought, and fine.

I helped Mama put supper on the table. We all ate, then she and I cleared dishes to the counter and wiped down the eating table. We'd wash up later.

The quilting business piqued my father's interest. He wanted to tell me my squares were unattractive. Not only did he want to tell me, he wanted to prove it with a quick survey of public opinion. Ten squares were complete, and he spread them on the table. He pointed out his favorite, second favorite. Third. My brother, who lives with them, followed suit. His and my father's tastes are nearly identical, and both chose squares my mother had sewed—one pink and flowery, another with a rusty tone, the color of scorched sweet potatoes. Back in the '70s, dresses of this color were popular. Our friend Lewis, whom we've known much of our lives and who is like a brother to me, had eaten with us. He chose three florals. On one count he differed from my father and brother. His first place looked like kitchen curtains we once had. Silas picked one of mine.

Daddy wanted Mama to name her favorite, but she is a mender.

If our differences were simply a matter of preference, they wouldn't matter, but the men in my family can't understand what is wrong with me that I don't see what they see. Why can't I see the God they know? I said Mama's squares were pretty, but that I liked these bolder colors, these hot browns and vivid yellows, patches of cloth that have snipped off the feathers of a printed swallow-tailed bird. I said to the men that our tastes were different, and that was a good thing.

Even with only five of my squares stitched, I could see

what this quilt would look like, and it would be magnificent. It might take a year to complete, but it would be worth every stuck finger, every hour of work, every argument.

"Let's cut tonight," Mama said. "I can sew when you're not here."

"You don't have to work without me," I said. "We'll get it done."

"I enjoy it."

When the men left the kitchen, Mama and I took out our paper patterns, cut from shopping bags, and tested the five or six pairs of scissors we had collected, hunting again the two sharpest pairs.

"What will go with this green?" she asked me. I plundered through the cloth we had brought down from the sewing room.

"How about that piece I just had? The blue and green gingham. Here."

Another time Mama laid six or seven pieces of cloth adjoining and wanted me to say what went with what. She told me that when she was a girl and her mother was quilting, Grandmama would bury herself in material, stacks everywhere, in the back bedroom. Beulah was very particular about what matched. It had to be the right shade of pink.

"Mama, is this corduroy too heavy for the quilt?"

She took it, fingered it deliberately, looked at me with her warm brown eyes. I couldn't get used to her glasses.

"I *think* it'll work," she told me.

I remembered a good story. "I was talking to Mrs. Spell the other day," I said. "You know who I mean, Deanna's mama?"

"Yeah," she said, with that sweet, sweet smile. She was maneuvering straight pins meticulously through fabric.

"She used to take care of her daddy-in-law when he was old. He lived right there in the house with them, and she was the one took all the care of him, cooked and helped him with his clothes and all. They liked each other and she didn't mind doing for him, so when he died she was tore up, she said. She said she couldn't stop crying."

"Hmmm," Mama said. "I don't remember her daddy-in-law living with her. I knew he lived out in the area. But I didn't keep up with them, of course."

"She told me that the day of the funeral, right after he was buried, a little black dog showed up at their house. They live in the country, you know, way out Poor Robin Road, and she said she knew all the dogs in the neighborhood, and suddenly there's this little black dog looking well fed and everything. Right after they got home from the funeral, one of the children came in and said there was a little dog outside and the next thing Mrs. Spell knew, the dog had come to the back door, which was screen, and pushed it open. The dog walked in the house like he knew the place."

"She thought it was her daddy-in-law, didn't she?" Mama said.

"That's what she thought."

"Come back as a dog?"

I nodded. "He stayed a few days, then disappeared, she said."

"I don't know."

"Me either."

In a long, cozy silence, Mama studious in her spectacles, we fluttered through the cloth.

"Have you ever known a man who quilted?" I asked her.

"No," she said at first, then remembered. "Yes, I have. The Gaskin boys. All of those boys quilted."

"Did you ever see a quilt they made?"

"Yes, I did. They were good quilts."

"Were they flowery?"

"As far as I can remember, yes. Like other quilts."

"Did the men work in the fields like other men?"

"Sure," she said. "They quilted at night. Their mama taught all of them how."

"I guess most men would scoff at the idea of making a quilt."

"I guess so."

"Some of the best cooks I know are men. They could probably make beautiful quilts too."

"I don't know."

"Wonder why some women quilt and some don't?"

"Laziness, I think." She paused to look at me. "I don't mean to speak badly of anyone, but people will say they don't have the patience to sit and sew. But they'll want somebody else to make them a quilt."

As the weeks passed, our stack of quilt squares grew, until the basket was so heavy we quit lugging it down-stairs each time we got together. Mostly now we just cut squares, because Mama got so many of them sewed in the between days. Sometimes we cut shapes for an hour, then sewed for another hour. One day Silas and I dropped by and Mama said she had counted the squares and we had eighty of them, more than enough for a queen-size quilt. Enough for two quilts.

That night I picked out the squares that I wanted for my quilt, and Mama took the rest. We hauled mine to her queen-size bed and laid them out, trying to keep the attic fan from blowing them around. Outside the screened windows the car noises were quieting; I heard cicadas in the trees. I put the two most beautiful squares, the ones with pieces of swallow-tailed kite, midway down the quilt so they wouldn't be hidden by pillows. I chose four with turquoise for the corners. Then Mama and I floated above the bed with squares in our hands, like two monarchs, arranging the garden below, careful to balance the red salvia with the green coontie with the orange fireweed, not too many dark- or light-colored squares in any one area. We arranged, backed up to study the quilt, rearranged.

To cover the bed, the quilt needed to be six squares wide and seven squares long. Forty-two squares. I positioned my favorite square where I would be able to gaze at it when I lay down. Finally I was satisfied. The quilt would be gorgeous, exactly what I wanted. We dismantled the arrangement carefully, for this was how we would sew the squares together, left to right, top to bottom. Each stack was a row.

Two weeks lapsed before I showed up to begin sewing the squares together. This work went faster, because now we were seeing the whole thing come together. The quilt was soon bigger than our laps, spreading across the couch and then across the room, and we bundled up its corners while we worked. At the end of one evening, we were half finished.

The next Sunday evening, we finished the quilt-top. We took it upstairs and spread it out on the bed to admire. We'd gotten confused sometimes while sewing the squares together, and their sequence was not the one we had arranged so painstakingly. By chance, though, the colors turned out to be well balanced, and the quilt-top was beautifully designed. One by one, the men trudged up to admire it, grudgingly.

"Turned out better than I thought it would," my father said with a nod and a quick smile.

It was not the turquoise forest I had dreamed it would be, nor the plum thicket. It was so much more than that. I couldn't stop looking at it. The quilt was the perfect picture of my mother's love for me, and mine for her: steady yet surprising, sweet yet firm, well sewn and practical, yet a bright-colored work of art even a violet-green swallow would be proud to nest in. She and I were woven into beauty.

A Natural Almanac

While here I stand, not only with the sense
Of present pleasure, but with pleasing thoughts
That in this moment there is life and food
For future years.
    —William Wordsworth, "Lines Composed
      a Few Miles Above Tintern Abbey"

A farm's is a meditative kind of existence. One could live many places happily, but some situate you closer to nature and the intricacies of survival; closer to the seasons and the cycles of moon and sun and stars; closer to the ground, which chambers water and is host to essential ingredients of life.

To pay attention to the world, where forests bend according to the wind's direction, rivers bring baskets of granite down from the mountains, and cranes perform their long, evolutionary dances, is a kind of religious practice. To acknowledge the workings of the world is to fasten ourselves in it. To attend to creation—our wild and dear universe—is to gain admission into life. One can live at the bone. This I wished to do.

Details define the farm: the arrival and departure of birds, wildflower blooms, habits of animals, ripening of fruit, passing of cold fronts. The more attention we pay a certain place, the more details we see, and the more attached we become to it. That's how it's been for my friend Milton, a naturalist who has lived over fifty of his seventy-odd years on the family farm near Osierfield, Georgia.

Imagine what he has seen there. Some years ago, he attended a conference in the Midwest and was homesick within a couple of days. "I wouldn't trade the whole state of Kansas for the farm," he said.

East of my house, beyond the dirt road, rises a five-foot bank of peach-colored clay, and above it a fencerow of young oaks. Beyond them the sun rises every morning, streaming out of the flat field like a gigantic epiphany. One morning at breakfast, clouds began to open up and show pink and orange in the east. "Look, it's heaven!" Silas said.

The only thing in this flat and stoneless land that aligns with the equinoctial risings, in March and September, is a leaning pine fence post. I have seen the orange sun sit there, as if to burn the post down, attempting to mark a monumental event on the flimsy leavings of our civilization. A historian friend, Dan, sketched the line of mountains circumscribing his Montana home, and on this range he notes the sunrise points on solar holidays. Of course, the equinox could be marked by a restaurant sign, or a rooftop vent, or be blocked altogether by condominiums. But here it is not. Biannually, the fence post flares like a torch.

The equinox heralds the two most pleasant times of year on the farm: March through May and September through November. These are four months of flawless weather, the time to schedule reunions and weddings if you want them to be perfect.

January and February are often characterized by bitter, wet, pipe-freezing cold, down into the low twenties, and on many winter nights Silas and I sleep in front of the fireplace. The sun rises toward the tall tulip poplars and magnolias along the branch, to the southeast, its light wan.

Yet even in the most frigid months, a day will surprise

you. One early January, a friend called from Montana
to say that four inches of snow had fallen and more was
coming down; I was in shorts and tank top, raking longleaf pine straw in the yard, piling it around the base of the
pomegranate, a subtropical fruit. Mixed with the needles
were hulls and leaves of the pecan, also subtropical.

I had been digging up one of Grandmama's flower
beds, responding to some urge triggered by the smell of
earth baking in the low winter sun. The musk of over-
turned dirt, with roots running through it and pecan hulls
rotting under the trees, drove me wild, and I was consumed
with the urge to dig through the new irises, knowing the
following night might be bitter. Midwinter, purple martin
scouts returned from South America. One February 13,
driving Silas to school, I noticed a dozen killdeer in the
rye field, where all winter there had been two. By evening
twenty-five had gathered, and the next morning they were
gone, heading northward to raise summer broods of young
killdeer in grass-pasture hollows or stream-gravel scoops.

Fickle March vacillates wildly between chill and warmth,
until half the clothes you put on in the early morning you
peel off by midday. But finally it is spring.

If I can be so bold as to name a time of full glory for
a place, spring is it in south Georgia: azaleas loud with
fuchsia, pink, magenta, and flame; water oaks with their
pools of viridescent shade; sweetshrub, coral honeysuckle,
and dooryard quince wildly extravagant in their blooms; a
patch of lavendar phlox. White azaleas. Wild cherries and
sassafras bloom, one wide open, one timid. Only the pecan
trees wait.

The beauty is like a drug—you want to sleep and read
and rest and laugh and watch the breeze ripple the clothes

on the line. A trip to the mailbox is dizzying—the air is full of fragrance and the private lives of birds. I bring the mail to the rocking chair on the porch, wind murmuring in the pines, where I find myself an hour later, the mail read but I am dreaming, listening to the brown thrasher chicks whose mother has built their nest two feet outside the porch screen. I can see through the white ring into the mother bird's eye, as if into all secrets. For how many human generations has this line of brown thrashers nested here, by Grandmama's porch? I have not had peace like this in years. Even in gratitude I am greedy.

The problem is with spring's length. If I am honest, I admit that spring lasts about two weeks, a wildly glorious fortnight.

Every day something new unsheathes, first blue violets in the yard and longleaf pine anthers, swollen purple and bristling with pollen. Pollen mists the air and Chickasaw plums bloom. Then the sun rises closer to due east, between certain oaks along the fencerow.

One evening, March 31, a chuck-will's-widow, a buff-brown nightjar whose song is often mistaken for a whip-poorwill's, called from the edge of the field. It was fresh arrived from Florida, and I was excited to hear it and hoped it would stay, but I didn't hear it again. I wasn't sure which day the kestrel that perched on a certain wire for months wheeled away. On one day of high and unusual winds, a flock of cedar waxwings appeared out of the white sky to take cover in a pecan tree. There the birds sat, brown and round, preening and smoothing mussed feathers. I counted twenty.

The grandsir-graybeard blooms, and snakes abandon winter quarters. The first ruby-throated hummingbird returns to feed on the trumpet creeper blooming up the pine tree, and kingbirds again perch on strands of barbed-wire fence, flouncing their ruffled tails. This is the time when enough pokeweed shoots up to cook a mess of poke salat. The rising sun eases toward Shug Baxley's house to the north. With hardly more than a taste, sweet spring is gone.

June is turncoat, the mild breezes of spring dying beneath the unbearable weight of July and August as summer overtakes the land. The heat is astounding, oppressive, the air like hot, clear soup. The sun bakes everything tough and brittle. On the worst of days, the thermometer hanging under the porch roof, out of direct sunlight, reads 100 degrees. In summer I run early in the morning, although even then the temperature is already in the nineties. As I pass the branch, biting flies swarm out of the woods and I feel like a running horse. Though I gallop, still the yellow-flies and horseflies buzz my calves and thighs, managing to prick me. Bulbs of sweat break out of my pores and stream down. This is impetigo weather, soaking-wet weather.

When the air turns hotter than body temperature, something happens. The blood turns sluggish. Nobody wants to eat. We drink quart after quart of water and still it's not enough. We sleep under two fans.

Folks who have less tolerance for the heat might say we have ten months of hell down here, and two months of temperance. I distinctly feel four seasons, although they are increasingly topsy-turvy, with droughts occurring now in what used to be wet seasons and too much rain falling at the time of the year we need it least. The unpredictable effects of global warming have made for some odd seasons in south Georgia. We had three years of drought (1998,

1999, and 2000), especially during the summer months, passing week after week without rain. Rainfall hit record lows for a year, then another. The summer of 2000 was so dry I mowed only twice instead of the usual weekly ordeal. Azaleas withered, and blueberries dessicated on the bushes. Everything looked thirsty and pathetic, whittled down; the weak wind wailed for relief.

That July I was away for a week when temperatures were combustible. One day the mercury touched 106 degrees. When I returned, the ground looked like fall, covered with drifting reefs of leaves. The leaves on every water oak in the yard had turned utterly brown—not fall brown, but paperlike, flammable, a dead brown. I swept the front walk as if it were autumn. But the light was summer. The grass was withered and sere, like greenish needles sticking up through the leaves.

Finally that summer a queer blue cloud streamed in from the west. The wind began to blow fiercely, knocking leaves off the trees so forcefully that their falling against the ground and against the window panes sounded like rain a long time before the water arrived. The air was purple and full of brown scraps of paper.

What is sacred about weather is that it descends out of nowhere. Even when we predict the weather correctly, its forces are beyond us. Its power will forever be beyond us, no matter what of weather we see coming, so that even the science of meteorology cannot fully answer our questions or soothe our fears. In weather we realize our vulnerability, that nothing can insure our security. Storms can come without our prescience and vanish without warning, heedless of our prayers. As is true of life, we will never completely understand the weather or be able to create the atmospheric conditions that make rain or sunshine or cloudiness. Lightning bolts will streak earthward out of the blue. No part of weather can be fully replicated, nor would we want it to be, and so it will always remain omnipotent, bearing down on us out of the heavens.

With a fantastic racket of thunder and lightning, clapping and popping as if to rend the fabric of sky, the parched earth received water. By morning the brown, shriveled resurrection fern on the limbs of the pecan tree stood upright, very green and alive.

Late summer I spend all day in the yard, bending and toting and turning and pushing. I dig the garlic, harvesting some but replanting most, adding sheep manure, then matted pecan leaves. Even the dirt smells like garlic. I clip three wheelbarrow loads of overgrown vegetation, azaleas from around the walk, an errant crepe myrtle that hides oncoming traffic at the edge of the driveway, dead limbs off the catalpa. I pile mountains of pine straw in flower beds and around the bases of the ancient pine trees.

One such day, two beautiful orange kittens showed up. They were twins, almost identical, with cute white throats and the most wonderful personalities. Silas would love them when he returned from visiting his father's house. Unfortunately, their favorite spot to nap was in the pots of flowers around the doorstep. The two of them wrestled in the grass.

Peaches ripened on the tree—they were falling off, in fact. I ate them standing beside the tree, taking off one glove. They were delicious, with ivory-colored flesh like marble, the juice cool. They would not last long and even as I squatted, licking my fingers, I mourned them, as I did the big purple plum that bore and shed its fruit within a week. The plums rained down, the ground below carpeted with wasps and rotting fruit, and I was too busy to make jelly. An ephemeral joy. Toward evening, I went to the garden and broke off an armload of basil, picked and washed the leaves, then made a blenderful of pesto. I used some of the garlic in it.

Fall is a subtle affair of gradations, for there is no great splash, no height of color, no ostentation. Fall is a gentle, patient process that for the most part goes unnoticed. Some would say our fall is nonexistent; I would say the constant flow of tiny spectacle is endlessly fulfilling.

Goldenrod is the first unmistakable sign of summer's overturn, coming as early as late August, turning saffron yellow from the bottom up. Fall's flowers are yellow and purple—tall stalks of false foxglove hung with lavender bells, shooting plumes of dog fennel, meadow beauty. Tiny spangling asters convert a field into the Milky Way.

Strands of wild grapevine drain the green from their leaves, and the five-pointed stars of sweet gum turn yellow, maroon, russet. Along the roads blazing leaves hit underneath the truck. Tulip poplars drop their lemon yellow hands. Dogwoods wax golden, then peach, finally offering red-coated seeds that the robins will fuss over when they arrive late November. Fall settles heaviest in the wettest places; cypresses go to rust. Maples turn fireball red.

Then one day you look and the landscape is dull, its wildflowers and grasses dead and decomposing. Only the pines and the evergreen oaks are left with speech. Another winter. Citrons, uncovered by first frost, lie along the edges of fields, reminding passersby that the days of watermelon are over. I light the first fire of the season.

On a November day, I gathered a bucketful of pecans

in slanted sunshine. The pomegranate bush was not much taller than I was, its whips thick with red-tinged leaves and bent like fishing poles under the weight of a single fruit that seemed to be waiting for an animal to come by. One of the pomegranates had split open while it hung on the tree, revealing fleshy ruby kernels, and I stood there and ate it like corn on the cob, except that it was jewel red and juicy sweet.

After a long drought, one December, typically a dry month, finally rain came. It was raining, raining. Shadows of animals streamed across the shining roads. For days we heard the murmur of rain into rain, tapping first into the leaves, then into the deeply saturated ground and the expanded wood of trees. The road into Okefenokee Swamp became a levee. *The earth is still fearsome,* I thought.

Rain trickled out of the gray, lowered sky, and another year seeped into the ground.

The pomegranate in flower.

Raising Silas

Between West Green and Broxton, Georgia, a giant cedar tree alone covers a corner of Lone Hill Methodist Church Cemetery like a misshapen green archangel. It is the national champion of Southern red cedars.

The tree is a forest unto itself. Beneath its branches is deep cool. Resurrection fern, growing hairlike on sun-touched limbs and along much of the trunk, withers in drought but after a rain revives, each fern leaf vibrantly green and erect. Walking up to the cedar is like coming side-on to a wooly mammoth. Where the fern does not grow, the tree is finely shaggy in the habit of ancient cedars. Some of its limbs touch the ground, and the tree covers close to 100 feet. Tribes of animals could live in the tree, oak snakes and squirrels and cedar waxwings. And although the tree is full of life, it lives among the dead. I wanted Silas to see it.

∞

Silas and I spent three days in Tallahassee, where we used to live. For two days, nine-year-old Silas played with buddies while I worked freelance for a magazine there, and the third day, New Year's, we visited friends.

In three days, Silas watched a total of six movies. He played hour upon hour of computer games, and celebrated his friend's birthday at a video game restaurant for young people. New Year's Eve, he and three of his young friends had a slumber party and stayed up until 2 A.M., the first time ever I went to bed before him. He used his twelve-dollar savings to buy two new action figures.

When it came time to drive the four hours home, back to Georgia, he was jumping with neighborhood kids on my friend's trampoline. "I'm not going," he said flatly. I kept loading the truck, strategizing. On the farm we have nature, slow in its revealing, and solitude. How could those compete with a neighborhood of children? Should we stay another night?

I looked up once from organizing the truck—we'd bought supplies we couldn't get in Baxley—to see a neighbor boy named Derek, three years older, push Silas down on the trampoline. When Silas rose, protesting, the boy tripped him.

"Silas," I called, straightening out of the truck, "you're welcome to fight back." The children instantly snapped their attention toward me. Had I said what they thought they heard?

"You're welcome to whip his butt," I called. The children looked at me, wide eyed and solemn, trying to understand.

"I don't believe in violence," I said, "but I don't think anybody should push someone else around."

"Mom," Silas said in a don't-be-ridiculous voice. "I couldn't beat him. He's bigger than me."

"Maybe not," I said, "but you're welcome to try."

I went back in for a bag and when I emerged my ridiculous suggestion had somehow worked to ease the bullying. Another child, Kevin, whom Silas had known since he was a baby, had challenged Silas in fun and they were tangled good-naturedly on the trampoline, Kevin on top.

"Hump him, hump him," said a bigger girl, pushing Kevin's butt up and down.

Those words made Kevin mad, and he went at Silas with fury, locking his head and forcing it repeatedly forward into the canvas. I thought he'd break Silas's neck.

"Silas, time to go," I called calmly. "Tell everybody good-bye."

This time he didn't hesitate.

Their world, my world. This boy, my son. I so wanted him to be a child of stars and dirt, not jiggering images of aliens and laser guns. Town life was enticing, with its toy stores and theaters and malls. Among those: four-lane highways, intense development, crime, high rent, traffic, people moving fast. To think in terms of city versus country, pitting lifestyles rather than social mores, is illogical, but I have a childhood mapped out for Silas that doesn't revolve around electronic entertainment and a culture hyped on sex and money. Still, I know child rearing is more complex than that.

I remembered a night back in Georgia, after school let out for the Christmas holiday.

"Who can I ask to come over tomorrow?" Silas asked from a full bathtub.

"Chris?"

"He won't come." Chris didn't like to leave his family room with its two TVs, both going, one hooked to a movie and the other to Nintendo.

"Jesse?"

"No way."

Jesse bored Silas. His Christmas present was a Bible and even at nine he was very devout. "He does everything

I tell him to," Silas said. "There's never anything he decides to do."

"Seth?"

"He hits me and doesn't stop when I say 'Stop.'"

Once I was talking to Sandy West, an octogenarian friend who lives on Ossabaw Island, off the coast of Georgia, about young people growing up now. Ossabaw is undeveloped; Sandy inherited the island and sold it to the state at a reduced cost, in order to preserve it forever. For all her life Sandy has shared an entire wild, glorious barren island with osprey, alligator, and wild hog. She worries that because of overpopulation, our young people will never know privacy, that they will always have to be entertained. Sandy worries that fewer young people know the smell of a book or the feel of one. "I feel about books as if I were a drunk," she said. But the real tragedy by far, Sandy believes, is their loss of a relationship with the natural world.

"They have never known total darkness or total stillness," she said.

Sometimes in the country I think I am depriving Silas, saying no too often, trying to push back something bigger than all of us, something that has brainwashed us. I am the mother with one finger in the dike, holding back glitz and materialism and sex hype. The tribe is gone—Silas has no swarm of cousins (there are two), no great-grandmother rocking by the fireplace. What we trade to live on the farm is a soccer team, art lessons, the coffee shop in Montana where we ordered hot cocoa and cranberry bagels after school, snowboarding, skate parks, festivals, natural history museums.

One day Silas went home after school with his friend Clint while I paddled Ebenezer Creek near Savannah with friends. I saw prothonotary warblers, solitary sandpipers, coots, white ibises, great egrets, little blue herons. A few cypresses were so big we could back our kayaks inside to take pictures. I glimpsed the tail of a snake as it disappeared into a hollow tupelo, and where we stopped for lunch, a tiny treefrog with peach and green markings. Afterward, when I picked up Silas early evening, he began to cry.

"I don't want to go home," he said.

"Baby, it's a school day tomorrow. You can't spend the night with a friend on a school night."

"I mean I don't want to go at all," he wept. "I don't like that house. It's too big and lonely and just me and you there."

"I know," I said.

"It's time to leave here."

"What do you mean?"

"It's time to leave Georgia. I want to go back to Missoula, or Tallahassee, or anywhere. I mean, I want to leave tomorrow."

"We can't do that."

"And you never do anything with me. You pitched the baseball until I hit it and then you left. You're always doing something else."

"I'm sorry. I'm busy a lot."

"I don't even mind leaving my friends here. I just want to go. You can't imagine the fun I have with my dad in Vermont. They don't have the rules like here." He didn't mean his father's house, he meant the place in general, that the people there had fewer rules.

"Honey, what are you needing that you don't have here?" I asked this question thinking that maybe something in particular was wrong, and I could go out of my way to fix that. Did he need more friends? Different friends? Did he need soccer? We could drive to Savannah, if that's what it took to find a soccer league.

"What's wrong with it here?" I asked again.

Through his tears, he said a line astounding in its profundity, a sentence I turned over and over in my mind. "Here there is no imagination," he said. I remembered it vividly the next summer when I heard Barry Lopez say, "Fundamentalism in any form is the sign of a failed imagination."

I don't dare wonder aloud whether we can make it, whether I will be able to piece an existence for him—before he is grown, his childhood gone—where the world is whole and in tune with the essence of life. But I will not give up.

ଡ଼ଉ

I took a different route home from Tallahassee, up through Douglas, so I could pass Lone Hill Cemetery. As we rode along, we exchanged a candy called an atomic fireball back and forth. When the ball of candy got too spicy for Silas, he handed it to me and I sucked on it awhile. Sometimes we had to hold it in our fingers.

Near Pavo, we passed a plowed cornfield that looked as if it were covered by a black wool blanket—but then the edge of the blanket lifted into the air. It was a throng of birds—thousands of red-winged blackbirds. We pulled off the road. A rafter at a time, the birds rose, flew across the highway, then rebounded, stringing between two fields. Shifting, they shaped themselves into shimmering optical illusions, like the changing patterns of a computer screensaver. At one point they

arched over us like an umbrella, or a mosquito net.
It was an exaltation of birds. They pivoted and hovered and sifted, their red wing-patches flashing in the
gray day.

"Come home," they sang.

The day was almost done when we reached the cemetery. "Why are you stopping here?" Silas asked.

"To show you that tree over there. Let's walk over."

"Walk all the way over there?"

"Yeah. Four miles is a long way to walk," I teased. The
tree was not 100 feet away, across rows of graves. A sign in
the cemetery proclaimed, "Thou Shalt Not Litter."

"Mom, why are you always bringing me to graveyards?"

"I'm showing you a tree. This is a national champion
red cedar. It's the biggest red cedar tree in the entire country. Look at this. Some of its limbs touch the ground. See
this one limb here? The biggest cedar tree I've ever seen
was as big as this *limb*."

"Sssssshhh," Silas said. "I hear something."

I hushed. Silas, wearing my big denim coat, looked
back over his shoulder. Evening was coming on, the temperature dropping.

"Leaf rattling," I said, and continued. "Here are the
graves of an entire family buried beneath the tree. Look at
their death dates."

I passed from grave to grave, kneeling at the head-
stones to feel the weathered granite. The gravestones,
though darkened by weather and moss, were yet readable.
February 23, 1870. February 19. February 26. February 18.

Intent on the gravestones, I was subtracting in my head
to figure out the tragic sequence of events. The silence
of the story never fails to tear at me, wanting to be told.

Champion Southern red cedar in
Lone Hill Cemetery.

"This is the father. He died first. This is the mother beside him. Here's a six-year-old, and an eighteen-year-old."

"Listen," Silas said, turned away. He listened. Then abruptly, "Mama, let's go."

"OK," I said, and twisted back to the tree. "You're a grand old cedar," I said to it.

"Why's it so big?" Silas said, as I paused with my hand on the trunk. "Like, fertilizer?"

"I think it holds the grief of that family. Did you see how they died within days of each other? They died in an epidemic. Yellow fever, someone said."

Silas and I clasped hands as we zigzagged slowly through the graves, back to the warmth of the truck and the remaining hour home.

"Back there I kept hearing noises," he said. "From all directions."

I lowered my voice, said sotto voce, "We better get out of here." I was teasing him. We were in the truck now, cranking up, and safe.

"Mama, don't talk about spirits anymore," he said. "It makes me scared." Upon admitting his panic, he started to cry.

"It's because you believe in them," I said. "I believe in them, too, but they don't scare me."

"Don't talk about it," he said.

ଊ

"Look at the moon!" Silas yelled when we turned the dirt corner of the farm. It was a gold sickle dangling over the bottomless head that feeds Ten Mile Creek, the road like a slowly closing gate that clicked shut behind us when I pulled into the driveway and cut the engine.

The minute we opened the truck door, our ecstatic unpedigreed dogs were all over us. The headlights showed they'd chewed up more plastic toys and brought deer bones to the yard while we'd been gone. The house was frigid, our breath white.

I unloaded our bags. On his own, Silas wadded newspaper in the fireplace and layered pinecones across strips of fat pine. He struck a match and pretty soon had a warm fire brightening and softening the icy living room.

I was looking at the Christmas tree, still up, and thinking of the evening Silas and I erected it. We had gone walking across the pasture into our own spare woods, looking for a tree, but the pines had longish needles, and they didn't branch. Many-branching was what we needed. So we brought the saw and drove riverward, looking along fencerows and highway right-of-ways, where young trees were doomed, until we ended up where thick electric lines from the nuclear plant cross the county. It was near dark and hunting season had started, so we didn't want to go into the woods. At the edge of the Georgia Power swath, growing hugged into a thirty-foot pine, we found a lovely double-trunked cedar about six feet tall. We took one trunk with only a few strokes of the saw.

We set it in a bucket of rocks filled with water and hung our modest ornaments on it. The room was cold. We made hot cocoa and worked by the fire, then brought our sleeping bags and before we slept I read aloud for an hour from *The Wind in the Willows*.

There is an unmistakable feeling you get when a day or an evening is perfect. Sometimes it's perfect for one person and not the other, but there's a certain feeling when it's perfect for all present. Silas and I have the same ideas about a good day, and we appreciate one when it comes along. Most days are good, but only a few are perfect. That evening was perfect.

Now, more than a week later, we lounged in front of the fire and the tree again, shelling pecans and talking, until the clock headed toward eleven. Silas rescued a coal-red nail from the embers with a pair of pliers and experimented with it, drilling holes through a plastic milk jug, playing that he was a blacksmith. Before we came here, he wouldn't strike a match, afraid of getting burned. We heated cocoa and before bed I read more of *The Wind in the Willows*.

The next morning, I looked out across the hoary fields at the tender, rosy light of new day. When I am away, I cannot imagine this place, nor guard it intact in my mind, but when I gaze upon it, I almost choke with love for it. That winter day, the only thing holding up the woodshed was the yen of my heart to see it there another day. The line of grapevines was a tangle of brown sinew since the leaves had loosened their attachments and drifted away. Behind the log outbuildings, the pasture grass stretched frostily to the woods.

Here are the tools Silas needs, I thought. *Fire will make a grown man out of him—the sun's fire, igniting the moon's fire, becoming his fire.*

Despair

There should be a word that means the opposite of epiphany: instead of sudden light, a darkening that sends one running to escape the gloom. It was this feeling of falling into darkness that convinced me that my experiment in rural community had faltered. After awhile, I began to fail and to know I was failing. I felt that I would again have to leave the place that owned me.

"I think you have only one chance at *place* in this life, your life," Joy Williams wrote. "A place where your spirit finds a home, a place you cherish and want to protect. All this can take a lifetime. And you can miss your place."

Everybody tells me I feel too deeply, especially about wildness, but often I can't tell where my body ends and the earth begins. What became painfully clear was how much wildness we had already lost in Georgia. As the forests dwindled, so did my spirit. How can a place produce a person that it cannot sustain?

Someone years ago told me that failure in a person can be traced back to one incident in which that person was belittled or hurt. It is the moment when that person accepts hopelessness, when the urge toward improvement, toward light, dies. A child's failure in reading, for example, may be traced to a particular moment when a teacher ridiculed the child for mispronouncing a simple word. "One wrong turn," Greg Brown sings, "is all it takes. . . . One wrong turn leads to the next."

With the nature of origins and essences, anything can be traced to a moment.

I trace my despondency to one word out of a news anchor's mouth the morning after election day during the second year of our return. The word was "lost."

Amendment 1 was a 1998 ballot initiative, created and driven by visionaries, to provide a funding mechanism for preserving land in the state. The Turner Foundation was backing this initiative to create a land, water and heritage fund. The proposal was a fairly innocuous, apple-pie kind of thing. Money would be generated by a tax on the real estate transfer fee, an idea that made a lot of sense—let development pay for saving land. For a $100,000 land deal, the extra cost would be $1000 to the buyer: peanuts. The result would be clean air, clean water, green space, and wildlands.

Along with so many others, I worked hard for the amendment, talking to groups, making phone calls, and sending out pleas for its passage. "If each of us gets ten people to support this, it can pass," I said. The week of the election, I was elated to find not only my letter of support for the measure in our local paper, but two others. Jimmy Carter appeared in television advertisements calling for a conservation fund. I dared to hope while all around me forests fell to the chain saw.

I voted early on election day. By evening results from rural areas showed the amendment failing by about 45 percent. Even then I was not disheartened. I went to bed Tuesday night thinking that Atlanta would pull us through. I woke the next morning to terrible news. "Amendment 1, the push to create a conservation fund, lost with 46 percent of the vote," the radio said. Failed.

In the awful plunging that follows loss, I could not
speak, could not answer the telephone when it rang. *What
now? How are we going to buy Moody Swamp and Varn's
Forest and Bulltown Swamp? How are we going to create a
wildlife corridor that connects Georgia to Florida? How are
we going to keep America from vanishing before our eyes—as
it is fast doing—not just wildlands but our history and our
culture?*

The lost initiative threw me into utter, unremitting,
inconsolable despair. Everybody was talking hope because
it was what we were supposed to do: we were supposed
to find that bright tunnel toward hope. The answer was
to remember how far the environmental movement had
come since Rachel Carson, everyone said. The answer was
acts of ceremony in community. The answer was imagination and art. If enough of us limited our reproduction and
consumed less and created an ethical system we might
stop the hemorrhaging of wild species from the planet.

These "answers" weren't worth the atoms of breath it
took to speak them or the paper pulp to write them. So,
I thought, we should look around and admit, Damn if
we haven't lost this battle. Good-bye, dear earth-world.
Good-bye, beautiful forests. Good-bye, Bachman's sparrow and flatwoods salamander and red wolf. Good-bye,
Sumatran rhino and golden bamboo lemur and Chinese
river dolphin. Good-forever-bye.

How could we keep avoiding the darkness that seemed
so inevitable? Pieces of beauty are not the whole. A tiny
remnant of forest, an edge, is not a forest. Seeing one
indigo snake in a life does not make up for the thousands
disappeared.

"If you have any hope to offer," I wrote my friend Rex Boner in Atlanta, a man who had saved thousands of acres of land, "I need to hear it this morning." The pain was not imaginary; it was deep and wrenching.

The only path to hope I could find was the woods themselves: fresh air and ancient trees, birds singing, a creek running to a river. This is the medicine that restores. But if I lived in a place where wildness every day died a little more, where was I supposed to turn for hope?

Finally I burst outside and ran two miles, entering a thin wood, maybe eighteen acres, that follows Ten Mile Creek below the farm. I crashed through the underbrush, touching poplar and magnolia trees and apologizing to them. Absorbing their strength. Touching galls and scars left from turpentining and also decaying stumps of trees. Listening to the steady silence of beings much older and more wounded, but more faithful—ever faithful to the blue sky above and to the water underground—than I.

Rex called to say that Ted Turner had announced, "Losing is not an option." Meaning, I think, that voters would see the initiative again.

At evening I walked the dirt road alongside the cotton field waiting to see the full moon rise, because I needed to be reminded of certainty. I lingered a long time out in the frost—a front was passing—and the moon never came up. It got to be six-thirty and then seven, way past time, and the moon never rose.

My word, I thought, remembering cultures that believed the sun would not rise unless they danced and sang it up, or recited poetry so lovely that the sun desired, for another day, to shine. I climbed the red maple Uncle Percy had planted when he was a boy, to the top, and even from that vantage saw no sign of light on the horizon. The moon refused to rise, and it served us right.

All night the sky was overcast.

Although I was not aware of it at the time, aware only of a feeling like a cold sledgehammer flattening my chest, it was in that moment of the radio announcer's news, the jolt of a single word, that I joined Silas in his desire to leave. This was not a fleeing or a retaliation, but a recognition of a direction I had been journeying in for months. It was a breathless attempt at survival, because in that moment I knew that as wildness died around me I, too, would die. Hope for the landscape had become tangled with a lack of art that was heartlessness, and with loneliness.

The loneliness frightened me—an endlessness of mute days where I searched for community, human and wild. I searched for art or for the path that leads to it, searched for the wildness that sustains me, searched for a way to rise brilliantly, as the sun rises, full of faith and hope.

Mama and Daddy called on us a few times a week, bearing fruit or anything surplus they had, as did Dell, and we dropped in on them, with a novel Mama might enjoy, fresh-baked muffins, or an interesting bit of news. At their house, we were encouraged to eat, even if it wasn't mealtime. Mama kept pots on the stove; she would heat leftovers or cook whatever we wanted. Well-read and thoughtful, Daddy always had a new idea or scheme to discuss. Their attention for us was undivided. Often I left Silas with them while I ran errands. Mama would quit all chores to play with him.

Our town had no coffee shop or other hangout. If I ran

into someone, such as my cousin Sue or Silas's teacher, it was at the library or the supermarket. I missed public dialogue such as I'd experienced other places. I missed depth of connection. Most days I found no one I could talk to about the joy in my life, or the terror.

At times after I returned to my homeland, I knew I had found the sense of belonging I desired, as I did when I stopped by the pre-kindergarten classroom at school to hug Carlin, my brother Stephen's son, to watch surprise and joy wash his dark-browed, serious face that resembled so much my own. Or bringing in wood on a cold winter dusk, wearing overalls, heavy workshirt, and boots. I would duck into the log chicken coop, now half rotten and leaning badly but functional enough to store firewood, and return to its open doorway with dusty lengths of oak. I would heap them into a wheelbarrow Uncle Percy had made. The sun would be setting in flamboyant pink and salmon strips across harvested and drab winter fields where kestrels hunted. The grace of it—the simplicity—filled every crevice of my heart until I would weep at the glory of such a life. In those moments, I knew the fullness of history and of return.

That winter after the initiative lost, rain fell, slight and unabated, dolorous. Day after day I traveled within the rooms of the wood house. The days were blank squares on a calendar that hung against the washroom wall, its pages shriveling, its paper fading where sun looped through the window. As the months passed, an unseen balance tilted me toward darkness. I had returned to the farm not knowing what I would find. What I found was silence, sometimes good and necessary, sometimes looming huge. Often I could not fill the space I moved in. *I have looked and looked for a home,* I thought to myself. *What kind of life is this?* I came to rest in a clean and flanneled bed and dreamed of people nowhere to be found.

"I have not yet come to terms with how utterly alone I am in this world," I wrote. "Every day is like a long envelope traveling toward its destination. The envelope is empty. Even wrens and squirrels have their own circles of intimacy. But people have changelessly been born at the edges of the world, their lives spent crossing that wild territory between yonder and nothing, between occasional visitors. What did they tell themselves they must not expect?"

Why the trials, I would ask myself, *if I were meant to be here?*

Wrapped in silence, I would hear a horn. Sometimes the letter carrier, Lee, stopped to talk, especially if he had a package that wouldn't fit in the box. He blew his horn as he entered the yard, leaped out, and headed with purpose up the walk, as if he were in a big hurry. He hollered, "Hulloooo," and rapped on the door, which was open unless it was winter. As he handed me the mail he started a conversation that he didn't seem eager to end. I became certain by things the letter carrier said that he noticed the mail coming to the house. On any day the arrival of mail was a highlight, and a dash to the mailbox was expectant, considering the prospects of delivery—letters from friends, a book, an unanticipated parcel. The mail meant community too, a wider one. It was sometimes the only connection I would have in days with the bigger world.

"Hello, Lee!"

"Hey! Do you know somebody in Portugal?"

"Yes. An old friend."

"A boyfriend?"

"Not any more. Did I get a letter from Portugal?"

"A postcard," he said. "I'd like to go there someday."

"Me, too."

He'd ask how I was, and I'd say fine, how was he? He reminded me that he wanted the first copy of the book, should it publish. Then he was gone, leaving me more grateful for his visit than he knew.

❧

"Because of you and Mama," I told my father. "I would never want to leave. But my life is not working for me. I'm lonelier than I've ever been. I've looked in lots of places for home. I thought I could find it back here."

"You've only got two options," Daddy said. "Stay or leave." He told me a story about a woman from Chicago who moved to Baxley with her husband. As the years passed in Baxley she continued to miss her Chicago home and to praise it, until her husband died. Not long afterward she sold everything she owned, packed up, and returned north. But the Chicago she found was not the Chicago she had left, the one she had imagined for years. In two weeks she repacked her bags and returned to Baxley.

"Happiness has to come from inside," he said.

"I don't know how to find it," I said. "If I knew, I would."

"Happiness is my God," he said.

"That works for you," I said, "but it hasn't worked for me. My religion—where I find spirit—is in nature, and every day I see more of the woods cut, more gone."

Then would come a messenger from the wild: one February morning while I was working I heard clucking and looked out to see a flock of wild turkeys in the field. The turkeys foraged slowly toward me, almost to the edge of the yard. So close, I had a great look at the male turkey displaying to his females, spreading out his glorious, shimmering fantail and beating it against the air, then strutting about, head high and tail feathers out.

One afternoon when I carried a rusty seeder to the junk pile behind the barn I saw a gray fox. She came from the inelegant brush pile growing there, too close to the oak trees to burn. The fox had a lot of red on her, as gray foxes do, and when she saw me, her big feather duster of a tail sliced through the air and *poof,* she vanished.

An hour before, I'd gone to the clothesline to hang laundry and noticed the pair of nesting bluebirds behaving oddly, flying to the opening of their birdhouse and falling away, pausing on the ground or on the box's roof, only to fly at the birdhouse again. As they fluttered at the hole they cried out in distress.

Snake, I thought. *There's a snake in the box.*

I had to knock the roof off with a hammer, because it wasn't the opening kind. Curled inside was a four-foot oak snake. When I hauled it out, I saw two lumps along its length—bluebird chicks. In the box were two chicks, their feathers tinged blue-brown, one crushed to death and the other still alive, huddled in a corner.

The dead one I tossed to the ants of the field. The other I restored to its bowl of twigs. The snake hadn't crawled far so I picked it up and carried it across the pasture to the tree line, knowing it would be back. Thus I was presented with the necessity of figuring out with faltering brain and two clumsy hands how to keep the snake from swallowing the last baby bird. The best idea was to find a metal skirt for the pole. Looking for tin, I had found the broken seeder cluttering the shed so I had hauled it to the junk pile, which is how I had glimpsed the fox.

I could have grieved the loss of the baby bluebirds, but one was left, and the adult pair would nest again. The skirt on their pole would keep the new babies safe. How could I lament when we had oak snakes and bluebirds and even gray foxes?

∞

Over decades the South has bled people who were thoughtful about the land and society. They couldn't take the racism or the Bible thumping, and they left. They never came back. Somebody, I thought, has to fight to protect the ravaged places. If a place loses the ones who care, the ones who can make a difference, what kind of doom does that spell? If the Southerners who love the wild leave the South, well, what happens then?

The days continued to fill with longing—for friends, for like-minded people, for change, for wildness, to be a great writer, for power and efficacy. It seemed a squander of spirit to long so much. If the conquest of longing was possible, I wanted to conquer it. Or, I wondered, were we born to yearn for greater things, for a better world, our heads turned toward possibility?

Mornings, watching the carousel of dawn, with the day unsaid and unseen, I would lie in bed and hope would come careening out of the prairies of dreams. I knew in those moments that hope was living, always alive, in our bodies, like scraps of wild forest. To save ourselves, we must gather the pockets of hope. We must reconnect and lengthen and fortify them so that a replication can happen in the world outside ourselves. I know we are creatures of light. Spirit demands that. We have to turn toward joy.

Angels, Arise

After dark, when the summer moon has risen, I stagger outside and into the pearly light of the garden. Some nights seven or eight saucer-sized white blooms will have burst forth from the moonflower growing up the back of the weathered shed. They almost glow in the dark. I stand in front of them like a sleepwalker, breathing in their incredible perfume.

Then I walk through the garden, past the hairy-leaved eggplants, their fruits hanging heavy and purple, past the beetle-stung wax beans, past the tall, prickly okra with its outpouring of green pods. I ease past sunflowers and zinnias, past cleomes with blooms head high, and angel's trumpets. In the moonlight, the garden lives a quiet tranquillity. I look up at the pale flickering stars, beacons in the universe, and from the black, shrouded woods, one corner of the earth, I imagine the sound of trumpets.

From this garden by day, I watch a male summer tanager filching Chickasaw plums. The female is shyer. In the water oak that shades the rosemary and the pineapple sage, a great-crested flycatcher calls, perhaps to the beautiful, noisy, red-bellied woodpecker on the pine. A pair of blue grosbeaks nervously snitch seeds at the feeder.

I am living a dream, a rural, agrarian, half-wild, place-bound dream.

∞

When I was a girl, a weekly publication from Atlanta called the *Market Bulletin* told the story of who I wanted to be. It was a thin, tabloid-size newspaper published by the Georgia Department of Agriculture, hardly big enough to wrap a bream but much welcomed in a household cut off by distance and by my father's censure of worldliness. This paper was fiercely read by me, a girl desirous to understand life, who looked for that understanding in what was available. I still get the paper—it's free—and a recent issue says it is volume 84.

Look around and you see agrarian lifestyles disappearing. Subsistence farmers are dying of old age, and their children are piddling around the farm, keeping a herd of cows or putting an acre into blueberries, gentleman and gentlewoman farmers who tend land in their spare time because they enjoy it; many are giving up all semblance of farming and are selling out.

If you were to read the *Market Bulletin*, however, you would never know any of that.

The weekly publication is much the same now as when I was young, ten or twelve pages long, between 1,800 and 2,000 ads any given issue, in what looks like 6-point type. To advertise is free, but the ad must be no more than twenty words, and no one is allowed more than one ad per issue. The average ad is less than a half inch deep and little more than two inches wide.

The categories include: farm machinery; bees, honey, and supplies; ag seed for sale; flowers for sale; farm employment; feed, hay, and grain; rabbits; fertilizers and mulches; fish and supplies.

Under "oddities," someone will be selling gourds, lucky buckeyes, homemade lye soap, several large black walnut trees. Under "alternative livestock," a more recent category, you'll find halter-trained llamas, emus (very tame), female ostrich, pure elk. In the category "poultry/fowl for sale," you can buy guineas and ducks and geese and peacocks and quail and pigeons and swans. And, oh my, the breeds of chickens: leghorn, Araucana, bantam, Dominique, Brahma, Rhode Island Red.

The sellers' names, phone numbers, and the names of their towns are given at the end, in bold. A lot of these Georgia towns I've never heard of. Kite. Chula. Alamo. Talking Rock. Ellabell. Franklin. Maysville. Locust Grove. Hephzibah.

In every issue a few pictures of people show off something: a tomato growing upside down out of the bottom of a hanging five-gallon bucket; somebody's grandbaby propped in front of a ninety-pound watermelon that was grown in a flower bed; four-foot-long elephant ear leaves; a twenty-pound cabbage; eighteen-foot-high mammoth sunflowers; a Buff Orpington egg three times the size of a store-bought egg.

One day, in a spume of enthusiasm, I called the Atlanta office of the *Bulletin*, full of questions. Is there any other state in the Union with anything like the *Market Bulletin*? Have any new categories been added over the years? Any taken away? It was a busy day for the managing editor. "Lots of states have them," he said tersely. I heard him shift from the speaker phone to the handset. "Georgia was one of the first, I think. It started in 1917."

"Have you ever looked back through the early issues? What kinds of ads are there? How are they different from now?"

"I've looked. I can't remember any advertisements in particular. The prices were cheaper, of course."

"Can you remember any trends? Like more mules being sold then than now?"

"I wasn't looking for trends."

"Did the people advertising in the '20s simply use their address so they had to contact each other in person, or by mail?"

"We had telephones in 1917," he said. "Didn't you know that?"

"Not where I come from," I said. A man who'd be ninety if he still lived declared to my father once that in 1920 there weren't twenty telephones in Appling County: they had two-digit numbers. My parents didn't get a telephone until 1959, and the following year my grandmother—the one whose house I live in—got one. I remember when our county used five-digit dialing.

"Oh, I imagine people in rural areas used an address."

"Will you ever go to email addresses?"

"Some people list their email address now," he said shortly. "Look and see. Listen. I've got a lot of other things to do. This is purge day. Maybe you can call back and talk to someone else who's been here longer than I have."

That's Atlanta for you, I thought. No time to chat.

In the early 1980s, after I moved to a twelve-acre homestead in north Florida, I began growing heirloom varieties of vegetables, both to keep old varieties alive and to stay independent of monopolizing seed companies. Heirloom plants are traditional, open-pollinated varieties whose seed, unlike hybrids, may be saved by farmers and gardeners for future use. Traditional heirloom varieties produce the same crop, year after year. Hybrids, on the other hand, are first-generation plants produced by crossing unlike parents. Growing them is seductive because they exhibit inexplicably vigorous and uniform productivity, called hybrid vigor. The seeds of hybrids cannot be saved, however, since those seeds, grown out, revert to one of their various ancestral strains. By hybridizing, seed companies can keep gardeners dependent on their products.

With the advent of seed companies and our dependence on them, many traditional varieties of vegetables, planted year after year by family farmers, have been lost. I joined the Seed Savers Exchange, a national network of people growing heirloom crops in order to maintain threatened gene pools and keep alive the waning skills of seed saving. Members exchanged nonhybrid seeds, everything from amaranth to watermelon, for postage only.

In 1985 (I would've been twenty-three), I sent a letter to the *Georgia Market Bulletin,* asking to know about old varieties people still grew and inquiring about a kind of squash I'd heard about. The squash itself grew two to three feet long and over six inches in diameter, like a stout, slightly curled club. It was dark pinkish orange and scrumptiously sweet. Candy roaster, the farmer had called it. Was this a new species, an odd squash invention, or had it been around awhile?

Bertha Woody of Ellijay wrote: "I found in the paper where you wanted to know about those candy roasters. I have plenty of those seeds. I raised 13 good ones this year. They sure make a nice pie. I thought I would let you know they are still around. P.S. I have a son living in Orlando, Fla."

Frances Campbell of Paducah, Kentucky, wrote: "I saw your letter in the *Market Bulletin.* I was born in Luthersville. My daddy still lives at Grantville, Ga. It's down below Newnan. I love all kinds of odd flowers and vegetables. I don't have a lot of the old-timey vegetables that you wanted. Would send them if I did. I have the peter pepper (hot) and cow horn pepper. I wondered if I sent you the money would you send me a banana tree? Or tell me of a place down there where I could order things like that. I've got a pineapple that I started from a pineapple. Also an avacado. Thanks so much. Love, F. P.S. I was born July 21, 1933."

Back then, when I was a young woman in north Florida, not yet a mother or even a wife, I poured my heart into gardening. I'd work all day at it, until it got too dark to see. I was mulching apple trees up the hill when my son's father-to-be came driving down the road, lost. He stopped, and I had to leave off piling ruined hay around the fruit trees to give him directions. When he came back a few days later, beginning our courtship, I was kneeling between chard plants.

It was beautiful, that garden, with a circular plot for herbs; long, raised beds for lettuce and kale; mounds for melons and squashes. I didn't have running water back then, only rain buckets under the eaves of the house. One day after a month without rain—the buckets long empty— I wept in the dusty garden. We won't go another season like this, my sweetheart said.

He helped me haul loads of manure from a nearby horse barn, and sawdust, and bags of leaves from neighborhood curbs in town, as well as heavy barrels of fish heads and guts from the fish house. We ran water lines downhill from a neighbor's well. Thinking about him working with me in the garden so many, many years ago, when we were yet free, before things ended with pain and perfect finality, I missed my son's father.

The garden was living art, a verdant jumble. Moon-and-stars watermelon, a time-honored green melon splotched with big yellow moons and small yellow stars, sprawled through the wild persimmon. You could eat the skin of hand-size Japanese melons. Lettuce-leaf basil and holy basil and sweet basil grew lush. Varieties of tomato you'd never heard of, and so many flowers: Mexican sunflower, nicotiana, strawflower, cosmos, cleome. Unicorn plant and castor mole bean. Scarlet runner bean. I grew cotton.

I saved seeds, dried them, and packaged them in tiny manila envelopes to ship here and there. To people outside the Seed Savers Exchange I sold them for a dollar a pack. I exhibited heirlooms at the Florida Folk Festival. I sold seeds of roselle and moon-and-stars watermelon and candy roaster squash, plants you couldn't find in seed catalogs anymore. Luffa, velvet bean, mullein, globe amaranth, bushel basket gourd. People would stand at the table for a long time, peering into baby food jars of wild coral bean seed, tiny droplets of tobacco seeds, knots of brown cotton.

"I'm so glad to see you again," one wiry old Cracker gentleman exclaimed. "I only came to the festival this year because I thought you might be here." He hovered over the seeds, as if the sight of them restored something unnameable to him. "Conch cowpea," he said. "We grew these when I was a boy. Haven't seen them in years." He bought a few packs. "We used to grow this cowhorn okra when I was a girl," an older woman told me. Or these Jacob's cattle beans. Or German Pink tomatoes. People would buy a few packs of seeds, a bar of lye soap, a bottle of herb vinegar, or a luffa sponge.

I have a fading photo from the folk festival in 1988.
I am sitting behind a table lined with seeds, talking to a
festival-goer, cradling my newborn son in the crook of
a crossed leg. He would have been two weeks old.

After that, there was sadness. My fragile marriage
didn't last the year, and for many years to follow I had
no garden—no time for one, no plot of land, no energy.
I wandered far from the happy young woman among
flowers who kept bees.

Me selling heirloom seeds at
the 1988 folk festival.

When I returned to Georgia, Uncle Percy said I could
use the original garden plot at the edge of the cotton field. I
gardened there the first few years, never producing much.
We had entered a three-year drought, and the ditch beside
the dirt road wicked water away from the plants' roots.
The soil, overworked from years of exhaustive farming,
stayed poor despite loads of mulch and manure. Plagues
of insects fled the sprayed cotton, and sometimes spray
drifted into the garden.

Later I moved the garden to the rich soil of the backyard, where the smokehouse had been, closer to the well
and to the kitchen. There it thrived, providing us with
spinach, lettuce, squash, tomatoes, peppers, herbs.

The next year, wanting more beauty and more ex-
travagance, I ordered plenty of flowers from the *Market
Bulletin:* moonflower, an immense-flowered, heady evening
glory, twelve seeds for a dollar. I planted it so it grew up
a broken hayrick beside the shed, where I also planted
cypress vine, loved by hummingbirds. I ordered the seed
from Betty Bryant, who sent a note: "The vines die in
the fall and usually reseed in May, but save seed until
you see how well yours reseed. I always plant about May.
Good luck!"

The woman from whom I ordered two-inch-across
marigolds for organic pest control said: "Mama plants hers
in a box or planter next to her mailbox. Real pretty."

Martin gourd seed arrived with a photocopied sheet of
growing instructions, complete with directions for hand
pollination, which you must do, the man said, "if the little
gourds die before starting to grow.

"The gourds are pollinated by a moth during the night.
Due to pesticides and predators, the moths are sometimes

missing: therefore you have to become a moth. Just before dark is the best time for this procedure."

With the angel's trumpet seed came a sheet of pure poetry: "As La Bella Luna's beams strike the earth, the Angel's Trumpet springs open and releases a heavy scent. The perfume attracts moths that brush against the stamens, spreading pollen in an act of procreation that lasts but through the night in a span of life and love even shorter than that of the mayfly." The gardener mentioned O'Keeffe's painting of *Datura arborea,* and at the top of the page, on the left, excerpted a couplet from John Donne:

> *At the round earth's imagined corners, blow*
> *Your trumpets, Angels, and arise, arise.*

On the right he typed:

> *Blow*
> *Gabriel*
> *Blow.*

Every Thursday I count on opening the mailbox and finding the *Market Bulletin,* because it tells me that more people than I imagined are growing self-seeding petunias and gathering swarms of bees and cooking at home and selling mules and needing a source of chicken manure. They may not live as far from town as they used to, and the farm may have shrunk—where they live may not even look like a farm—but there's plenty of country out there, and people living in it. Living the way I have dreamed, with a mockingbird versifying from the sweetshrub and hummingbirds chattering over the salvia.

Waiting for the Tide

T he first time I laid eyes on James Holland was in December 1998, at a public meeting in Jesup regarding the state's plan to monitor water quality in the Altamaha River, which drains a quarter of Georgia and is the second largest system, in terms of water flow, pouring from the Atlantic seaboard. Two rivers, the Oconee and the Ocmulgee, converge thirty miles northwest of Baxley to form the Altamaha, a wide, dark, sedimentary river that over the centuries keeps modifying its course and forsaking oxbow lakes in the wide floodplains alongside it. Our farm is located about seven miles from its banks.

The Jesup meeting had been ill publicized—purposefully, we thought; I was surprised when thirty people showed up. These weren't well-heeled, college-educated, liberal idealists. They were manual laborers, dressed in boots and work clothes. They loved to fish.

And they were angry. They'd seen too many degradations of the river, they were quick to point out—increased pollution and sediment and algae and exotic species. They were tired of the state's environmental protection agency not doing its job.

James Holland looked about sixty, his chestnut hair sparkling gray. He kept asking hard questions, like, "What are you doing about nonpoint source pollution?" and, "Why aren't you testing in the estuary?"

"Who is he?" I whispered to a bearded man nearby. He told me.

"What does he do?"

"He's a crabber."

Since we were forty miles from home on a school night, my son and I left early. Halfway to the truck I heard someone call, "Excuse me!" It was a man from the meeting, not the crabber.

"I got off the front row to chase you down," he said. "Where are you from?"

"Baxley."

"We're going to do something about the river," he said. "We've got a grant to start a group, and we need people from up your way to get involved." His card read Robert DeWitt, R & R Seafood. Until then, I often thought I was a lone duck, the only person in a hundred miles who cared about wildness.

∞

A month after the Jesup meeting, mid-January, I was in the small coastal town of Darien, at a meeting to organize Altamaha Riverkeeper. Near Darien, three or four wide arms of river braid into a gorgeous blue-green delta, embracing Lewis Island, where a grove of ancient cedars too remote for loggers to reach grows older every year.

James Holland ran the organizational meeting. He wore his hair slicked back at the hairline, revealing a broad forehead grooved deeply by twenty years on a crab boat in full sun. He was a big, vehement man with eyes that were unnerving in their intensity—not the kind of man to cross.

"My reason for being here is necessity," he told the

twenty people gathered. "I am watching my way of living going down the drain. Used to, I could harvest 1,500 to 1,800 pounds of crabs off 100 crab traps in a day. Now, on a good day, I'm lucky to get 160 pounds." The crabbers have tried limited entry (160 crabbers are permitted by the state), he said, and have required traps that let small crabs escape, all without success.

"From live coral reefs on up," he said, "marine life is being destroyed by inland pollution. I'm ready to do something about it."

Blue-eyed DeWitt, the seafood dealer who had followed me out of the Jesup meeting, rarely spoke but was equally emphatic when he did. "I've seen the river come from one of the most productive shad fisheries to no shad fishery," he said. He grew up on the Altamaha. Blue crab catch for 1996 was the lowest reported in twenty years statewide, he said, and brown shrimp was 25 percent lower than the twenty-year average.

Water quality in the watershed had been declining steadily. Nutrient levels in the lower basin had approximately doubled over the previous thirty years. The degradation was blamed on erosion caused by clearcutting along stream banks, on agricultural and forestry runoff, on altered drainage patterns, and on point source pollution. I marveled to hear such terms coming from the mouths of farmers and shrimpers and crabbers. You'd never know by listening that James Holland had only a ninth-grade education.

"The largest populations of short-nosed and Atlantic sturgeon south of Cape Hatteras are here," said Gordon Rogers, fisheries biologist turned contractor. He talked about the endangered spiny mussel, endemic to the basin, found now only in the drainage of the Ohoopee, the most pristine of the river's tributaries. "We don't need to be maintaining the Altamaha. We need to reverse the damage."

Altamaha Riverkeeper would be based on Hudson Riverkeeper, a watchdog organization founded in 1966 by commercial fishermen determined to improve water quality in the nearly dead Hudson. Since 1983, when the group hired a full-time riverkeeper, it forced more than 150 violators of clean-water laws, through litigation, to spend over $1 billion to restore the Hudson River.

After the meeting, I stood outside in the sunshine with James. A quarter of a mile away, the Altamaha threaded through salt marsh. "We're gonna take that river back," James said. "It belongs to the people." At that moment, he told me later, he was the happiest man alive. It was in that moment that both our lives yawed. James would become a fierce activist, an outspoken advocate for a functional watershed. He would be much recognized for his courageous work. His name would travel far. As for me, in that moment I began to collect a community around me, focused on a vision I believed in wholeheartedly. I had been scooped up in a beautiful net filled with people who would become good friends, James among them. Loneliness dwindled.

Within a week, a board adopted a mission and a set of bylaws, then elected officers. James found office space, distributed membership forms, and applied for nonprofit status. Our group sent out press releases with a new phone number, letting people know of our mission: to preserve and restore the quality of water, habitat, and flow in Georgia's largest river system, including its tributaries.

Two days later, James called to say we needed a meeting upstream, in Baxley. I was to gather as many people as

I liked, but at least eight, to whom he and Robert could
come talk to about Riverkeeper. Our group needed power
to be effective, and that meant reaching out for members.

∞

I've seen lots of activists at work and have never seen
anybody mobilize people the way James does. Maybe it's
the almost rude certainty with which he speaks. Or that
he knows exactly what he wants and asks for it. He makes
a lot of phone calls. Even when he could do a task alone
with less effort, he takes time to involve people on many
levels. He uses established friendships to contact strangers
through someone who knows them. And he worries at a
problem until he has an idea of how to solve it. He finds
someone who can help him. He asks for help. If he's told
no, he asks again or finds someone else.

At 8:31 Sunday morning, the phone rang. "Were you
sleeping?" James boomed.

"No," I said. "I was lying in bed, reading."

"I was laying in bed at four this morning, waiting until
I could get to work." He interrupted himself. "I just talked
to my first cousin. Her husband's a professor in Athens.
Which shows that all my folks didn't turn out like me.
She'll get our press release to the university newspaper.
I want you to mail it."

"Okay." I took down the address.

"Include a short note to my cousin, so she knows a
human being sent it." Abruptly he switched the subject.
"Listen, there's this scientist studying the Gulf of Mexico.
Forty percent of his water samples contain human viruses.
What the hell's going on?" He asked this as if I were

supposed to supply an immediate and satisfactory answer—
as if I were responsible, even. I stayed quiet.

"I don't think it's septic tanks," he said. "I think it's
treatment plants. Medicines and antibiotics show up,
heart medicine in particular. Like tests for caffeine in
water. About 10 A.M., the caffeine shows up from that
morning's coffee. If it's happening there, it's happening
here. We've been telling them about this shit. Pardon my
French, but we've been telling them." By "them" he meant
the Environmental Protection Division (EPD) of our state
natural resources agency. "For years I've been trying to tell
them we're losing our fish, our shrimp, our sea life."

"I'm so glad you've been paying attention," I said, hon-
estly grateful, "and that you care about these things."

"Listen, I've got to go crabbing. I've been waiting for
the tide."

∞

When the tide comes in on the Georgia coast, it comes
with a vengeance. On a full moon, it can be as high as
eight feet, covering the tips of the spartina so that you
can't distinguish creek from marsh.

One evening on their way to a meeting in Hazlehurst,
the next town west, James and Robert met me for supper.
James told us how he got involved in environmental issues.
Years before, someone invited him to a coastal meeting
put on by EPD.

"I didn't understand a thing they were saying," he said.
Determined he would never again be ignorant of the
issues, he borrowed textbooks and scientific reports and
began to read about water quality.

"I say to EPD," he laughed, "you created me, now you're gonna live with me." He sobered when he thought of the task he'd taken on, piecing an environmental community together where there had never been one. It required fearless leadership, an immense amount of educating, and lots of help. The headwaters of the Altamaha extend north to Atlanta.

"This sucker is mammoth," James said.

In Hazlehurst someone drew James aside and told him that two pipes needed investigating. One, the informant thought, drained raw sewage into the river; the other contained "white stuff." The informant told him to check these pipes at nine on a Sunday morning.

The next month, forty people attended our Baxley meeting. They talked about the fact that the sandbars used to be white as sugar and now they were stained by algae, that last summer the algae were so thick the water looked like spinach stew, that because of sediment buildup the river was shallower than it had ever been, that people were scared to eat the fish.

Robert DeWitt's brother was in the front row. He'd been sent by Rayonier, a huge paper mill that pumps water from and into the river near Jesup. Rayonier has a permit to pollute. A Jesup restaurateur had told us he couldn't publicly promote Altamaha Riverkeeper because "Rayonier runs this town. They'd put me out of business." As Rayonier's chemist, the brother took a storm of notes. The brothers stood together, one on each side of the podium, locked in argument. The hardest work comes when blood is divided. Yet, surely, in this kind of dissension is also hope.

We signed up a few new members—fifty-five, fifty-six, and fifty-seven.

With two or three grants in the works, we advertised
to hire a riverkeeper. We intended to monitor, to educate,
to lobby, and to litigate, if necessary. In mid-February
a scientist trained twenty of us to take water quality
samples. At the first session, a thin black woman in heels
showed up. She lived on the water near Everett City and
had read about the training in the paper. Admiring the
courage it must have taken this woman to come, I smiled
at her a lot. After an hour, she started to smile back.

One evening after a call from James, I had a surge of
energy and I went dancing through the house. "I'm in love
with those crabbers," I sang. "I'm in love, in love."

What I was in love with was possibility. This far upstream, the river isn't influenced by the tide, but I was
rising with another tide, an awakening. Hope sprang where
none was before. Within six weeks, Altamaha Riverkeeper
had 125 members. It happened so quickly, this new environmental community that had seemed light-years away.
We floundered at times, losing one board member to strife,
but by early April of 1999 we were 200 strong.

Within three years we would have a director, an office
manager, a riverkeeper (James, who no longer crabs). We
would have about a thousand members, and over half a
million in grants. We would win our first lawsuit against
a manufacturer dumping arsenic, cyanide, and copper into
the river in excess of what its permit allowed. We would
secure two other legal victories against municipalities that
were discharging excessive organic pollutants into the
river. Altamaha Riverkeeper staff would conduct over 350
site visits in response to water quality complaints. Other
lawsuits were pending.

Now I had a community, ever widening and strengthening. We weren't close geographically, since we were spread throughout a watershed, from Atlanta to Darien, but we were joined by a dream. Already, water quality in the river had improved by many parts per million because of Altamaha Riverkeeper. The tide comes in, the tide goes out, and the river will come cleaner out of Georgia.

In This House We Are Not Separate

The morning we encountered a snake in the house I discovered a daddy longlegs in the blender. "He better be glad I looked before I switched it on," I told Silas.

"Ugh," he said. He was watching the cat, Suzy, who crouched near the screened kitchen door, by a counter cabinet. Silas tiptoed over and peered into the corner by the cabinet.

"A snake," he said almost matter-of-factly, although it was the first one we had ever witnessed inside the house. His voice was free of alarm. I bent over and looked. The intruder was a harmless yellow rat snake. The reptile was small, maybe three feet long, easing between the cabinet and the door, looking for an escape. It exited where the corner of the warped screen door didn't meet the jamb.

"How did you notice it?" I asked Silas.

"I saw the cat acting peculiar," he said. "I went to see what was the matter."

"Well," I said, "I'd rather it visit in the daytime than at night."

I could think of five places in the venerable house where you could look directly out through a hole, into open air. There was one under the kitchen sink, where the drainpipe opening was cut two inches too big; another in the floor, where the water heater pipe led out; another in the back bedroom, where a floorboard didn't meet the wall. There was also a puncture I couldn't account for in the living-room floor; and a gap where the dryer vent should exit.

Field mice used these portals, and gigantic cockroaches, kindly called palmetto bugs, and anoles. So did diminutive sugar ants and cotillions of ladybugs. So did moths, wasps, and bees. Following a message trail laid by one of their outriders, armies of fire ants marched single file up the brick cornerposts of the foundation to swarm the dirty laundry, looking for pockets of oily sweat. A Carolina wren, singing her descending spiral, had to be chased out of the dining room. She must have flown through torn porch screen, looking for a secluded nesting spot, then entered through the front door.

The house was abominably open to the world. Windows didn't fit their sashes, doors missed their frames by an inch. Wall cracks allowed spiders and flies, especially on overcast days, to sneak inside. A green treefrog, emerald with an ivory line down the side, squeezed through a chink. I discovered it hunting the little bugs that spun around the lamp in the evenings. When it called, *quank quank,* the sound was startling, resounding off the living-room walls.

Summers, chimney swifts roosted in the unused chimney. Mockingbirds and woodpeckers knocked and knocked on glass panes, questioning their own reflections. "No," I said to them when the glass began to rattle.

Nor were we separated in this house from the weather. The house was bereft of even an ounce of insulation, which might also have blocked some of the holes through which the creatures entered. The house was built before fiberglass. The temperature outside was about the temperature inside, although sometimes on a raw day it stayed colder

indoors longer on account of heat lag. The colder the
weather, the bigger the cracks, until it seemed one could
slide swords and scabbards through them.

The house offered three heat sources. One was a fireplace in the living room, which had an insert and blower
or it would have been useless. I was ceaselessly coaxing
and stirring and feeding the fire. Uncle Percy rigged a
wood rack under the living-room window, so I carted
wheelbarrowloads of wood to fill the rack, and dragged
the logs into the house through the window. A gas space
heater warmed the southwest room, my study. The oven
helped in the kitchen. We had no furnace. No speed-dial
thermostat with heat pump. No central heating and air-
conditioning. We had a goosebump bathroom, breath-in-
the-air bedroom, froze-toes kitchen.

I found an anole half frozen in my study. It was a drab,
static brown. Easily I captured it and removed it to a ca-
mellia that caught the first golden sunshine, so the anole's
blood could thaw and its hide go green. "You're welcome,"
I said.

Real winter came, with gray days, when the temperature didn't exceed forty and I had to leave the spigots
dripping so they wouldn't freeze and burst. Piercing and
relentless, the cold crept around the edges of the bed with
its seven covers, including two quilts. Morning arrived too
quickly. One January night the temperature plummeted
to twenty-five degrees and the daytime temperature never
climbed above freezing. The next night the thermometer
dropped further, to twenty-two degrees. The fireplace
was going continuously, burning, burning. The heater and
oven were on high, and still the house was glacial. We
moved about in snowsuits, like skiers.

Even on the most bitter nights—especially then—the
field mouse who frequently darkened the hole beneath
the kitchen sink tumbled pecans from the basketful by
the fireplace and rolled them into her hollow between the
studs of the wall. Sometimes she squatted and whittled a
nut open by the fire, loudly gnawing out the meat. Late
at night, I often spied her edging along the baseboard,
rounding the open door to the kitchen, and I wondered
idly whether to bait a trap. If only she'd be quieter at
night. I found her nest of little pink babies in a drawer
of sweaters and unkindly carried the woolen cradle out
to the field. "You're field mice," I said. "Good luck with
the hawks."

In summer the house felt like a sauna. With every window propped open and every fan whirring, including the
attic fan, the heat was wearing, irritating. On such days, I
stripped off shorts and sleeveless shirt two or three times
a day to pour cold water over myself in the bathtub, but in
minutes the water had evaporated and the coolness gone.
Some nights the heat did not lift and I lay under a fan, on
sticky sheets, sweating.

In winter the creatures came in for shelter, and in
summer they came because they could. Most nights we
slept under netting to escape the mosquitoes sweeping
through holes in the screen wire of the porch or bumping
through open doors. One unusually warm January 3,
I noted, we had to rehang the mosquito net that we'd
stored two weeks before. Every winter I vowed that I
would not last another in this old house, and every summer I said the same. Insulation would be good, I said, or
at least some way to keep the critters in their places. "Not
in the house," I said to the blue-tailed mole skink, who

found the palmetto bugs delectable. Although I declared these things, the truth was that I loved living with only a permeable screen between us and outdoors. In the openness of our house, I didn't feel separated from the rest of life. It was a fine habitat.

Gator Trapper

M y friend Ann called to say the gator trapper was leaving Racepond at seven that evening. "He's gonna catch that gator in the pond. I'm afraid it'll get one of the dogs, or somebody's child, one day," she said. "Meet us out there, about nine."

Ann lives in town, but her farm is way out in the country, fifteen or twenty miles from town, a long way down a dirt road, past two unrailed bridges. I arrived by nine to find the gate locked, usually an indication that nobody's home. Could they have locked the gate so they wouldn't be disturbed? Had they already gotten the gator and gone?

The night was moonless and pitch dark, and the pond house was three-quarters of a mile away, through a pasture, through a wood, across two earthen dams that form a pond. Unable to see even my hand in front of my face, I set out, and gradually my pupils widened until I discerned the gray of worn tracks through the grass, fencerows of wild cherry and sweet gum, water that found its own light. I walked steadily through the darkness, loose jointed and wary, often with an arm out to shield my face from the titi, or leatherwood, a shrub that frequents swamps and low woods, gnawing at the water's edge. Along the lake, frogs hollered for help.

Nearing the pond house I saw no lights, heard nothing. Where the sand hill sloped upward to the camp, I began to shout softly for Ann. If the trappers had gone already and she was there alone, I didn't want her shooting me. No reply. Nobody. I didn't even stop to rest in the darkness, simply turned and started the three-quarter mile trek, and in one of those rare, lucid moments my thoughts rose above my body. Dark woods stretched far on all sides, and I was small. "What in hell are you doing way out here in the woods alone at this time of night?" I asked aloud.

Help, help, the spring creepers yelped.

Recrossing the second dam I saw a pair of headlights coming in, followed by another. The road makes a deep S there, and Ann's carlights caught me against the pine trees, only my shoulders and head visible above titi. I grinned and waved. In overalls I must have looked like a strange woodland revenant materialized from fetterbush.

Ann stopped her vehicle and I got in the back, where Campbell, Ann's little boy, was.

"I can't believe you walked in," she said.

"Why?"

"You don't even have a flashlight."

"You're just getting here? It's way after nine."

"I ran into them at the store," she said.

"How many of them are there?"

"Two."

By now the night had taken on the surreal quality where anything could happen.

A voice from the passenger's seat: "Weren't you afraid of snakes?"

"Ms. Charlotte! You're in here too?"

"I brought Mama to see the gator," Ann said.

"No, ma'am. I'm not afraid."

At the camp, the road was chafed yellow-pink by the

tires of four-wheelers. The two-acre lake lay beyond. Ann parked in such a way that her headlamps shone on the dirt ramp and some distance across the adumbral water. It looked like a mountain lake, so set was it in the landscape, so nestled. The world appeared to end beyond the light.

The trappers galloped up in a black Dodge pickup and pulled beyond us, backing down the ramp. On the door panel of the truck, an official sign read DNR with a logo of the state of Georgia and, underneath, Nuisance Alligator Trapper. A johnboat protruded out of the truck bed.

The door sprung open as soon as the pickup stopped, and a man whose face I couldn't see alighted and without ceremony began to work at his equipment. In the head-lights, he was astonishingly wild looking, tall and lean, with a bone-silver shank of hair that hung against his back. He was wildly beautiful. His chin jutted a fraction too much forward, as if in some ill-spent past he had fallen against it hard enough to snap his neck but had not.

"Good gracious," I breathed to Ann.

"Wait until you see the other one," she said. His helper came around the truck, a man even taller and more handsome.

"Wow."

We climbed out with Campbell, acting like concerned landowners. Because she had to walk with a cane, Ms. Charlotte opted to stay in the car. The headlights were on.

"Y'all, this is my friend," Ann introduced me.

"Howdy," the one who looked native said. "I'm Jackie Carter. This is David Thompson." He talked very slowly. He had strapped a light such as coal miners wear to his head, and on his forehead the bulb looked like the lovely eye of a dragonfly, enlarged and replicated in glass. He was careful not to shine it in our eyes, which meant he had to look slantwise to see us. I felt my face lit by reflection.

"A pleasure," I replied.

The silver-haired man, Jackie, started pulling out things—a bamboo pole, a metal noose, a headlamp for his buddy, rope, a roll of electrical tape. He was serious. He had an alligator to catch. We watched in silence until Ann asked him, "What was the biggest gator you ever caught?" and he talked while he worked.

"It was over in Ware County," he said. "It was eleven and a half feet long and weighed 680 pounds."

"I'm glad it wasn't me tangling with that one," Ann said. More silence, broken again by Ann. "You cook gator meat?"

"All the time. Fry it, boil it, cook it on a grill."

"He's telling you right," said David. "He can cook."

"I've been cooking for myself so long I cook better than most women," Jackie said. He was taping the rope attached to the noose to the fishing pole. "We had bear meat for supper. With mashed taters and hot biscuits. I make 'em from scratch. I make cinnamon rolls too."

I eyed him closely, and he was watching me, too, albeit sideways. He didn't miss much, I could tell. Even while he talked he played his light around the boat's edge, his eyes dancing and darting like two brown sparrows that wanted to know everything.

So he wasn't married. And he couldn't be a total redneck if he liked to cook.

"My friend here is a writer, and she'd like to go out with y'all," Ann said. "Is there room?"

Jackie was silent a long minute in the darkness. He looked toward two upturned johnboats on shore.

"You got a boat that don't leak?" he finally asked Ann.

"I believe so."

"Ours has a big split in it." Both men laughed. "It leaks bad."

"You got a plug?" Ann said. "Mine might need a plug."

"We got a plug."

In the darkness, they righted the small boat on shore, then began to rig it.

"How'd you get that leak in your boat?" Ann asked. They both guffawed but wouldn't say.

"We borrowed a friend's wooden boat one time," Jackie said. "A gator bit a chunk out of it. I mean a big chunk."

"This gator isn't going to eat a hole in my boat, is he?"

Jackie moved alongside the truck, where his boat lay. "See these here teeth marks? That was gator." Deep, angry scratches marred the aluminum along the lip. "They'll grab ahold and bite the boat, but they can't put a hole in a metal one. We had a gator pull one under one time. But that was the worst of it."

"I'm not sure I want to go out there," I said. "Not to bring a gator back."

"You could sit in the middle," Jackie said.

"You'll be all right," David said. "What do you write?"

"Mostly about nature," I said.

"Send me something, sometime," he said. "I run the Charlton County paper. Me and my wife." I looked at Ann but her face was veiled in shadows.

"You catch gators by night?"

"He's the gator trapper." He motioned toward Jackie. "And a good one. I help him out occasionally."

"How big do you think this gator is?" Jackie asked Ann.

"I don't know," she said. "Four or five feet. I'd like to get it out before it gets any bigger."

"I'm not going out there without a life vest," I said to Ann.

"There's one at the pond house," she said. "Let's go get it."

When we were out of earshot of the trappers, I said to her, low, "Whhooeee, Ann, them's some purty men."

"Purty, hell, that's boyfriend material. Especially that tall dark one. I believe that's about the best-looking man I've ever seen."

"Did you hear him mention his wife?"

"That don't matter," she said, talking big. She was teasing, of course. She's well married.

"I like the long-haired one," I said.

"Baby, I believe we've got us a couple of wild men out here in the woods," she said. We chuckled, low and happy. "This is more fun than eating boiled peanuts naked on the courthouse lawn."

"I've got to have something to take notes on," I said. "I've got to write about this."

"Here's a paper bag," Ann said. She scurried around the rough, concrete-floored pond house, looking for a pen. I tore the brown bag into uneven squares and stuffed them in my shirt.

"What are you taking for a light? You can't write in the dark."

"Yes I can. I can do a lot of things in the dark." I grinned and winked.

"You owe me one for this," Ann said, hands on hips. "A big one."

Back at the lake I clambered into the middle of the

boat, where someone had flopped down a cushion. Jackie
stepped into the bow, checking equipment around him.
David turned on the trolling motor they had latched to
the stern and eased out into the lake. Nobody spoke. In
the light of their lamps, I watched small bugs, tiny moths
and unknown winged beings partial to wild lakes, careening about their faces. Jackie knelt in the bow, moving his
head back and forth, constantly playing his light along the
shore of the big pond. He was alert as a deer, watching
everywhere. His light tripped over the surface of the water,
illuminating stumps near the edge and shrubs strangely
shadowed in the weird artificial beam.

David leaned forward, murmuring. "Once he gets the
gator, he gets wild with the pole until he gets the noose
free. He yells 'pole' and I grab it. Don't let him hit you
upside the head."

"Okay," I whispered, not knowing what in the world he
was talking about.

"It hurts when it hits you," he warned. "I've been hit a
few times. Now I try to grab it quick."

"Okay," I said.

We were cruising almost soundlessly. Jackie never
relaxed or stopped turning his head back and forth, and he
extended his right hand out at arm's length, fingers straight,
so that without looking backward once he directed David to
the right, around an island at the back side of the lake, then
to the left. Everywhere Jackie looked, I looked.

"There," both men breathed at once. Jackie rotated
his hand palm down to slow David. Finally I saw a pair
of lucid eyes at water level. Gator eyes reflect red directly
back to a light source. Jackie directed the boat with hand
motions until we were twenty feet from the gator, then

pressed his palm outward as if to push against an invisible wall, the sign to stop. The boat glided forward in its own wake; Jackie had the long fishing pole with a noose on the end stretched in front of him, guiding it toward the gator's jaws. In one quick motion he lowered the noose and swept it over the gator, who swam forward into it. Jackie snatched, the noose tightened, and all hell broke loose. By this time I was lying in the bottom of the boat.

I heard David call "pole," but I was oblivious to what was happening with the trappers, so riveted was I by the cauldron of water boiling alongside the boat, spraying three feet into the air.

"I didn't get him good," I heard Jackie say. "Just by the tail."

I eased erect. "Is it coming off?"

"I don't think so."

I got a good look at the gator. "It's a baby," I said.

"About four feet," Jackie replied. The alligator might have been small but it was fierce, throwing its body this way, then that. The rope caught it midway down the tail. Alongside the boat, it arched skyward, snapping and hissing. Water flew. The alligator lashed against the boat and rocked us, a maelstrom of ferocity, then grabbed the aluminum rim in its mouth, teeth screeching across metal.

"Damn," I said. I usually don't curse. The gator banged the boat with its tail, fighting. "Are you bringing that thing in here?" *Wham. Wham.*

"No. We tow them in. He'll wear out in a couple of minutes."

"Start back?" David asked.

"Yeah. I've got him." *Wham.*

On shore Jackie tugged the alligator from the lake and

in one quick motion was atop the reptile, wrestling its snout to the ground. He didn't want help. He pinned the jaws flat with one hand and rummaged in his pocket for a large rubber band, cut from a tire tube, and corded the jaws shut. Then he trussed the alligator's legs backward. The reptile couldn't move, couldn't snap. Only the tail was still dangerous, and we watched for it.

The trapper got out a measure. The gator was four feet, six inches. "You never know what size gator you're gonna find when you get to a place," Jackie said. "Sometimes they say it's ten feet long and when you get there it's half that. Sometimes they say it's small and when you get there it's an eight-footer. Usually, the higher the fear, the bigger the gator."

I drew another scrap of paper from my shirt and wrote that down. The higher the fear, the bigger the gator. I couldn't see a thing.

"What will happen to this one?"

"I'll take it to the swamp and turn it loose," he said.

"Okefenokee?"

"Yeah. I live right there by it. I turn them loose at Kingfisher Landing and then they have to fight for their lives with the big gators."

"What about the big ones you catch?"

"They go to an alligator farm."

"And then?" I asked.

"Some of the big females are used as brooders."

He remembered something. He turned to Ann. "I brought the meat you ordered," he said. I knew right then what happened at the gator farm.

"Hot dog," she said.

"Isn't there someplace you can take them and save their

lives? We need more wild areas where they can live. We need gators in the wetlands. Florida gators were on the endangered list for years and years because of overhunting."

"And now they're everywhere," he said. "Eating people's dogs. Not long ago one ate a kid down there."

"Gators aren't dangerous unless they've been fed by humans," I said. "If people feed 'em, it's a death warrant. I've got a friend wades all the time through swamps getting to bird rookeries, gators all around."

"Believe it or not, I like gators," he said. "They're one of my favorite animals. But people don't want them laying up in their ponds, and they call me. They're afraid of them."

"People need educating about gators."

He didn't say anything.

"Is that a male or a female, reckon?" I asked. I knew how you find out and I wanted to see if he'd do it.

"Turn your head, ladies," Jackie said dramatically, and he stuck one finger into the alligator's cloaca.

"Female," he said, and smiled, and the men flopped the trussed gator into the back of the pickup. The entire operation had taken less than a half hour.

Inside the pond house, Ann offered the men a drink, which they accepted. They looked around at her collection of faded "Posted" signs and turpentine equipment and Creek Indian points while she fished out her checkbook and paid for the meat. I can't remember a thing that was said. I was thinking about what I was going to do. I withdrew a piece of the brown bag from my pocket and wrote my first name on it and my phone number. Without a word I handed it to Jackie. I couldn't read a thing from his face. He took the number and nodded, never missing a beat in the conversation.

Back at the truck, he lingered after Ann had driven away, back to town. David was already in the truck, waiting. I stood nearby. Jackie fidgeted with the ropes that secured the boat, checked the straps, moved a paddle. Finally he stood, too, a few feet from me, waiting. I didn't know what we were waiting for.

"It's a pleasure to meet you," he said. He reached out and quickly touched my hand. "A pleasure."

Later, I would unwad the torn squares of paper bag. They would be filled with odd, jumbled sentences whose letters and words ran together, as if they'd been written by a drunk. One would say, "The slowest talking man I ever knew was Cooter. He tried out for Hee Haw one time and they turned him down because he talked too slow." Another, "He's contemplating getting ahold of my leg." The long-haired man would unfold a square spelling out the name of a woman. If we knew the future, hope would become extinct in this world, so we are allowed to try, to imagine, to wonder.

The truck doors slammed shut and the gator trappers were gone. Under a sky brindled with ashen clouds, the lake drowsed, motionless.

The Rural In-Between

For eight years, I lived in Sycamore, a community in north Florida, on a divided farm that had been sold in pieces to back-to-the-landers in the 1980s. Houses and gardens and orchards, mostly hidden, were scattered along our branching sand road; my friend Irwin and I were land partners on a twelve-acre triangle that went from old field pasture to deciduous forest to remnant Appalachian ravine. The community gathered for Sunday volleyball, potlucks, clothes exchanges, baby showers, and also funerals. In spring we held plant exchanges.

Sycamore was three miles from the one-horse town of Greensboro (a post office, a convenience store, a hardware store), seventeen miles from Quincy, with its two groceries and weekly newspaper, and forty miles from Tallahassee, a university town and the capital. In Sycamore I learned to live simply and cheaply. I learned how to garden and how to take a dole of day-old bread from the Catholic mission for migrant workers, and how to make a smidgen of money last a long time. But the cultural poverty I could never overcome. Human beings are curious creatures who long for stimulus and for knowledge, and we are by nature gregarious. Tallahassee drew us with its concerts, movies, book groups, libraries, dances, benefits, readings, and parties.

In the same way, when we came home to Georgia, the port of Savannah drew Silas and me. Savannah is an

hour and a half from Baxley, a beautiful drive through
Fort Stewart Military Reservation, where the forest stands
tall—well managed, burned regularly, returning to wildness. The reservation takes almost an hour to cross. Two
painted white lines girdle the trunks of red-cockaded
woodpeckers' cavity trees. Once, on the road, I found a
bobcat fresh dead, not even stiff, and I dragged it into
the woods, memorizing the wildness frozen on the lovely
cat's face, the tiny tufts at the tip of each ear, the other-
worldly markings.

In Savannah we bought books. Silas looked at the latest toys. Often we ate out at a Greek or Japanese restaurant and then wandered the waterfront, along River Street,
listening to street musicians, dropping coins in their styrofoam cups, and ogling portrait painters at their easels.

Although we purchased as much of our food as possible at the grocery in Baxley (the cashiers had gotten
accustomed to our cloth bags), often what we wanted
they didn't have. So in Savannah we bought groceries at
the health food store near colonial Forsyth Park, gorgeous
with its drooping live oaks and Spanish moss and benches.
Tofu and tempeh. Organic produce. Eggs from free-range
chickens. Fruit-sweetened cereal. Soymilk. Brown rice.
We bought teas and beans and vitamins and nonsaccha-
rine toothpaste and biodegradable soap.

Each dollar we spend is a vote, I believe, and I wanted
to vote for a cleaner earth, better health, family farmers,
pesticide-free food. Sometimes the bill was a couple of
hundred dollars, and we stacked the perishables in a cooler
and headed home, drinking kefir and eating fruit popsicles. We left invigorated by the historical and cultural
mecca of Savannah, with its cobblestone streets and young

artists with outlandish-colored hair and trailing, bell-bottom pants.

Often our friend Alan took us out in his boat when we went to Savannah. We explored the archipelago of state-protected islands off Tybee Island, and the saltmarsh creeks of that labyrinthine landscape: fishing, kneeboarding, tubing, casting for shrimp and mullet, sunbathing, swimming. The ocean was an edifying foil, as if through one eye we saw the farm, with its boundaries, and with the other, the unfathomable possibilities of the sea. We visited the edge of the world, characterized by the turn and tag of tides; we lived in the interior, in a place that was as unchanging as a place erected from trees could be.

Sometimes in Savannah I thought of Baxley, 100 miles away, and I said to myself, "That is another world." When Alan visited us in Baxley, he would joke, "Well, I've set my watch back a hundred years." He would call himself a Yankee, although he was born and raised on Tybee, because he came from a place far away not in distance but in sensibility. I hear people say they'd like to retire to a small town, disgusted as they are with traffic and crime and pollution in a crowded city. It would have to be a college town, they say. In many ways, we have abandoned the rural in-betweens.

००

One day I ran into Sandy Brobston in the grocery store. She and her husband, Stan, had moved back home to be near Stan's brother Henry, just in time for Henry to be diagnosed with colon cancer. He was dead six months later. They stayed on, two kind-hearted, educated, hopeful people who care. Stan is on the arts council. He joined

a service club so he could do something about litter, a
terrible problem in the region, and he designed signs that
were put up across the county: "Illegal to Litter."

Sandy loves to cook exotic meals and will drive no-
table distances to find ingredients she needs, but mostly
she spends her time volunteering at the hospital gift shop
(they raised enough money in the past year to buy a new
radiology machine), making wild jams, or working in her
herb garden.

"You can get the big pasta shells for stuffing in
Hazlehurst," she told me. "I buy coconut milk here."

"Here?"

"It's in the foreign food section. They don't have many
things, but they have coconut milk."

We talked for an hour in the store, with so much to say.

These two people are vital assets to our community;
they are not expendable. Should they happen to move away,
their absence would make a big hole. The place would miss
them. What I see, everywhere, are a few people trying to
bolster communities, trying to keep them intact, reaching
out, organizing. If more of us had the courage and tenacity
of Stan and Sandy Brobston to work for a better place, no
one would call us backward. A visitor would set his watch
forward when he crossed the county line.

Toward the Promised Land

Ushers had closed the double swinging doors to the sanctuary when I arrived at the First African Missionary Baptist Church for its Christmas candle-lighting service, and through the thin foyer wall I could hear the pastor praying. Another young woman came through the front door, herding two smartly dressed children and dragging along a sharp wind; we stood together waiting to be allowed in.

When the prayer ended, we entered the worship hall; I entered timidly, head slightly bowed. I took a seat near the back. The choir was singing and I looked around. In the golden dimness, the church was modestly elegant, its aisles carpeted red, a decorated tree behind the pulpit. The church could hold a few hundred worshipers, and it was about half filled. Noticeably missing were young black men, although many young women had come, with children. Elders sat among them, and stable, middle-aged couples, people who had been raised in the church and had raised their own children there. I drew a couple of looks, but not the attention I expected.

I was there at the invitation of Dr. Juanita Nails, who served on the town's arts council, where I met her. She was an administrator at the high school, and she sang with a glorious a capella group called the Baxley Trio. I finally spotted Juanita up in the choir loft. The choir, dressed in canary yellow robes with blue kente-cloth stoles, sang, swaying softly, and the churchgoers sang with them. I have never heard an elk bugle or whales keen, but I doubt any sound is more deeply moving than our own species singing. After the hymns, the singers came down and dispersed themselves into the pews, joining families. I saw Juanita take her place at the far front.

The pastor, well versed and eloquent, delivered his sermon. I do not remember his message, or the section of the Bible he spoke on, but I know I listened. Often my eyes filled with tears, because that is what church does to me; I am touched by people acknowledging spirit, desiring it.

As soon as the sermon ended, a pride of youngsters got up and went to the back, where a good deal of bustling was audible above the hymn that accompanied the passing of collection plates. The pastor announced the Live Nativity. To organ music, a teenage boy and girl marched down the aisle side by side, dressed in satin robes. Younger children—shepherds and wise men—followed them, wearing robes, cloth tied about their heads.

At the edge of the pulpit, as someone read the story of Jesus' birth from the Bible, the youngsters reenacted it. "And unto Mary a child was born." Someone handed her a pretty brown baby, swaddled in blankets. The children played their roles earnestly, somber in front of the church, enacting a story essential to their parents' faith.

Powerfully I have felt the deep wound that divides races here in the South. In my town we say the black community or the black swimming pool or a black church. How in the name of earth and heavens do we continue so divisive? I've learned that the way to end racism is not through affirmative action or government programs, although those help, but through personal friendships. When we eat at each

other's houses, spend time together, enjoy each other, no
matter the skin color, that's where real change starts.

In the cafeteria at Altamaha Elementary, where white
and black tiles alternate, some of Silas's classmates invented
a game. "If you step on the black tiles, you love niggers,"
they said. My son told me he went and stood on a black
tile. I have never been more proud.

I especially remember three things about the service.
One was a bright-eyed boy—he must have been four—
sitting behind me. Sometimes I felt the barest of nudges,
and I tilted my head, and the child would be leaning
toward the pew I occupied, pretending he had touched
me by accident. When I beamed at him, he would examine my face. I would direct my attention to the pulpit
again, only to feel another brush past my shoulder. Once,
silently, I reached out a hand to him and gently touched
his arm in return.

The second part of the service that I remember well
was called Spiritual Interpretation. Three slender, middle-
aged women, dressed in long-sleeved leotards and midcalf,
swaying skirts with iridescent sashes, came out and twirled
to a song they broadcast from a cassette tape, swooping
and turning and reaching their arms heavenward, then
sweeping them down, bending at the waist. It was nothing
less than modern dance.

I thought about the arts council then, trying to bring
more attention to the arts in the county. Rural, poor
communities can't afford to think about art much, and
often the artists leave to find bigger places where they can
be their free, avant-garde selves. So far, the council had
sponsored what we called the Ditchwater Jazz Festival,
where the high school jazz band played and the Baxley

Trio sang and a Dixieland group from Atlanta tooted big horns. We'd had a community production of *Cheaper by the Dozen*, a community acoustic jam, and a community coffeehouse. We're always searching for local talent in our little town.

But here it was. Here was theater, music, literature. Here were three dancers using the art form of their bodies. Would the First African Missionary Baptist Church open its Christmas service to the entire community? Why not invite everybody, black and white alike, to celebrate this service side by side?

The part of the service that I remember most was the candle lighting. Everyone made a big ring around the sanctuary, along the walls. It was a very large circle. Now everybody could see me, and I stood in the circle happily, taking a place easily among people of a race that had been oppressed by my own. The church members were more than kind, welcoming me into the line and demonstrating where I should stand and what I should do.

Deacons passed out candles. We swayed to organ music past other deacons who offered fire and lit our candles, hand to hand. The lights lowered further, and soon the darkened church was a moving circle of lights, each light lifting someone's face in it, a room of encircling faces, intent and ceremonial. We sang, "Jesus, light of the world," over and over, although I still can't get it out of my head that we were singing, "This little light of mine, I'm gonna let it shine. Let it shine, let it shine, let it shine." Over and over, gently flowing around the circumference of the room. Then we blew out the candles and sat down.

When the last hymn had been sung, I moved out into the flow of worshipers to give Juanita a hug, and she embraced me. She was embarrassed, she said. When she was singing her solo spiritual, at the top of her lungs, moved by her faith, she hadn't realized I was sitting in the back. "I wouldn't have been so—." She searched for a word to describe herself. "Had I known a visitor was here, I would have been more moderate, more contained."

"It was perfect," I said. "You're a great singer."

Then other people stopped to extend their hands and thank me for coming and say they would love to have me come anytime.

Isn't that what we all want, to have each other? To stand in a grand circle, each holding aloft our own wavering light, hearts wide open? To know the feeling of forgiveness washing through us? To defend each other? To hear each other's stories?

Every day we move toward reconciliation is a step toward the promised land.

Log Trucks at the Crossroads

Every week or two, it seemed, another forest I knew went down. A strip of gorgeous tall pines along the highway south of town was laid flat. The pines were maybe seventy-five feet tall and hid the pine plantation behind them, and I loved driving into town from that direction. I could pretend it was a real forest, deep and wide.

Every time I went to town I counted the log trucks. Cruisers were beating the roads looking for timberland, offering unheard-of prices, trying to keep the chip mills in stock. We were in the middle of a timber cycle like the one that swept Southern forests at the turn of the century, when most of the old-growth cypress and longleaf pine was logged.

The Southeast had become the woodyard for the rest of the country, with timber companies shifting interests from the Northwest. Trees grow fast here in the long-summer South, and the industry goes largely unregulated. From 1977 to 1997, harvests in the thirteen Southern states increased by 50 percent, from 6.8 billion cubic feet to 10.2 billion cubic feet. Today, two-thirds of the wood harvested in the United States comes from the permissive South.

Not only landscapes were being transformed rapidly, but Southerners' attitudes about the changes were also. People no longer sweepingly supported the timber industry; forest destruction was less popular. Investigative

journalists were beginning to look at the timbering, and
I would hear people freely acknowledging that the rate
of logging had them worried. Efforts had begun to slow
the timbering through sustainability studies, activism for
policy changes, and public education.

∞

As forests are cut, they are replaced by pine plantations
that are more agricultural than sylvan. Between 1950 and
1990, 70 million acres of natural forest dwindled to 30 million. In 1950 pine plantations were almost nonexistent; in
1990, they covered 30 million acres.

In 1991, for the first time since records began to be kept,
the removal of softwoods outpaced net growth across the
thirteen states of the South. The trend continues, with the
removal rate of hardwoods, too, now approaching the growth
rate. We are cutting more than we know. We blame the
rate of loss largely on chip mills, plants that grind whole
logs into small wafers used for particle board and paper.
These have tripled in number since 1985, with more than
155 currently in operation. One chip mill can obliterate
3,000 acres of trees in a year. The Dogwood Alliance, a
coalition of nonprofit, grassroots forest protection groups
based in Asheville, North Carolina, has raised hell about
chip mills.

Drive any transect across the South and the view will
be about the same: clearcuts, pine plantations, development. And signs: "Large Log Trucks Entering and Exiting
Highway." It's rare to glimpse a precious bit of woods that
has regenerated on its own and functions as forest, with
ground cover, native canopy trees of all ages, the magic of

birds, and the vanishing tails of animals. Trees represent the spirit of a place. To cut too many is to strip a whereabouts of its soul.

A short time ago a Minnesota friend who was raised in Georgia fifty years ago drove, on a visit home, from Brunswick to Baxley. "I don't see what you mean by forests being cut," he said to me. "All the way here I saw trees." A comment like this frightens me. We may forget what our forests were like and think that brush and scrub produced us. If the trees that surround us are five and ten years old, we miss a lesson in maturity. The land I drive through exhausts me.

Nor has the cutting stopped at pines. Loggers are going into shady bottomlands and along fragile mountain slopes for hardwoods, and into sloughs and creeks—into wetlands!—for the slow-growing and noble cypress, which mostly becomes garden mulch.

In 1998, 2000, and 2002 the Timber Harvesting Southeast Exposition, a consumer and trade show, was held in Baxley. Loggers from across the country swarmed into town to learn about new tree-cutting equipment, acres and acres of it.

"This is the Center of Destruction," I moaned to my friend Susan.

"No," she corrected me. "The Center of Redemption."

ಞ

During the first year we were back, a forest in front of Altamaha School got cut. Midweek I met my neighbor coming down the school steps. She was seventy and lived over on U.S. 1.

"Used to, you couldn't see the school from the high-way," she said. She's a quiet woman, and she shook her head slowly back and forth. "And if ever a person needed money, he doesn't," she said of the owner of the property.

Every day, as we passed, my son and I watched tree-toppling machines snip off huge pines, loaders pile them as if they were popsicle sticks, and trucks haul them away. The first casualty was a juvenile raccoon, hit on the four-lane.

The next day we noticed a turtle upside down a foot from the center yellow lines. I made a U-turn. It was a female gopher tortoise, about three years old, and it had been hit but not fatally. Where her carapace was cracked on the left side, she was bleeding, but not badly, and aside from a broken and scuffed shell, she was uninjured.

We brought her home and set her up in a box to heal, gave her greens and an apple (gopher tortoises are vegetar-ian) in case she wanted to eat, and a saucerful of water. That day she didn't move about but her head protruded from its carapace and she drank. That night we took her to my father's house to repair her shell with epoxy.

And then we looked for another upland forest for her.

∞

In early 1999, at the urging of the Dogwood Alliance, a host of federal and state agencies consented to a Southern Forest Sustainability Study, to be administered by the Forest Service. Public meetings were held across the South that August. I attended one in Tifton, Georgia. I had faxed a letter to the editor of every local paper across southern Georgia, saying that if people were concerned about forests they should attend the hearing. Arriving early, I sat in a chair and waited. Timber industry representatives began to enter.

"How did you find out about the meeting?" I overheard one timber executive ask another.

"I saw a letter in the paper," she replied.

"Me too," another said. For the five activists who showed up, 150 employees of timber companies signed in—not the loggers on the ground but the executives. These tree-cutters could have driven bulldozers and loaders to Tifton and come inside wearing gloves and smelling of pine sap, chain saws in hand. But their cologne came out of bottles and they had replaced the saws with notebooks. They wore name tags that identified the companies they represented. My name tag had only a name.

"It doesn't matter how many timber people show up," an activist said to me. "We're putting them on notice."

Everywhere I get a chance to speak about our forests, in libraries and bookstores across the South, I say: "If you remember nothing else, remember this: *A pine plantation is not a forest.*" The pine plantation may briefly sustain deer, squirrel and common birds until the thickly sown trees shade out ground cover. After that, plantations are ecological dead zones. In plantations, the trees are one age, one species, and planted in rows. Herbicides have been applied, and the tract has been bedded—plowed in wide furrows—allowing commercial trees to be grown in lowland.

Ten years ago, five years ago, I would not have gotten the response I now get to my sermonizing. People listen wide eyed and they nod. Sometimes they raise a hand and express their own grief and dismay at the loss of our landscapes, the loss of unique cultures. People are slowly awakening to what is happening around us. Loss of woods. Wholesale conversion of natural forests to plantations. Fewer wild animals. Fewer places to hunt. They see with their own eyes what is happening and they are troubled, even horrified.

I understand then that we Southerners are not going to sit back and watch every bit of our forests get cut. Logging is necessary, but in order to end our gross neglect of the land and limit wholesale destruction of wild habitats, we will act against greed to retain some of our glorious and endangered ecosystems.

We are finally saying no. No, timber corporations. No, clearcutters. No, forest products industry. No, chip-mill builders. No, cypress wetland loggers. No.

Pine flatwoods are disappearing in the South.

Milton

If I had to pick a person who represents the Southern landscape, with its deep pine flatwoods grace, it would be Milton Hopkins: naturalist, farmer, tree planter, great-grandfather, friend.

To explain who Milton is, I will describe our first meeting, which took place many years ago, when I was still living in Florida. A biologist I knew told me I should meet Milton. "He's a Georgian, like you," the biologist said. "A farmer, and a great conservationist." I called Milton to ask if I could visit. "I could come Sunday afternoon, after church is over," I offered.

"Young lady, I'm not a churchgoer," he answered. "Come anytime."

On a Sunday afternoon, following Milton's directions, I drove to a Georgia town I'd never heard of, Osierfield. It was hot, the clouds flat bottomed and blackening below, but piled high and white as mashed potatoes at the top. I crossed Big Brushy Creek, the Willacoochee River, the Satilla River. Osierfield is ten miles from Ocilla, a town that looked as if it hadn't changed since the 1940s, brick storefronts with angle parking on both sides of a wide main street. An elder woman in church clothes, a green Sunday hat on her head, walked home from church.

Osierfield is nothing more than a speck in the road, split by a railroad track, with one store and a few abandoned buildings. The courthouse is a frame building about the size of Mama's kitchen, painted white. A voting sign on the door warns against campaigning within 100 feet.

Milton lives two miles away, in what had been the Osierfield train depot, which he had relocated onto his farm in 1974, as I later learned. I pulled up in his yard, enchanted with the architecture of the depot, its red-painted tin roof and the round room lined with windows. No longer did these windows face up and down a sooty track; they looked onto a yard full of pines, an aging water oak, a prize sugar maple, and more unusual trees. A tapioca dropped nuts everywhere. An iron dinner bell hung on one pole and a bleached cow skull adorned another.

When a dog commenced barking, a big man came out, grinning. He looked to be six feet tall, in his sixties, and strong. His face was tan and round as a walnut, shaped, it seemed, by good humor. He wore silver-rimmed glasses, cotton trousers, and a T-shirt.

"You made it," he said. "Come in, come in out of this heat."

While he poured a huge glass of sweet tea, I glanced around. His kitchen used to be the ticket office. Now the kitchen sink was below the ticket window that opened into what was once the white people's waiting room, Milton's living room. It was filled with natural history paraphernalia, amid the rocking chairs, long sofa, and lamps: a hummingbird nest made of lichens and spiderwebs; a ceramic vase of sweeping, iridescent peacock feathers; duck decoys; a carved turtle; bird sculptures. Every inch of the walls was covered with enlarged photos of flowers, framed antique documents, maps, wildlife paintings.

On one wall hung an eight-by-ten photo of a deadly coral snake that Milton said his son Bubba had found. "They're rare around here," Milton said. After they examined the snake, Bubba took it back where he found it and released it.

Milton's tea tasted like Grandmama's, sweet and icy; I was raised on the stuff. What was once the colored waiting room was now Milton's office, with collections of bird eggs, bones, shells, animal skulls, and mounted butterflies. "I love the out-of-doors," he explained simply. "It's been a hobby since I was eight or ten years old."

Milton asked if I'd eaten. It was 1:30, and I hadn't. He heated vegetable soup he'd cooked that morning: carrots, tomatoes, beef from the farm, peas, okra, corn. Antique colored bottles crowded the wide windows, one of which was stained glass. In this part of Georgia, not even many churches have stained glass.

Milton is a farmer and an anomaly among a group of people who are traditionally conservative. He row-crops 600 acres with his son Bubba and grandson Donnie: peanuts, corn, and this year, for the first time in years, 100 acres of cotton. "Farming's a good life," Milton said. "You work like hell a few months of the year and watch birds the rest of the time.

"There's an insa-tie-able desire for cotton around the world," he said. Milton speaks in his Southern tongue, omitting certain letters, especially R, mostly at the ends of words: Oshafield. At times he mispronounces big words, a trait I've noticed in people who read more than they talk. He lapses into memories. "Some of those cotton pickers used to pick 400 pounds a day," he said. "Once, in 1961 or 1962, I worked alongside one female picker; by day's end she had over 400 pounds, I had 124. That was my last try at cotton picking."

We lingered at the round kitchen table. I was taping the conversation. I needed to hear this man say something, and I didn't want to miss it if he did. I wanted to be able to hear it again and again. I didn't want to forget it, whatever it was, if it was said.

Milton Newton Hopkins was born in Fitzgerald, Georgia, the son of a postal clerk, one of five children, four boys and a girl. Milton wasn't yet fifteen when he began collecting specimens for a well-known northern naturalist. His great childhood friend, Bob Norris, whom he met by chance one day in the woods, went on to become both an ornithologist and a botanist. Milton studied ecology and zoology at the University of Georgia under Gene Odum, the father of ecology. He was most interested in birds. He thought to be a caretaker on an island, like Blackbeard, off the Georgia coast. For a year in the early 1950s, Milton studied avian malaria in mourning doves at the malaria research station in Baker County. At the time malaria was still a major health problem in the South, and avian malaria was similar to the human strain. Milton's project was funded by Robert Woodruff, of Coca-Cola fame, who had seen malaria's curse at work in his plantation hands and vowed to put money into controlling it.

Sometime about 1951 Milton returned to his father-in-law's farm at Osierfield to work; he had helped there off and on since he married a few years before.

"I thought it was going to be temporary," he said, "but I've been here forty years."

I interrupted him to ask about Osierfield, if it was a

dying town. He chuckled and told me that it used to be a bustling farm town, but that markets had shifted. Children had moved away and never come back. Osierfield had lost its post office in December of 1967. "It's just not smelling," he said. "It's been dead a long time."

Milton never abandoned his biologist's training. He participates in annual Christmas bird counts on the Atlantic barrier islands, including Sapelo and St. Catherine's. He accompanies groups of university students into the field and sometimes leads field trips into wild areas. He is an active member of the Georgia Ornithological Society and author of *The Birdlife of Ben Hill County, Georgia, and Adjacent Areas.*

He keeps what he calls a field catalog of unusual sightings from the farm. "If you stay in one place, anywhere, long enough, you're going to see some interesting birds," he said. He's seen a scissor-tailed flycatcher and a Eurasian ring-collared dove. Once a golden eagle stayed out in the cornfield for three days. It hunted and ate, and when it had flown, Milton retrieved a single golden feather. He told me all this.

Suddenly he rose, went to his desk, and brought back a jar. "Here's you some plum jelly I made," he said.

"Chickasaw plums?" I asked.

"One of the *Prunus.*"

He told me that the red-bellied woodpeckers love them. It's odd to see one flying across the yard with a big red plum in its mouth, he said. He once saw two gopher tortoises eating plums.

By this time he and I couldn't contain our joy in each other's company. When we started to talk, the words squeezed out through grins. Milton told me that his farm

lies in the middle of a migration corridor for sandhill
cranes. They come over by the hundreds, more in March
than in October. The local people think they're geese because they fly in Vs. Milton said he's offered his binoculars
to show people the long legs, but they won't look.

"Them air's geese," they say. The cranes often land in
a big, open peanut field and stay there of a morning until
the thermals start.

"What do the people around here think of you?" I
asked him.

"They think I'm a kook," he said.

But he didn't want to talk about that. "There used to be
a spiny clam," he said, "occurred locally in big rivers. It was
three or four inches long, with six spines protruding from
the sides of its shell." In the late 1960s Milton and his son
walked barefoot along the Ocmulgee sandbars, collecting
a dozen in a few minutes. "A couple of conchologists were
through here a number of years ago," Milton said, "and we
tried without success to find even one live one."

The spring-fed House Creek, near town, used to
have a four-by-two-inch mussel that grew pearls. The
pearls, though rarely perfectly round, shone with lu-
minance. "I'm sad to say I think pollution's got them,"
Milton said. "I've seen nothing but dead ones lately. Want
to see the farm?"

First he showed me the farm office. A bumper sticker
on the door read, "Farmers Are Out Standing in Their
Field." The office is part museum, with boxes of rocks and
shells, divers bones, arrowheads, rattlesnake hides, and
hornet nests. One section features all kinds of turpentining paraphernalia—tools for boxing trees (debarking

a section of trunk in order to collect sap for turpentine making); tools for scooping; tools for sharpening; turpentine cups (hurdy, bird's eye).

"Is turpentining still practiced?" I asked.

"Over in Homerville someone keeps two- to three-thousand catfaces," he said. Catfaces are the long, resinous scars left after the trees are boxed, or debarked.

The office also serves as a huge library, divided into sections, one for birds, another for snakes, another for books written by Georgians, another expansive section on Southern history. "A small subsection of the library is on Indians," Milton said. The phone rang then. He had been standing and looking the other way. Suddenly he turned to me and grinned apologetically. "I think I'll let that go," he said. "I use the telephone mostly to call out."

We got in the truck for the farm tour. "We could take the funeral car," Milton said. "It's a '78 Cadillac. I call it the funeral car." Grinning like mules eating briars, we rode with the windows up and the air-conditioning on, circling through the fields, looking for the cows. We finally found them in the last field, settled in the shade: Hereford, Angus, Brahman.

"Granddaddy used to come out and play the radio for the cows," Milton said. "He turned the radio up loud in the car and the cows would all gather around it. Once Bubba cut off a milk jug and put it around a little batt'ry radio. He played loud jive music to the cows." Milton paused. "They looked consternated," he said.

He had spent the day before gathering corn. Thirty thousand bushels were already in the bins. "That's a good feeling this time of year."

"Thanks for spending the afternoon with me," I replied. "Do you have the time?"

"I'm so damned glad to be out o' that corn patch for one day," he replied, smiling. These days, he did the hauling. While he sat waiting for his grandson to combine and dump a load, he would read. During the corn crop, he'd read eight or ten issues of the *New Yorker*, first the cartoons, then some serious reading.

"You know what, I was listening to Italian opera in the field yesterday," he said. "Public radio has good symphony in the morning."

In a very short time, Milton became dear to me, a godsend. In him I found the model I had searched so desperately for, a person who ignores social pressures to pursue a life he believes in—full of books, nature, and art. Caring little for monetary gain or public recognition, Milton lives by his convictions and his curiosity. He is a man of honor.

I visited whenever I could. After breakfast, in cool weather, we walked the farm to the beaver pond, wearing two shirts and a jacket, our breath hanging after us in the nippy air. The farm was quiet, and though it had not been cold enough to drop frost, a certain stiffness lay upon the wet stalks of dead soybeans, harvested but not plowed under. From the east the sun crept toward us, painting the sky. A small trove of chipping sparrows flew out over the field, and we listened for sandhill cranes passing. If we were lucky, we might see them on the ground, landed for the night. We passed through flocks of sundry birds that Milton would identify.

"The work of belonging to a place is never finished," wrote Scott Russell Sanders. Nor is Milton, with more

than seventy years in one vicinity, finished. I think sometimes he is the place personified, his eyes gleaming with
redstarts and monarch butterflies, his heart the wings of a
sandhill crane. He boils peanuts and makes mayhaw jelly.
He sits quietly below the trumpet vine, watching the mat-
ing dives of ruby-throated hummingbirds. Every atom of
his body belongs to this landscape.

Bird Dreams

After Silas and I returned home, we visited Milton more often. The hour-and-a-half drive to his house was well worth his company. All humans need intimacy. We need to be understood. We had a true friend in Milton. When we visited, Silas chauffeured us around on "the mule," a mechanical buggy, through fields and woods, looking at the world. We tramped the corn rows hunting arrowheads. We fished in the farm ponds. We pulled sweet corn and picked off peanuts. We cooked and ate, talked and laughed. We exchanged books and articles. Milton sent us home with whatever produce was in season—blackberries, kumquats, tomatoes, green peanuts, grapes—and with grits, cane syrup, honey, kindling he'd chopped.

Those days on the farm, I told Milton about bird dreams I'd been having. He told me stories of recent trips, like one to the Outer Banks, where thousands of snow geese and hundreds of tundra swans swarmed the coast. Often we took field trips: to Okefenokee Swamp, to Broxton Rocks, to visit his friend Bob Norris, to Mule Day, to Cypress Lake.

One day he showed me Oscewitchee Creek outside Fitzgerald, fed by the Boils, two beautiful, ice-cold, spring-fed creeks Milton frequented as a young man. Green-eyed Susans bloomed near royal fern, a ribbon snake swam away, and overhead, Mississippi kites wheeled.

By the time Milton was fifteen, he had already begun

to collect herpetological specimens for Dr. Francis Harper, the renowned naturalist who explored Okefenokee Swamp and eventually published an annotated version of William Bartram's *Travels*. In his youth, Milton spent all his spare time identifying and collecting frogs, toads, and salamanders; he dropped them into mason jars filled with formalin and shipped them north. "I swore to myself I'd do my dead-level best to search far and wide in our area for new specimens," he said, "for Harper's satisfaction of what was living hereabouts and for my own satisfaction, for I dearly wanted to know the names and habits of the critters inhabiting our area." Harper forwarded the specimens to the Academy of Natural Sciences in Philadelphia.

In 1944, at Oscewitchee Springs, Milton discovered a tiny, unusual fish, which he mailed to Harper, and in the time it took to receive a reply, he joined the U.S. Navy. The letter from Harper, dated March 13, 1944, came to the Navy barracks. "The jar of specimens came a couple of weeks ago," Harper wrote, "and I want to thank you especially for this last lot.

"The real prize is the rainbow-colored darter. I doubt if that species has ever been collected in the coastal plain of Georgia. Fowler has not yet made it out, but thinks it may even be a new species." In the same letter Harper thanked him for his service to the country.

A letter dated ten days later begins, "Yesterday Fowler showed me a fine drawing he has made of your darter. He has decided to describe it as a new species and to name it after you." The fish was classified *Poecilichthys hopkinsi*, or Hopkins darter (the name has since changed to *Etheostoma hopkinsi*). It has since been collected in the Savannah River drainage and is known commonly as the Christmas darter.

Milton was an avid correspondent, and he and I began a correspondence that has lasted for years. He would write when he saw the first kestrel returned for winter in the bleak rural farmland of south Georgia, or when the robins returned. One year, he first saw them on November 18. I saw them a week later in Baxley, on Thanksgiving Day, their arrival itself cause for celebration and thanksgiving. They would be plundering the woods of the South.

"The Okefenokee trip was fine," one letter said. "I sat alone on the tower overlooking Seagrove Lake, peering over many square miles of Chesser Prairie for over one hour, and let the birds come to me. White Ibis 75+. Great Egret 35+. Great Blue Heron 5. Sandhill Crane 4. In a flock of white waders over a mile away and with the naked eye I distinctly saw a pink bird. I'm sure it was a wandering Roseate Spoonbill but could not pick up the bird with binoculars.

"I thought of my friend, Francis Harper, who was in the same area in 1912 on a Cornell expedition, and wished I could have witnessed some of his observation before all the primeval Cypress had been cut and when the Ivorybill Woodpecker was a fairly common sight."

Milton began to send me short vignettes of natural history and life on the farm, stories he wrote sitting in his farm kitchen in the evenings. In one, called "Buzzard Trapping," he talked about the days when turkey vultures were thought to be predators of quail, although they feed on carrion. In those days they were trapped in wire cages, baited with a dead calf if the farmer could find one. "Do buzzards find carrion by sight or smell?" he wonders in the essay.

"On returning to Osierfield Farm in 1951 I duplicated a buzzard trap in the corner of a hog pasture. At its completion I lay down in the middle of the pen, facing skyward and shielding my eyes from the sun. Believe it or not, several turkey buzzards were soon overhead. I hadn't noticed any while building the pen. They began circling lower and lower until they were 50 to 100 feet above me. I was convinced my inert body had attracted them."

"The stories are wonderful," I told him. "You should publish them."

"I write mostly on winter days," he said, "to leave the stories for the children. I bought a word processor, but that thing intimidated me."

"Send them to me," I said, "and I'll type them up."

Before long, Milton had 300 pages of what he called *Tales from the Depot.* We found a small but big-hearted publisher, Saltmarsh Press, who wanted to bring them out. After many months and many meetings, Milton's book was completed: *In One Place: The Natural History of a Georgia Farmer.*

When I look at Milton's book, I think what a magnificent gift he is to my life. Milton has modeled a way of life it is possible to live, even if few others care for wild things, even if those things are being rapidly destroyed. In addition to guidance, he has brought a wondrous love to my life, one that is permanent and true. Everybody needs someone to teach her the meaning of the word "beloved."

The Bread Man Still Stops in Osierfield

Milton pointed out the courthouse of Osierfield, Georgia, as if he could still see the sheriff swaggering out through tumbled and crumbling bricks. "The post office was there." Virginia creeper sprawled inside and outside the building, cascading out gaps where windows used to be.

"Dr. McElroy's turpentine commissary was right over there. And the town ended here." Milton still regarded the town as it was in its heyday, and he saw the people who occupied it then: the postal clerk, his father-in-law, neighbor Meeks with his pet bear.

Now the town begins and ends at the one operating business left, the Osierfield Grocery, a brick building with a faded Texaco sign and a dry pump outside. What had been a thriving farm town is now nothing more than a collection of decaying buildings, about forty people tucked about on country farms, and one country store. Madie Denton runs Osierfield Grocery, as she has done for thirty years, since she bought it from her aunt and uncle as a new divorcee. Madie lives with her three children in the back of the store.

"It didn't use to be this quiet," said Madie. "Used to be, it was in and out, in and out." We had stopped, for old time's sake, for a bottled soda and a candy bar. The red drink box was the antique thick-walled chest type, with an opener at one corner.

Crackers, soda waters, corn chips, potato chips,
sunflower seeds, peanuts, oatmeal cookies.

Madie is tiny, almost frail, with a sweet, heart-shaped face. "The farms didn't close down," she said. "They started buying equipment that didn't call for hands."

Farmers still frequent the store, especially early of a morning, coming in to talk of news and have a cup of coffee and a honey bun. Evidence of them has settled around the easy chairs and upturned buckets. On a gas stove a hubcap collects cigarette butts.

"I have racked my brain," said Madie, who remarried years ago. "And my husband has, too. What can we put in the store to keep it going?"

Bottle of bleach, nuts, spool of white thread,
one box of cinnamon.

"People" is the only answer, of course, and the bigger question might be, "What can we put in the town to keep it going?" or "What can we put in the people to keep them home?" Towns all over America are asking themselves these questions as people flood to cities to shop, to recreate, to live. "Now there's not much for the young people to come back to," Madie said. "Lots lived on the farm. If they ever go to college and get a taste of something else, they don't want to come back. And now all the country schools have closed and the children are transported to town."

There in the country, eight miles from the next nearest small store at Ambrose, fifteen miles from the nearest supermarket in Fitzgerald, Madie has about anything you might need.

Juice, ice cream bars, popsicles.

The bell on the door chimed and a young farmer entered with two field hands. He grabbed a lemonade; the others rustled up drinks. Milton knew him and asked how the crops fared.

"Well, peanuts are looking pretty good," he said. "Cotton ain't doing too good." Farmers rarely use statistics, only nuances and chance and hope. Madie totaled his purchases on the oldfangled cash register that really rang. For eighty-four cents she had to hit the eighty cents and the four cents. Three dollars and something.

"Charge?" she said, and he nodded.

"Madie'll charge anything to him except beer," Milton whispered. "She knows his daddy'll pick up the bill."

On the counter was a chewing gum dispenser that came from L's drugstore. L is her husband, a pharmacist in a nearby town. That's really his name, the single letter. Wire-closed glass jars were filled with three-cent candy. Behind the counter, plank shelves displayed cigars, tobacco, aspirin, mouthwash, snuff, lighters. The top shelf Madie couldn't reach anyway so she crowded it with vintage soda bottles and cans: Royal Crown cola, Red Rock ginger ale, Sundrop Golden cola. She had tacked photos of her grandchildren to the shelf.

Correction fluid, packs of tacks, envelopes of headache powder.

Along the aisles I noticed she had one or two of everything. "Grocery items are about a thing of the past," Madie said. "It's snack food."

Pudding mix, cake mix, five or six salt boxes, jelling agent,
pork and beans, baking soda, one box of vanilla wafers,
tea bags, dried black-eyed peas.

A clay turpentine pot dangled on a wall, next to a resin scoop. A paper hornet's nest was mounted in a corner. I met Milton on a back aisle. He was reminded of a joke. "What does a man consider to be a seven-course meal?"

"I don't know!"

"Six sweet potatoes and a possum," he said.

Eggs, milk, cheese, two cherry pies in the freezer.

Farmworkers came in several times a day, Madie said, and sometimes the train stopped so the railroad workers could take a break. Out here in the country, they weren't holding up any crossings.

"You don't get rich, do you?" I said to Madie.

"It's hard to get rich in a small town," she quipped good-naturedly. "Everybody's watching."

General purpose fuses, battery terminal, fishhooks,
extension cord, trotline, buck lure.

"Another problem is salesmen," Madie said. "I don't do enough business for them. Isn't that pitiful when a truck goes right by here and they won't stop?" She pursed her lips when she said "pitiful." Texaco stopped delivering gas because Madie needed a new tank, costing $45,000. "We sold 100 gallons a month," she said. "You know what I'm gonna do? I told L, we're gonna put us a sign on that pump that says who's responsible."

At least the bread man still stops.

Madie is one of the hidden angels all over the country, striving to hold small rural communities together as the forces of globalization work to tear them apart. A virtual commingling cannot replace a real one. Knowing your neighbors is as important as patronizing local businesses is as important as knowing the elements of the bioregion.

Up near the front of the store, below a corkboard of community photos, was a small shelf of books, all paperback, by authors such as Robert Ludlum and Danielle Steele, with titles such as *No Account for Love* and *Temperature in the Tropics*. A sign nearby read "How to Check Out a Book." Madie saw me looking. "This is a Coastal Plain Regional Library Book System stop," she said proudly. "The bookmobile stops once a month."

For a few years she organized the Osierfield Reunion, an afternoon picnic where neighbors sat around picnic tables outside the store and talked. "We've had over one hundred people here," Madie said.

Madie's store is a primer in community repair, and from her you can learn lessons you need to know in how to stay alive in a predatory world market. Her hints for business owners might be:

- Keep chairs in your store so people can sit a spell and talk.
- Put up a billboard for people to hang notices on so they can connect regarding what they need.
- Advertise in the local paper. Keep a copy of the paper in the store.
- Help organize events that draw the community together, that make it unique.
- Every time you have to make a business decision, ask yourself, Does this unite or does this alienate people? Does this sacrifice quality of life for the making of money? Charge fair prices local people can afford.
- Sell local products.

- Display in your store those things that make your region unique. Honor your place. Honor your history. Honor your people.

Madie now lives not far down the road from the ghost town of Osierfield in the renovated schoolhouse. Milton is in the old depot. A marble column that held up the post office is part of another house nearby. It is as if the residents of the disappearing town are hanging onto pieces of it, because that's what you have left when a community falls apart, pieces, and between all the pieces, you have the ghosts who knew the place when it was less rudimentary and more whole, who are eternally present, inhabiting the town's hollows like wind and weeds. Each morning early Madie drives her old truck to the lone business left operating in Osierfield, Georgia, and opens her doors one more day.

Uncle Percy Leaves Home

I knew it was cancer from the start, but how do you tell a person who does not want to know? When Dr. Bedingfield prescribed antibiotics for the symptons of infection, Uncle Percy believed they would help. Then he became convinced that the pain sprang from his prostate, and he visited a second doctor for prostate trouble. The prescribed medications also did no good. Always there would be some reason to stop taking the medicine— it upset his stomach, it made him powerful thirsty, it made him nauseous.

"Did he do an X ray of your lungs?" I asked, and Uncle Percy said no. He went to a third doctor, a prostate specialist. I researched the symptoms of lung cancer and found Uncle Percy had all but one. He was short of breath and had lost his appetite, but he had no pain in his lungs.

"You have no pain in your back?" I asked.

"No, it's down here." He touched his kidney area, below the lungs. Maybe something *was* wrong with his prostate.

"You should stop smoking," I said gently. "It can't be good for you."

Mama called. "You'll never guess who came for supper last night," she said.

"Who?"

"Percy."

"Uncle Percy?" I had to know the details: where he

parked, what she prepared, what he ate, how long he stayed. We knew something was really wrong.

I became more tolerant with him, and more forgiving. I would sit and talk when I needed to work. I invited him to accompany me to readings. After one in Folkston we ate at Okefenokee Cafe, whose "No Smoking" sign he eyed nervously when we entered.

I was giving a reading in Savannah the night the cancer overcame him. He had gone to visit Uncle Bill and Miss Jo. It was out of character for him to appear at someone's door. Instead of sitting on the couch he fell onto it.

"Percy, you're not doing good. Maybe you need blood or something. Let's get the doctor's wife to come over," Uncle Bill said. The doctor lived the next place over. The doctor's wife, a nurse, said, "Let's take him in for tests," and that night chest X rays showed a massive tumor in one of his lungs.

Three weeks later he was gone.

Those three weeks were awful. I was in the middle of a book tour, with readings almost nightly, flying here and driving there. My aunt Coot took over. Between travels I watched restlessness and despair bloom in Uncle Percy's eyes. The skin tightened around his bones, and his eyes sunk in his head. Now a wraith, he roamed from bed to easy chair to sofa, searching comfort. His desire to cling to the world of flesh flowered even as he saw the world slipping away, until the doses of morphine were so intense they forced him, wild eyed, toward another reality.

The community did not abandon him but brought food and visited. One somber afternoon I was sitting alone with Uncle Percy when Preacher Elzie Carter knocked.

"He'd love to see you," I said. "He's in the back bedroom."

"I didn't come to see him," the preacher said, apologetically. "I'm tenderhearted. I don't want to see Percy suffer. I just want to know how he is." Two of Elzie's brothers had made preachers, and one of them performed my parents' marriage.

"It would mean a lot to him if you spoke to him," I said. "Just for a minute." I led him, reluctant, through the house, into the back room where Uncle Percy lay, weak and drugged. Although Elzie had come to say good-bye, the two men greeted each other as if it were any normal Saturday afternoon. Elzie asked how Percy felt.

"Not a bit of good," Percy said.

"Sorry to hear it," Elzie said.

"I can't seem to find no rest," Uncle Percy said. He struggled to sit up.

"Lay back down, Percy," Elzie said. "Don't sit up on my account. I don't intend to bother your rest."

Elzie looked at me. "We've known each other all our lives," he said, and I nodded. "All our lives." He was close to tears. Uncle Percy lay gaunt and remote and drawn. Neither of them said much else.

"Percy, you want me to pray with you?" Elzie asked.

"I'd appreciate it, Elzie," Percy said, simply. Then Elzie prayed for Percy, who lay on his deathbed, Elzie's words a benediction that settled upon the sick man, who received the blessings as if they were rain on a parched field. Percy believed in prayer, and believed in the power of Elzie Carter. Elzie asked God to watch over Percy, to ease his pain, to

guide him. When he was done Uncle Percy sat up on the
side of the bed, and held out his shaking hand. "I shore
thank you," he said.

Elzie's eyes brimmed, and he said, "I'd better get along
and let you rest."

When he was gone I went outside and wept.

As the days crawled by, Uncle Percy withdrew
steadily from the world. He began to see Grandmama,
his dead mother, and to have conversations with her. He
would call to her from his sickbed. "Mama? Where are
you? Mama?"

He would turn onto his side, trying to ease the pain,
and lie silent. After a minute he would say, "I'm going to
town. Do you need anything?" He attempted to sit on the
edge of the bed, then fell back upon it.

"Maybe she's outside and can't hear you," I would say
to him.

"I heard her at the kitchen sink," he would say.
"Mama? Is Daddy coming in to eat?"

"I think so," I'd say.

Many times those few weeks, Uncle Bill, on his way to
the fields or coming back from visiting the trailer, found
me and poured out his grief. He was exactly the age of
Uncle Percy, his first cousin; he had known him every day
of his life. "He's not getting any better," he would say, and
tears would come to his eyes. "I hate to see him in such
bad shape." Not a day went by that Uncle Bill did not stop
to visit, even for a few minutes.

"He can't stay still," he said to me. "He's from couch to
bed to chair, then back to the bed."

"It's the pain," I said.

"I wish there was something we could do for him."

"You're doing it."

In a matter of a fortnight, Uncle Percy was desperately ill. His doses of morphine had been increased to impossible levels and yet the pain drove him in circles. It would not be long.

Late one night he died, in his room alone. Uncle Bill had come over to sit awhile, knowing the end was near. Uncle Percy was sleeping fitfully while everybody sat quietly in the living room, talking, except for Aunt Coot, who was resting in the other bedroom. Uncle Bill decided to go on home, a mile away, and get some sleep. "I think I'll go back and check on Percy one more time before I go," he said. When he got to the bedroom door, he knew everything had been recast. He turned and stumbled back out to the living room. Everybody looked at him.

"He's gone," he said.

I did not dwell on Uncle Percy's death. I knew he had been moving open armed toward it for much of his life. During the time he lay in state, I sobbed, rocked, prayed. *When the funeral is over,* I told myself, *you will not cry.*

Uncle Percy's funeral was huge. He didn't have many close friends, except for Uncle Bill, but a lot of people knew him, and even those who barely knew him came. That's the way it is with funerals in a small town. Grief racked me as I watched his Sunday school class lay him in the ground on the other side of Grandmama, where he belonged, in the cemetery where I had sung hymns at daybreak on Easter Sunday morning with the church. Then grief let me go.

Now Uncle Percy's spirit could wander the farm or the rooms of the house. He was liberated from the world, with its rusting motors and leaking roofs, free at last to know everything it was possible to know. My requiescat was that he be, with the new revelations, finally content.

Cypress Lake

Something in us longs to see a hundred thousand birds—
not imagined birds, but real ones. Such a spectacle of
numbers reassures us that nature has not been completely
conquered, that we have not set our foot against all its
magnificence.

In a cypress lake near Rhine, Georgia—a tiny
Southern town lucky enough to have had progress pass
it by—thousands of wading birds have been nesting since
the late 1960s, gathering each spring to fill the watery
thickets of small cypress with a garble of noise—squawks,
grunts, gurgles, and wails. The noise is enough to wake
the dead. Almost every tree in this tree-thick lake bears a
shallow bowl of sticks filled with eggs or chicks, guarded
by a beautiful statue of bird: snowy egret, little blue heron,
white ibis, cattle egret.

This is a place of wading bird origin, a cradle of
civilization.

Preacher Junior Caldwell is keeper of this holy place,
and for a few dollars he will carry you on a boat trip through
it almost any day of the week except Sunday, when you find
him at the New Red Hill Holiness Baptist Church over
near Milan.

It was my mother's birthday, late May. She was turning sixty-one and for a present I took her, my father,
and the three grandchildren who lived nearby to see the
rookery. We passed through Rhine and located the sign

for Cypress Lake on Highway 280. Could there really be
thousands of birds?

"You'll see all you want to see, I guarantee you," Junior
Caldwell said. "We've got more of everything this year.
The most blues we've ever seen." He was wearing light
blue slacks, a striped blue shirt, and sneakers. A local doctor had owned Cypress Lake and had hired the preacher
to caretake it and lead groups through it; when the doctor
died, the rookery was sold; the new owner kept Junior on.
He lived in a travel trailer near the picnic area.

He settled us on his ark, a pontoon boat rigged out
with benches and a roof, and we went puttering across the
115-acre wetland, leaving a dark trail swirling through
the lime green duckweed. We got into the bald cypress,
the boat slow and steady. Baby birds poked their heads
above the sides of nests. Their mamas and daddies perched
near them, or flew to and fro feeding them. A vee of white
ibises passed overhead, the motors of their wings drowned
in the racket of the rookery.

The children were bug eyed. This was better than any
toy store or amusement park.

Glossy ibis. Anhinga. Great egret. Great blue heron.
Lily pads floated in the tannic swamp, and a swath of
delicate pinguicula, the carnivorous bladderwort, bloomed
purple. Carolina ash fidgeted their helicopter seeds. The
snowys were pure white among gray limbs.

"I've seen some pink birds," said Junior. "And one time,
a red one. Right on that point one fall. It had to be either
a roseate spoonbill or a scarlet ibis."

Junior takes a lot of schoolchildren through the rookery
late March through September. This spring, already 800
to 1,000 children had visited. He was guiding one group,

watching a cattle egret drink from a low bush, when suddenly an alligator leaped from the water and snatched the bird under. Junior began to entertain our children with jokes and riddles. He recited the ABCs backward in less than five seconds. The children smiled. He asked them why the farmer built the hog pen behind the house.

"To put the hogs in," he answered. They smiled.

Junior Caldwell does not think about ecotourism, the nature-based tourism that allows us to both protect natural areas and make a livelihood from them. At seventy-two, he simply takes care of the rookery, like a shepherd with a flock. He watches. He marvels at God's creation. "I've been in here a thousand times, and every time I see something different," he said.

All around us, the birds. Without this, we would forget that we have been made from swamp water and sun, as have the birds, and that our bodies are simply crucibles for more to come, vessels through which life passes. We would forget this clamor for life. We would forget that we take nothing with us when we die.

Judging the Pork Cook-Off

L ate July, when I was in the library to work because my
computer was down, the librarian, Ms. Alice, came
up and asked if I'd judge the Farm Bureau's pork cook-off.
They do a cooking contest every year, she said, and feature
a different farm product. Some years it was blueberries
and some years tomatoes and some years corn. This year
it was pork.

What rotten luck, I thought.

I had not eaten pork in twenty years, but I didn't say
so to Ms. Alice. When Ms. Alice asked a favor of me, I
couldn't refuse. She was in charge of 4-H when I was a
girl and drove me to project competitions, where I never
won. Losing did not weaken Ms. Alice.

"Oh well," she'd say in her thick Danish accent. "It
dond matta anyhow. You did the best you could do."

We'd recite the 4-H pledge after her, heads to better thinking, hands to better service, knowing she meant
what she said. All her life she's pledged her heart to better
living. She led story hour at the library during summer
book club, where we listened to her read, colored pictures,
painted bookmark crafts, and ate the cookies she baked
for us. Ms. Alice taught me to crochet, and would have
taught me to knit and to tat had I been capable of learning. After thirty years, I found she was still doing story
hour at the library.

I once had a high school English teacher who was a vegetarian, the first one I ever knew. On field trips he'd order a cheeseburger without the meat. From him, I learned the reasons people might not eat meat, and the reasons made sense to me. After that, I was at best a half-hearted carnivore.

Ms. Alice told me that the cook-off was to take place that very afternoon, in less than an hour, in fact. One of her judges, the county extension agent, a person infinitely more qualified than I, had called a half hour earlier to cancel.

When Ms. Alice talks, excitement gleams in her eyes and she becomes very animated. I remember how angry she could get, too, if she caught us whispering while she read aloud, or if we used too much glue or too many pipe cleaners in our projects. She'd stand straight up and say, "No ma'am. You get right over here and clean this up." She came from firm people, and you'd never hear her described as weak-kneed or spineless. She has inordinately sturdy knees and a stalwart backbone.

"What about the home economist?" I asked. "She'd be perfect."

"She's out of town," Ms. Alice said.

"What about the mayor?"

"I've called everybody I can think of," said Ms. Alice. "He's in a meeting all afternoon. It won't take long."

"Okay," I said.

"Good." Ms. Alice beamed.

At the Farm Bureau we found the two other judges, both men. One was an investigator who wore a shirt that looked like a U.S. flag. It had taken a good deal of flag to make the shirt. The other judge was named Lafayette Butler.

"Where'd your mama get a name like that?" I whispered.

"I've asked her the same thing," Lafayette said.

The Farm Bureau women diplayed the pork dishes. Mercifully there were only five entries: roast pork, pork salad, Hawaiian meatballs, Brunswick stew (a regional soup of corn, tomatoes, and pork), and hogshead cheese. This is a congealed mass made from the boiled head, organs, and other remains of the pig, seasoned with salt and pepper. Grandpa Charlie, my daddy's father, loved hogshead cheese. He'd come by with a hunk of it and cut off slabs with his dirty pocketknife while he sat on the hood of his Biscayne, which left paint stains on the seat of his pants.

We were to take a small serving of each on our styrofoam plates and go into a separate room, the three of us, and shut the door. In the room we sat at three chairs on one side of a table. I was in the middle.

"I've never judged a cooking contest," said Lafayette. "But I like to eat."

"That's all the experience I believe you need," I said.

"Are we going by taste?" the other man asked.

"What else is there?"

"I don't know."

"How're we gonna do this?" We eyed our plates.

"How about one to five?" the investigator suggested. "One the best, five the worst."

"Sounds good."

We tried different dishes, taking small, intentional bites, studiously chewing. Did it make a difference which taste hit your palate first?

The pork was good. I was sorry that it was greasy and full of additives, and that swine are ill treated on the corporate farms, because I liked it. The meatballs contained pineapple and coconut, and the roast pork was served with bread so we could make sandwiches. I found even the hogshead cheese delicious.

"Wasn't your picture in the paper not long ago?" Lafayette asked. "The one with the trees?"

"Next to a huge tree?"

"That's it." The photo showed me standing beside a tree so immense that, even with my arms opened wide, I could reach around only a quarter of the tree's circumference.

"What kind of tree was that?"

"Cypress."

"Where is it?"

"Moody Swamp. We're hoping to be able to preserve it. We wanted to publicize how rare that forest is, with its huge matriarchal trees. You could see from the picture it'd be a shame to let Moody Forest get destroyed."

"How are we going to stop all the cutting around creeks and rivers?" he said unexpectedly.

I shook my head. "Tragic, isn't it?"

"I was born 150 years too late," he said. "I wish I could've been the first person through Georgia. I was an environmentalist before people knew what they were."

"I'm glad you feel that way."

"If there's a way I can help, call me," he said, and handed me his card.

"I will."

The Brunswick stew was everybody's number one. We differed slightly on second and third place. I voted the Hawaiian meatballs second—I strongly suspected Ms. Alice had made them, although they were entered in her daughter's name—and the men agreed. The roast pork took third. We exited together and handed Ms. Alice the results. The men served themselves second helpings, and I took one more piece of hogshead cheese.

From the pork-cooking contest I learned that many things are above dogma. Respect, for example. Love. The requirements of our place in a community may land us in the middle of odd, funny stories we never schemed for ourselves. What we are asked to contribute may lie outside the lines of what we imagine. Some of our participation we can't design.

A Thousand Lights

I have seen the farm in a thousand lights. The light of
winter is hollow and hopeful, and different from that
of summer, which is educated and intent on its business.
A thin and piercing midday is not the gray kneel of dusk.
The light of April cuts through a basket of greens, the air
a minor shade of leaves newly unfurled. June morning is
watermelon the moment before it is struck to the ground.

The light before a summer thunderstorm is blue tinted,
as if the air has been bruised, its violet petals crushed and
smelling of long-awaited rain. The earth darkens and
darkens, the sky full of boulders, and rain threatens to ex-
tinguish all light. Afterward, when thunder begins to lag
behind the strikes of lightning until it passes out of hearing, booming toward another horizon, light seeps beneath
purple clouds to reach the farm. If the storm ends exactly
at sunset, as sometimes happens, a miraculous scattering
of clouds in the drizzling finish of rain allows multicolored
light to rise like canyon dust in the northwest, where the
sun is setting those hot days, and bathe the tired trees and
weathered buildings in a sheen of golden pink. The well
curb glows. The wild cherry shimmers, lighting tiny drops
of filigree. The field goes full yellow.

August noon, parched and mean, makes of everything
a skeleton.

Then it's hurricane season and the sun retires behind
purple clouds for days—dreary gray days that weigh on

your spirit. Finally, in one great moment, the sun unfolds itself and opens a small spot to shine. Mostly, autumn light is happy, balanced on the branches of the trumpet vine, as if constructed of honey.

That's daylight. At night, there is the light of all the moon phases, and also the time when the moon is absent, a mercurial flickering of planets and stars. On a cloudy moonless night, there are the weakest of lights that seem to have no source.

When you enter a place, your eyes first note the characteristics of three dimensions, but not so much the proportions of light. Not immediately. One learns a place through its light. The longer I am here, the more ways I experience the farm, until there are a thousand farms, in a thousand lights, and I want to see all of them. In one week that I am away, how many have I missed? And given my ignorance and immaturity, do I witness all the lights that wrap this ground?

Where the Cutting Ends

Miss Elizabeth of Moody Swamp lived two years after I returned to Baxley. When I first got back, she was in a personal care home. She'd been stricken with pneumonia and hospitalized—the first time she'd left home except for one trip to Savannah years before—and the family decided she couldn't return to the cabin and live alone. She missed her home so badly that the mention of it brought her to tears. "It was a old wore-out place, but I loved it," she said.

Finally she insisted. "One way or another I want to go home." The executor of her estate, a mortician in town, added central heating, air-conditioning, and an indoor kitchen. One of her nephews stopped to chat one afternoon. "I want you to write a poem," he said. "Aunt Elizabeth has gone home."

Miss Elizabeth hadn't been much of a talker and had grown to be even less of one. She had round-the-clock attendants, and often I talked with her caregivers while she stared silently at the fireplace. We never discussed what would become of her forest when she died, because that subject was outside her configuration. She had been sheltered, and negotiating the future of a piece of land that had everybody's attention was beyond her means. We could talk about weather, flowers, people we knew, our health, the present. Not legalities. Not land. Not death.

During that time, I was meeting with people from the Nature Conservancy, and they were meeting with her executor. We were meeting with anyone who might be able to help us, who might be even a thin thread between the Moody family and the idea of conservation. I sent out a call for testimonies from naturalists and others who had visited the property, who could attest to its ecological value. Over the years botanists and foresters and biologists had seen it, and they were willing to write. I compiled these essays. We began a biological species list, trying to name everything that had been found living in Moody Forest. Many times I parked on the dirt road and walked into it, listing plants and animals. Endangered species would help.

One July Sunday I went into the swamp alone to see if an egret roost reported on the east side was a rookery. It had been a very dry summer and I was able to hike into areas I had known beforehand only as swamp, although the ground there remained wet and slurpy. Thick, sticky mud clung to my waders. Taking advantage of the drought, cypress seed germinated. Deep in the lizard's-tail swamp three wood ducks flushed, and an eight-foot alligator eased away through a duckweed slough. Red blooms of trumpet vine lay on the forest floor like a fallen orchestra. As I wandered the majestic forest, I thought of Jake Moody, surrounded by these same animals, ferns, wildflowers. I could almost see him coming through the tall trees.

> *Oh, Jake Moody, have you seen what I've seen?*
> *It was not a vision, it was not a dream.*

Big cat by the river with the cypress turning green.
Oh, have you seen, have you seen?

"We're going to save it," I whispered.

 တ

I was doing everything I knew to save the forest, yet it
wasn't much. It certainly wasn't enough. When I could
do nothing else physically, I fashioned an altar of an old
tobacco sack my friend Ann loaned me. It had come from
the Moody place. On the altar I arranged candles, pictures of the big trees, and objects I'd found walking on the
property—a raccoon skull, a cloudy glass bottle, mussel
shells from the adjacent river. I prayed. One day a month,
on the full moon, I fasted, because to starve the body is to
feed spirit.

My last visit to Miss Elizabeth was on a Thursday in
December of 1999. She was not ill at all, but two days later
she sickened unexpectedly, was hospitalized for pneumonia, and suddenly was gone: a person I loved, the last of a
generation, the link that held a virgin forest together. The
land passed to thirty-eight half-nieces and half-nephews,
many of whom were in their seventies.

The Nature Conservancy copied *Moody Forest,* the
book of testimonies we'd created, and distributed one to
each beneficiary. We began to visit the heirs, hoping to find
that they wanted the forest preserved, were willing to sell
it to the Nature Conservancy. I wrote letters to politicians
about the place, sent them copies of the book, toured a
couple of them through it. I called reporters, trying to
interest them in feature stories.

The process of settling the estate dragged like a

wounded dog through months, past a year. In beneficiary meetings, the family decided not to divide the property among themselves but to sell. They voted to put the land up for sale in a silent bid.

My brother positioned himself at the auction and telephoned immediately to recount what had happened. Seven timber companies bid on the 3,500-acre property. Four million dollars. Six million. Seven point six million. The last bid to be opened was the Nature Conservancy's, and a miracle happened.

The executor opened the envelope and called out its number, and that figure exceeded every other. Eight point two-five million. Amazingly, beautifully, after fifteen years of work to secure the property, the Nature Conservancy of Georgia had won. Wildness won.

"Oh my God. Are you sure?" I said to my brother. "Are you absolutely sure? Oh my God, my God." That moment I will recall as among the most blessed of my life. I have shed enough tears over the Moody Forest to fill a creek, through years of sorrow and hopelessness and hope and finally joy. Now it has been saved forever.

Our Town

To live in this world

you must be able
to do three things:
to love what is mortal;
to hold it

against your bones knowing
your own life depends on it;
and, when the time comes to let it go,
to let it go.

       —MARY OLIVER,
    "IN BLACKWATER WOODS"

I am a Southerner. Long ago I fell in love with a
Northerner, and the child we birthed is divided. Silas
decided to live in Vermont, where his father was, with me
or without me, for the school year. "When Silas is away,"
advised my friend Ann in Mississippi, who was forced
to live some years without her children, "fill the space
with love."

 I went to visit him. I was not smitten by Vermont,
although I like that region and have many friends there,
and my heart ached when Silas flung his arms wide
and said, "Look at the mountains. Look at the meadows.
There are flowers everywhere in the grass. Don't you love
it here?" One morning we ate breakfast at Ray's Diner,
a funky cafe made from a boxcar. The restaurant was
cozy and the waitress sweet; no less than four times Silas
asked me, "Don't you love it? How could you ever find

a place like this in Georgia? Don't you love the flowers on the table?

"Do you like it enough to live here?" he asked. And then later, "So you've decided we can live here?"

Back home, I missed him profoundly. Would he come back one day? Would I go live there? A place will wait for one's return, but a son's childhood will not wait. Every day I was in agony, yearning for my child, separated from him by love of homeland. I telephoned him every day, and every day, after I hung up, I wept. Torn and confused, I went to sleep crying.

I couldn't bear to think of leaving. Each day in the memory-filled house felt as if it might be the last, or among the last. It was as if I couldn't get enough of the farm. When I ran the road I knew that the place was mine, for the present, as no place had been before, and that it might be years before I again found that certainty of citizenship. Everywhere I looked I tried to memorize what I saw.

I visited Silas again in Vermont. I got there on a Friday evening, which was Gallery Walk for the town, when the art galleries stay open late. After we ate hummus in the Middle Eastern diner, we walked around in the dark cold. The streets were full of people of all ages, bands of teenagers, older couples, children in parents' arms. Silas's neighbor, Cindy, told us that the candy store had free chocolates, and that a band was rocking the thrift store. We got a taste of chocolate and went to the thrift store. The musicians in the band played old-time banjo and fiddle. A boy Silas's age was respirating the accordion with great concentration, knocking notes and keeping up only with effort. Silas knew him from a rock-climbing class.

Behind a rack of winter coats we ran into our friends Ra and Carrie. Carrie was trying on a pair of high-heeled black pumps. Ra, going through the quarter shelves, unearthed a set of noisemakers that I bought for no good reason, along with a pair of rain shoes that fit perfectly. After every song the shoppers clapped.

It could be a long time before we have a gallery walk in Baxley where half the town turns out. We may never be able to buy a falafel pita there, or stuffed grapevine leaves.

I've been taking a good hard look, however, at the quaint, charming towns where tourists flock. They are pretty, with their brick sidewalks, street-planters full of impatiens and petunias, and wrought-iron benches. They are progressive, with their cafes and their cappuccino counters. They are painted to look historical, and their art (murals on the sides of the buildings, painted wisteria vines) is as predictable as Fourth of July fireworks. I love these pretty towns as much as anybody. Their gingham curtains and antique shops partly satisfy our desire to know our history, to honor heritage, to remember times when towns mattered because the people living in them mattered. But I have come to learn that these towns aren't real. When they are full of tourists, the community usually is gone.

To welcome art in a town is to embrace imagination, and only an imaginative, artful place can welcome all its citizens and recognize in them a shared humanity. Yet art as facade is as useless as no art at all. What will our communities look like when we learn to love and accept each other, with all our differences, with all our similarities, in the fullness of the human imagination?

Our town isn't aesthetically pleasing by any stretch of

the eye, but it isn't artless. Our dreamers, paupers, alcoholics, millionaires, idiot savants, infirm, and a goodly share of geniuses save us from artlessness. Ours is a folk art.

∞

One morning, glancing at a local circular whose text consisted of free, small-print ads, I read this: FOUND. *Set of dentures in Dr. Dickens' office.* I smiled and perused further, coming upon another that said, *FREE. Cats.* Not housetrained, registered Siamese kittens but simply, cats. Fullgrown, mouse-wise, unspayed cats. I wondered where Dr. Dickens had found the dentures—under a chair or on the magazine rack?— and if they had been claimed. Had the people with the cats located homes for them?

The most interesting ad by far, however, was this: *For Sale. Fallen Star. Radiocarbon-dated to 15 billion years old.* *$52,000.* A phone number followed. I called Daddy. "You ever heard of such a thing?"

"No. You reckon they mean a meteorite?"

"Or tektite?"

Later, riddled with a double curiosity, he dialed the number. His friend Beverly answered. She had no such thing, she said furiously. Somebody had played a joke on her. She'd been fielding calls about a damned fallen star since the *Shopper* came out.

I am reminded too of the pumpkins I passed one day, piled out by the road in front of someone's house. A sign on a stake read *FREE. LIMIT 4.* I turned around and pulled in the stranger's driveway to take three of his pumpkins. I gave one to Mama, and I kept one. I tried to give the third to Robert, my sister-in-law's brother, who had stopped by looking for land to hunt on. He seemed hesitant about accepting the pumpkin.

"Would Laura cook it?" I asked. Laura was his wife.

"I don't believe Laura's ever had any dealings with a pumpkin," he said.

∽

Our town's beauty is raw and its charm mostly hidden. But there's something real about it, something down-to-earth. Neglected, threadbare, not so pretty, it has a soul. Its sorrows are obvious, as are its successes. Even if tourists on the way to the Golden Isles don't see it, there's something honorable and affirming about living in a place where the people work hard, where ability is valued above education, where clan means more than money, where every molecule of your body fits the landscape. Where home means something, and matters. Where every ounce of good thinking is needed. Where one person can make a difference. Where Silas's return would be celebrated.

The homecoming parade rolls every year down Main Street.

Finishing the Quilt

For over a year the quilt-top lay folded in my mother's
sewing room. "When do you want to finish your
quilt?" she would sometimes say.

"How long will it take?" I asked.

"It depends on how fast we sew. We could do it in a
week, with both of us working," my mother said. "I've seen
Mama and Coot put one in and quilt it in a day's time.
They'd finish before they'd go to bed that night. Mama
was a fast quilter."

"It'd take both of us a week working all day?"

"Part of every day."

"I don't have a week. Maybe when Silas goes back to
school." Maybe after Christmas things would slow up.
Maybe in the middle of winter.

For my mother, time had become something she could
not depend on. Her arthritis had worsened to the point
where it debilitated her for parts of every day, and there
was no cure. Her days began in pain that she appeased
with aspirin until she could function. She was no longer
the dawn-to-dark, work-like-a-man, never-stop mother
I had always known.

"Do you feel like quilting?" I asked.

"I don't have pain in my fingers," she said. "It's in
my feet now." She would slip her swollen feet out of
terrycloth, rubber-bottomed slippers to show me an

inflamed toe that had puffed to the size of a Jerusalem artichoke.

"My word," I said. "That looks painful."

"It's better than it was." She was, as always, positive.

"Where could we quilt?"

"Anywhere," she said, pulling her slipper back on carefully, but this was a nonanswer, since every room at her house was overstuffed with their collections.

"Your dining room?" I asked.

"I don't know if the frame would fit in there."

"Well, next time I'm by we'll try it."

We did. The frame, really four pieces of two-by-two-inch wood, ten feet long, rammed into hutch and china cabinet and wall on all sides.

"We need elbow room," Mama said. "We have to work around the outside of the frame." So the dining room wouldn't work. We disassembled the frame.

After Christmas, and all through winter, the work piled high, and daily a reason not to quilt thwarted my intentions. I was too busy. We had no room big enough. Then it was too hot.

ᘒᘒ

In late May, at the forty-ninth Florida Folk Festival, a miracle happened to me. The folk festival has been held in the tiny town of White Springs, on the banks of the Suwannee River, every Memorial Day weekend for the past forty-nine years. Since I first brought him as a two-week-old infant, year after year, my son and I have returned, I thankful for that one weekend to be steeped in lifestyles swiftly becoming extinct, Silas happy to listen to

the bell-tower chime playing "Old Folks Back Home" and
to lick homemade ice cream. A cowboy showed us how to
crack a whip. We watched a man hand-tatting a cast net.
I learned the Cajun two-step. A farmer demonstrated
how to grind corn into grits, and a girl barely ten years
old almost won the fiddling contest.

Through all the changes—divorce and grad school and
moving back to Georgia—the folk festival was a given in
my and my son's life. In fifteen years the only folk festivals
we missed were those that happened when we lived too
far away to attend. I have dozens of stories—of camping in the musicians' campground, where the tents are so
thick they look like a Bedouin encampment; of wandering until two in the morning from bluegrass to country to
old-time, the music drifting up through the lamp-lit and
moss-lovely limbs of live oaks. Or during the memorial to
Will McLean, Florida's darling balladeer, on a perfectly
still day, watching wind suddenly catch in the tall pines at
mention of his name. Goosebumps rose across my body.
Of eating pumpkin frybread at the Seminole camp. Of
hearing Gamble Rogers, who would later die attempting
to save a drowning swimmer, singing at the Old Marble
Stage.

But no story has more meaning to me than the one
that transpired at the forty-ninth.

I was sitting on the grass at midafternoon on Sunday,
listening to music at the main stage as the sun grew hotter
in the sky. Silas was not yet home from Vermont, and I had
come to the folk festival for the day, alone, packing a tote
with water, sunscreen, and my journal, to listen to music
and study the folk artists at work. Gospel choirs were singing and the audience was yet sparse, Sunday being the third

and last day of the festival. The climbing sun beat down until my dark hair felt it would catch on fire. I decided to move. Across the grass I saw a patch of shade.

When I got to the shade, a man dressed in black sat alone on a towel ten feet from a retired couple in lawn-chairs. I spread my blanket between them, a foot or two uphill. I took off my sandals. I sat through Tracy Sands (an Irish singer), Jesse Sam Owens (a guitarist), and the Green Grass Revival. The man to my right had been reading a book, *Zen and the Art of Motorcycle Maintenance*, but now he was packing everything away. He stood and turned to leave, then paused at my blanket, a move that would change both our lives permanently.

"Are you writing a song?" he asked.

"It's a poem." I smiled.

We talked for ten minutes, I thought, but Raven said later it must have been an hour, because he missed the music workshop he was heading to. We agreed to meet for the evening concert and sit together. We did: Nancy Moore Band, Chief Jim Billie, the Bellamy Brothers.

Almost as soon as I got home, the phone was ringing. Before a week was out, Raven rode his motorcycle over to visit. That first time he came, I took a phone call as he arrived, so without me he explored the outbuildings and the yard. Fifteen minutes later he entered the kitchen door with his eyes wet with tears.

"What's wrong?" I asked him.

"The clothesline pole," he said. I stared at him. The pole that held up the sagging line was a time-grooved length of heart pine that had once been part of a split-rail fence.

"It's so beautiful," he said.

I knew he gardened, grew herbs, kept chickens, built

furniture, turned bowls, and loved to camp and canoe—
all of these spoke highly of him—but in the moment he
saw the beauty of a rugged piece of wood propping up
a clothesline full of clothes, I knew he was the man I'd
dreamed and prayed into being.

"What am I thinking?" he said to me later, after we
both knew.

"You are thinking that we have only today to build on.
What we have built in such a short time is great, but it is
between only us. It is so new. One day others will know.
But that is all in the future."

He laughed. "That wasn't exactly what I was thinking."

"What were you thinking?"

"How happy I am you talked to me when I stopped at
your blanket."

After that, we spent every moment possible together.
If Raven had a day off, he left work at 4:30 P.M., spent the
next day at the farm, then got up at 4 A.M. to make the
four-hour drive back to Tallahassee, where he delivered
mail. Within two months Raven asked me to marry him
and I said, "I'd marry you in a greased minute."

It was as if the universe had spoken: *Here is what you
asked for, that you may do what is expected of you. You are
given great things so you may do great things.* I had never
felt such love. My heart split wide open. He was the most
beautiful man I had ever seen, or known. I had been
blessed beyond belief.

I wished that I could offer him wholeness—a pristine
farm and a thousand acres of virgin pine flatwoods. I
wished I could show him indigo buntings and Bachman's
sparrows within the range of a short walk. I wished the
farmhouse were perfect, so that when he entered the front

door he would know he was home. I wished that waiting for him would be a multitude of friends who were good, thinking, courageous people, and a family that welcomed a son-in-law with open arms. I wished that everywhere he turned he would see flowers in bloom and fruits hanging ripe and faces blossoming with love. Some of these things I could offer—my friends and family loved him immediately, for example—but most everything else had been compromised in one way or other, including me. Few old-growth pines remained at the farm and its fields were adulterated by pesticides and erosion. I offered it to him anyway. He took it as if it were what he'd always wanted.

Almost at the exact time I met Raven, my cousin Jimmy decided to sell his part of the farm, the section I lived on. While I was away, sitting beside a stranger I would marry, listening to folk music, Jimmy visited my parents, offering to sell to them. In a moment the moon of my life waxed full.

I had by then accepted a yearlong job at a university ten hours away and would have to leave the farm for long periods. Silas had decided to live with his father for another school year. Nothing was the same, nor did the changes indicate what my new life would look like, although I knew it would in some way involve the farm, my son, my family, my newly found beloved, and our dreams for the world.

ﬡ

In the powerful ripeness of summer heat, knowing we had to get back to it, Mama and I cleaned out the packhouse at the farm and finished the quilt. Even here the quilting frame barely fit, but Mama had a solution, one I couldn't understand from explanation, but only from demonstration.

Early one morning, after the thin dew dried from the grass in the soft horizontal sunlight that is bearable in Georgia mid-August, before the sun hits the roof of sky, Mama showed up at the farm. She and I pitched four chairs in a square in the yard, under a longleaf pine. We spread blankets on the ground around the chairs and perched the quilt frame (the four poles clamped together with C-clamps) on the chair backs. Solemnly, Mama unfurled a wide flag of white cotton in the grass as if we were about to make a shade tent for tiny ladies, or call some important truce.

A length of cotton is a beautiful thing, voile and translucent. Shadows pass behind it. A piece of white cotton resembles weather, mostly fog, and becomes a play toy for wind. Not to mention that it immediately brings to mind warmth and shelter. Imagine the human happiness when we first learned to weave, to make something big, warm, and useful from many smaller pieces, first vines and reeds, and then jute, then more delicate strands, like the fibers of yucca and hair of alpaca, until our fingers became too clumsy to guide the threads. Draped under the pine, within sight of the cotton field, the fabric seemed very much to belong to the farm, perhaps because it was a material returned in altered form to the place it originated. Like me.

Uncle Bill passed and tooted his horn.

Mama commenced doing what she called "sewing the quilt in," which required that we loop the lining to the frame temporarily, using package twine and a four-inch needle. The chairs kept falling over backward with the weight of the frame. I propped them up again and stood on one that especially wanted to tilt, only to have the chair diagonally across from it go down. Pretty soon all of the chairs were lying on the grass, and we were picking up the frame and starting over.

I thought I could hear Grandmama hooting somewhere off in the ether. The more the chairs fell, the harder she laughed. She had loved a joke, and to be tickled. She had an eye for anything to laugh about, and once she got started she laughed for a long time. Expert quilter that she was, she'd owned a proper quilt frame, and she would have found our struggle to keep all four chairs standing hilarious.

"Those chairs won't stand up by theirselves," she would have said.

Smiling, I dragged up cement blocks to weight the chairs. "There," I said. "They'll stay up now."

A ghost is like a quilt in that both are made of stories. Both are made to wear out. Both represent a life spent, and those parts left behind.

Mama and I rethreaded our robust needles and began to cord the cloth to the frame, over and under. When we finished, we had what appeared to be a cloth trampoline, or a giant embroidery hoop. Mama satisfied herself that the frame was perfectly square and sent me for the batting, the layer of processed cotton or polyester fiber that makes the quilt warm. She told me the traditional batting was cotton, and brown colored for some reason. When Mama was a young girl, Grandmama insulated quilts with cotton from the field. It had been ginned to remove the seeds, then had to be spread across the lining in handfuls that she patted even.

"Made out of pure cotton?" I asked.

"Plain cotton. That was all the batting they had. Back then people used quilts to keep warm. You needed them. Now they hang them on the walls to admire."

"This one will get used," I said. We had bought polyester batting, less natural but warmer on winter nights, and more durable. We unrolled it like a layer of rolled dough.

After the batting was tidy we laid down the top. We pinned it to the lining all around, using a thousand straight pins all pointing out, as Mama had been taught. It was like making a pie—crust, filling, crust.

There, hovering above the rich grass beneath evergreen, long-needled boughs, bearing the noted blue of sky, next to the mallow-pink of the cotton field with its yellow morning blooms, upbraided by jays and clucked over by cardinals, was our quilt. After we stood around and admired it awhile, we unfastened two sides from the frame and began to roll it up so that finally it looked like a stretcher, or a banner waiting to be unfurled at a town meeting. Now it was a thick secret.

Morning was over and it was time for Mama to drive home and cook dinner for Daddy. She would return in the relative cool of late afternoon and we would quilt again. Midafternoon, Silas and I donned bathing suits and turned the water sprinkler on the trampoline. Every time we bounced, droplets of water flew. We found a bar of soap and played soap hockey in the spray, sliding around, trying to keep the other person from scoring. As soon as we turned the water off, we were hot again.

At five Mama returned, this time with Daddy, the day sweltering, breezeless, with not a degree of relief in sight. We erected the four chairs again, but inside the packhouse this time, and we laid the quilt-stretcher on them and unrolled the quilt enough for two rows of squares to show. Even with its two windows and one door wide open, the packhouse was intensely hot, so hot you could feel the fine arm-hairs trapping a layer of heat. I was wearing loose shorts and a tank top and had clamped my hair off my neck; still, sweat issued from my armpits, ran down my sides, and flowed through the coulee of breasts and down the trough of spine. The packhouse had absorbed many days' heat; for nights in a row the earth had not cooled enough to cool the buildings. I toted fans to the packhouse and aimed them directly at us.

"What design do we use for the quilting?" I asked.

"Whatever design you like."

"What choices do I have?"

"You could quilt around certain of the shapes, or you could stitch in straight lines across the entire quilt. Or you could do what we call tack it, which is tie it here and there with pieces of embroidery thread."

"What do you usually do?"

"A half-box shape. That's the way Mama showed me and the way I do it."

"Like how?"

"You start at the lower right-hand corner of each square with a half-square, like a backward L. You go out an inch and stitch another row, and quilt the square a row at a time." Mama drew the design with her pointer finger on a square, a right angle repeated outwards at intervals of an inch until the square was full.

"Do the lines have to be exactly an inch apart?"

"Nobody would ever be able to tell if they were more or less. We'll judge it by eye."

"Then let's quilt it the old way."

"I think you'll be happy. Most people around here quilt that way."

Mama and I worked facing each other, sewing running stitches that tied the lining to the batting to the top. From the start I could see I'd never keep up with her. Her stitches were neat and quick, and she was even-eyed, her

lines running impossibly parallel. It was so hot I thought
the sweat dropping off me would stain the quilt, but instead
it trickled down my ribs and soaked my waistband. Vainly
I tried to position the fans so the wind hit both of us. Not
even three fans on high could drive the heat away.

"The tank ran out of propane yesterday," I said.

"That could be a blessing," Mama said. "It's too hot
to cook."

"When the gas man delivered, he had to come in because the pilot lights had gone out on the stove. He said it
was 102 degrees."

"Dog days," she said. "It's always hot during dog days."

Daddy had decided to renovate the packhouse while we
worked. He stayed busy outside, prying off cheap, painted
plywood somebody had nailed onto the front, exposing
heart-pine siding. He planned to replace rotting boards and
bring the original look back to the building. Sometimes
he called me outside to look at his progress, but mostly,
absorbed in his work, he left us to our talk. Silas and his
cousin Carlin were riding their bicycles around and around
the yard, and we could hear them laughing.

"How old were you when you first made a quilt with
Grandmama?"

"I saw her make lots of them. I was nineteen when she
showed me how."

"You remember being nineteen?"

"Kay was a baby. While I was pregnant, I sewed together
a quilt-top. It was squares put together, and I embroidered
Kay's name on the squares. She was two weeks old when I
brought her out here to Mama's every day and we quilted it."

"How long did it take you?"

"About a week."

"Where did you do it?"

"In the front room of your house."

"Did you roll and unroll it?" I asked, but she explained that if people have the room they leave the entire quilt frame up and roll only to get to the center squares that they are unable to reach from the edges.

I was slow. At the end of the first evening, I had quilted one and a half squares in a quilt that had forty-two. Alone, it would take me a month. Mama was on her third square. At the end of the second day, Mama helped me finish my row and we scrolled the quilt out another two rows and rolled up what was already quilted.

Mama talked about the women of Spring Branch getting together, Grandmama among them, to quilt.

"Where would they gather?"

"In the social hall over at the church. And I'm not talking one quilt. I mean they'd work on three or four quilts at one time."

"How many women would be there?"

"Sometimes a dozen or more."

"I bet they could finish a quilt quick."

"The young girls wouldn't do anything but thread needles," Mama said. "So as soon as someone ran out of thread, they had another needle ready and waiting."

Uncle Bill came by with Miss Jo, to check on cows, and they sat with us for a long while in the heat. Miss Jo thought the quilt was pretty. Mr. Shug, the neighbor the other way, came by to persuade us that the road should be paved. He had a paper he wanted Mama to sign, but she wouldn't because none of us wanted the road paved. Paving would bring more and faster traffic and would end neighborhood use of the road for horseback riding and evening walks.

On the third afternoon my beau drove to the farm from Tallahassee. He had left the minute he got off work and arrived late afternoon. I heard his truck before he got there.

"He's here," I said. By then we could see his truck through the open doorway, turning in the driveway. We all stopped what we were doing to greet him. I couldn't take my eyes off him. Mama and Daddy knew how much I liked him, and they liked him too. I knew by then he would be my husband. Daddy put down his crowbar and hammer and settled onto the door stoop to talk to Raven, who took a plastic yard chair nearby. Through the open door, Mama and I listened.

"We wanted to talk to you and Mrs. Ray about our plans," Raven said to Daddy.

"We've heard a little," Daddy said.

"I'd like to marry your daughter," Raven said. "We know we don't need your permission but we'd like to have your blessing."

"No, you don't need permission. You're both adults," Daddy agreed.

"I wanted you to know I'll take care of your daughter, treat her as an equal human being, and love her until the last beat of my heart."

"We don't know you well yet," Daddy said. "But from what we do know, I think we'd be proud to have you as a son."

"Everything has happened quickly," Raven said.

"A couple knows when they're ready to marry. Length of time doesn't matter. My brother Nolan saw a woman on the street one Friday afternoon and said, 'That's the woman I intend to marry.' By Monday they were married."

"How soon are you thinking you'll marry?" Mama

asked. She had said nothing before that, but had quilted with a happy smile on her lips. Raven looked at me.

"In the spring, we're thinking, when Janisse finishes at the university." I smiled at him.

"Where will you do it?"

"Where we met, perhaps. It's kind of halfway between."

In that moment I had most everything I needed—my family, my child, my husband-to-be. I carried the preciousness of them inside, fragile crane eggs, guarding them furiously. And I had my place.

Mama and I would finish the quilt and it would ever seem to me a dowry, because it represented all I could offer—mostly a dream, a dream of a life pieced from scraps, imitating a fragmented world stitched back together with ghosts and sapling trees.

Our wild card quilt, complete.

A Forest for the Children

Raven and I married on the spring equinox, on the banks of the Suwannee, where we met, beside the river that joined our two homes, south Georgia and north Florida. Silas, in his pocket two silver rings, escorted my mama down the boardwalk to a gazebo our friends had decorated with garden flowers and with the names of birds and trees printed on thick paper, hanging about. Egret, tupelo, towhee. My sister's son, Ian, ushered Raven's mother down the boardwalk. When Daddy started down with me, stepping slowly and ceremonially in time to our friend Michael's ethereal violin, with everybody watching, he began whispering.

"Kay hugged me," he said.

"Did you talk to her?" I whispered back. Each step had its turn.

"A little," he said. "Things are good, I think."

"Let's talk later," I said. After all, my husband-to-be, whose two grown daughters had escorted him to the gazebo, waited for us, surrounded by our bright-eyed friends, whose faces glowed and whose cameras flashed. There he was, my beloved, his eyes misty with tears. Raven and Daddy embraced.

The ceremony, led by Susan, committed us to each other, to our now-big family, to our community of friends, and to the land. We each thanked the other's parents for the gift of their child. We welcomed each other's family into our own. The community agreed aloud to uphold and support our marriage.

All of it was perfect, and most perfect was that my birth family, including all four siblings, came together for the first time in twenty years. That day, my father not only gained a son, but he reclaimed a daughter. When I glanced toward my family, I saw my brother Dell sitting close to my sister, Kay, laughing about something or other, and then I saw my father gazing at his son and daughter as if he couldn't get enough of their faces.

Toward the end, Susan opened the ceremony for community blessing and participation. Our friends stood and read poems or sang songs. Although we had asked for no gifts, they presented pictures they had sketched, a basket of herb plants, poems they'd written for us, bouquets of flowers. They wished us well. Christi, who worked for the Nature Conservancy of Georgia and was responsible for negotiating the Moody Forest purchase, came forward holding a bunch of bronze grasses and coppery pine needles. On this very day, she said, south Georgia basket weavers Henry and Mary Foreman were making a basket for us of Moody grasses and longleaf pine needles. I wept then.

Kay had stitched a magnificent pine tree quilt for our wedding present. She got up and opened the quilt out so everyone could see. Its background was tan cotton; centered in each square was a dark green tree, pieced of material printed with pine needles and cones. The quilt had taken hours of painstaking work. "It honors their love for each other and their love of nature," she wrote on the quilt's cloth label. "Let it be a warm reminder of that commitment."

This part of the story could have ended happily there, with Raven and me floating down the tannic river in our kayaks while our friends shower us with wisteria and rose petals. Or it could have ended with us coming back to a potluck feast prepared by our friends, spread on tables with white tablecloths high above the Suwannee River, beneath live oaks hanging with Spanish moss. The buffet was twenty feet long, replete with the finest dishes our friends could offer. This story could have ended with the cutting of the wedding cake made by a local baker, the same rose geranium cake she had served us the day we met, when she poured us a glass of her rosemary-infused wine. Our wedding night we spent singing folk songs around a campfire in the campground, and Leeann serenaded us in our tent later with a song. The next morning we gathered at Suwannee River Diner, whose walls were painted with local flora and fauna, for breakfast, and from there a smaller wedding party in canoes and kayaks paddled all day down the Suwannee River. The story could have ended with the native azaleas blooming wildly along the riverbanks.

It didn't. It ended much earlier, really, in the same moment that it began. Wholeness doesn't have a beginning or an end, but is a process, a long service to honor our humanity, our own and each other's. It's like making a quilt. We start with pieces of a good, well-functioning life, and all our lives long we try to put them together until we finally have something beautiful that functions, that is whole, that makes us happy. Even then it will need mending, but that is the work of humanity.

ﺗ

"What would you do today," Raven asked unexpectedly one day, "if you knew beyond a doubt that you would not fail?"

"Let me think," I said. "What about you?"

"I'd like to stand on the edge of the Grand Canyon, step off into it, and fly." I thought about what he said. I've never wanted to fly. I am earth bound, terrestrial. Then I knew the answer.

"I would return the earth to the way it was," I said. So Raven began to understand my dream for the earth, and to own it as his dream.

By now, Mama and Daddy had bought three or four pieces of the farm, so it was partially put together again. Concerned about the toxic chemicals used on cotton, and about serious soil erosion, we had ended the lease of the land to out-of-family farmers. Because Raven and I planned to live at the farm some day soon, we decided to start making it the home both of us desired. We'd fix up the farmhouse, plant more fruit trees, prepare the fields for organic farming. Raven worked as a letter carrier in downtown Tallahassee, Florida. For now, we would live in his log home in rural Crawfordville.

We needed to decide as a family what to do with the fields in the meantime. "If you don't do something with them," Uncle Bill had said, "they'll become pure wilderness." Some we decided to keep for food production. Some we would plant in cover crops. Some we would turn back to longleaf pine. We knew that we would never in our lifetimes see on the farm the kind of forest that survives on the Moody land, but maybe our offspring will.

Early one morning in the middle of winter Raven and I drove back from Florida to spend a day tree planting. When Mama and Daddy arrived from town, the two of us were already up and dressed in work clothes, gloves stuck in back pockets. First we crowded around the enamel kitchen table, pushing breakfast dishes aside, and drew a map of the farm: road, house, pastures, fields, stream run, the surprise pecan tree we discovered bearing in a fencerow. Around the map we marked where we want the forest to be years from now—coming up out of the hardwood bottomland, along the lower edges of the fields, where the erosion was worst. We'd do this slowly.

Daddy had picked up a thousand seedlings from the Georgia Forestry Commission, and they came in four bundles, each about as big as a foal. We piled them on the back of the pickup and drove out to the field. All day, using hand dibbles, we planted the trees one by one, making a hole in the ground with the dibble, pushing the seedling in and arranging its roots, then using the dibble to push dirt back against it. We stamped dirt firmly around each tree.

"Grow," I would say to the trees. "Grow for the children. Grow straight and tall and ancient. Spread far and wide until you cover this land."

We planted at random, wandering here and there as if we were wind itself, spreading seeds. Longleaf seedlings don't have trunks for a few years; they look like tufts of thick grass. Each has a long taproot. Carefully, we closed the bundle after we took a few saplings, so they wouldn't dry out. We worked steadily and happily. My niece Taira and nephew Carlin arrived to spend the day, and they planted, too, sharing a dibble, until they got tired and drifted away to climb trees and build sand castles in the field.

Mama and Daddy left with the children in the late afternoon to cook supper, and by the time my beloved and I finished planting, the sun was going down toward Alabama. We gathered our tools, then stood and surveyed the day's work. It was more than a day's work. It is our dream to rebuild community, human and wild, and it is the earth's dream to have its forests back. We are making the dream of the earth come true, creating the possibility of wholeness around us, so that our lives can be of a piece. We are living the stories that for years we will tell, how the root of one of the saplings was split but my father planted it anyway, and it grew as well as the rest. How the trees began to take root and exhibit new growth and turn a bright, flourishing green. How over 90 percent of them lived.

We are filling in the empty squares of the quilt.

Acknowledgments

Because he inhabits the deepest province of my heart, I acknowledge my beautiful son, Silas, who is grace and life to me, whose spirit is very bright. Nowhere is there a set of parents finer than mine, and I thank Franklin Delano Ray and Lee Ada Branch Ray for their omnipotent love and their unswerving generosity. Much love and appreciation to Dell, brother in more ways than blood.

Everybody deserves a friend like Susan Cerulean, who for many years has been a beacon of wisdom, who has helped me think rationally on a daily basis, and without whom I might still be lost in a wasteland somewhere. Rick Bass has remained a loyal and true friend not only in times of exaltation but also during great despair, and I will remain grateful to him until the moment I die. Abiding gratitude goes to my beloved Milton Newton Hopkins, a landmark in my heart, for unmitigated support. Thank you.

I was blessed to discover Wendell Berry's books when I was not yet grown, and his great thinking and sound character have inspired and guided me every day on this earth: I owe him an unsayable debt.

The poetry of Mary Oliver has comforted me.

Since 1999, an ever-swelling group of Southern nature writers has been gathering to discuss how we can better use our art to protect the landscape. I must acknowledge the importance of these writers and activists, who are friends as much as they are colleagues, in my life. Though a net must be cast wide to gather them in, they compose a vital circle of my community. They share my dreams. Without them, I would be made depauperate in the most essential of ways. They include Bill Belleville, Franklin Burroughs, Chris

Camuto, Susan Cerulean, Thomas Rain Crowe, Jan DeBlieu, Ann Fisher-Wirth, Lola Haskins, Julie Hauserman, Jim Kilgo, John Lane, Janet Lembke, Barbara Ras, Jeff Ripple, Renee Ripple, Betsy Teter, and Melissa Walker.

By sheer good fortune I was brought to the publishing house of Milkweed Editions, whose vision for the world and whose belief in the power of literature match my own. Emilie Buchwald, Milkweed's founder, has been my editor for two books now, and every day I count my blessings that her capable and loving hands shape this thinking. Emilie is a visionary, a bright star, a brilliant and compassionate woman who has given her life in service to this world. Without her, many mouths would still be closed and the world would be a darker place.

Hilary Reeves and Elizabeth Cooper have labored ardently on my behalf in the marketing and publicity departments at Milkweed Editions. They are ever cheerful and helpful and have surpassed duty to support and promote this work. Thanks to Laurie Buss, Ben Barnhart, and Ellen Hawley for superb editing.

Leigh Feldman is more than I thought possible in an agent: honest, fun loving, fierce when necessary. She is a sound, capable boat that rows me into the world.

Thanks to all the wise and good people who have founded and kept running environmental organizations in the South: Altamaha Riverkeeper, bent on protecting the mighty Altamaha and its tributaries; Dogwood Alliance of Asheville, North Carolina, a network of grassroots forest-activist groups whose mission is to stop industrial-scale clearcutting; Longleaf Alliance, an Alabama-based group dedicated to restoring the longleaf pine ecosystem; the Charlottesville-based Southern Environmental Law Center, legally protecting the South's natural resources through policy reform; Southwings, an environmental pilot service based in Chattanooga, for watching over the southlands like angels and, in particular, for flying me over a 10,000-acre clearcut near McMinnville, Tennessee;

The Nature Conservancy of Georgia; and all other groups guarding local communities and wildlands from the pressures of a global economy and intense population growth. Much gratitude to the funders and volunteers of these groups.

Thanks to my town and my rural community for holding open a place for me, and thanks to all my friends, who have been exceedingly kind and helpful, especially: Tom, Kay, and Ian Amsler; Bill Branch and family; Uncle James and Aunt Joan Branch; Norine Cardea; Jackie and Zachary Carter; Lynn Carter; Jeff Chanton; Dorinda Dallmeyer; Alice Coleman; Albert Culbreath; Claire Daughtry; Leeann Drabenstott; Sharon Fairbanks; Roger Hall; Claire Hicks; Neill Herring; Annie Ruth Moody Howard; Victor Howard and Margaret Birney; Wes Jackson; Elizabeth and Cecil Johnson; Jimmy Johnson, Steve Cowan, Wright Gres, and Randy Dewberry; Christi Lambert, Alison McGee, Christine Griffiths, and everyone else at the Nature Conservancy of Georgia; John Lane and Betsy Teter; Anna James Martin; Caleb Martin and family; Vic Miller; Jody Mingledorff; Gary Nabhan; Annette Osborne; Stephen, Tamara, Taira Shea, and Carlin Joshua Ray; Alan Roach and family; Kelley Segars; Ann and Alan Singer; Andy and Cina Duggan Smith; Breeze VerDant and Robin Reiske, Silas's other parents; Christopher Wall; June White; Tommie Williams; Myra Winner; Mick Womersley; and Sue Woodard.

A thousand thanks to friends from the Georgia Nature-Based Tourism Association; to POGO (Pinhook Swamp, Osceola National Forest, Greater Okefenokee) Coalition, working to preserve a corridor of wildland between Georgia and Florida; and to the board of Altamaha Riverkeeper, particularly Robert DeWitt, James Holland, and Deborah Shepard. I acknowledge gratitude to all the kind people associated with libraries, book clubs, bookstores, universities, literary festivals, and nonprofit organizations who have hosted me so graciously and generously, for readings and lectures.

Many thanks to Florida Gulf Coast University, especially Peter Blaze Corcoran, Bill Hammond, and Jim Wohlpart, for providing me furtherance to complete this manuscript.

I am forever grateful to my husband, Raven Burchard, who has brought the gift of great, inimitable love.

Janisse Ray was born in 1962 and is a native of the coastal plains of southern Georgia. A naturalist and environmental activist, Janisse has published essays and poems in such periodicals as *Audubon, Hope, Natural History, Orion,* and *Sierra.* Her first book, *Ecology of a Cracker Childhood,* was published by Milkweed Editions in 1999 and has won the Southern Book Critics Circle Award, the Southeast Booksellers Association Award for Nonfiction, the American Book Award, and the Southern Environmental Law Center Book Award. In 2002, the Georgia Center for the Book selected *Ecology of a Cracker Childhood* for its inaugural "All Georgia Reading the Same Book" campaign. Janisse lives on the family farm near Baxley, Georgia, with her husband.

*Of Landscape and Longing:
Finding a Home at the Water's
Edge*
CAROLYN SERVID

The Book of the Tongass
EDITED BY CAROLYN SERVID
SNOW AND DONALD SNOW

Homestead
ANNICK SMITH

*Testimony: Writers of the
West Speak On Behalf of Utah
Wilderness*
COMPILED BY STEPHEN
TRIMBLE AND TERRY TEMPEST
WILLIAMS

The Credo Series

*Brown Dog of the Yaak: Essays on
Art and Activism*
RICK BASS

*Winter Creek: One Writer's
Natural History*
JOHN DANIEL

Writing the Sacred into the Real
ALISON HAWTHORNE DEMING

*The Frog Run: Words and
Wildness in the Vermont Woods*
JOHN ELDER

*Taking Care: Thoughts on
Storytelling and Belief*
WILLIAM KITTREDGE

*An American Child Supreme: The
Education of a Liberation Ecologist*
JOHN NICHOLS

*Walking the High Ridge: Life As
Field Trip*
ROBERT MICHAEL PYLE

*The Dream of the Marsh Wren:
Writing As Reciprocal Creation*
PATTIANN ROGERS

The Country of Language
SCOTT RUSSELL SANDERS

*Shaped by Wind and Water:
Reflections of a Naturalist*
ANN HAYMOND ZWINGER

THE WORLD AS HOME, the nonfiction publishing program of Milkweed Editions, is dedicated to exploring our relationship to the natural world. Not espousing any particular environmentalist or political agenda, these books are a forum for distinctive literary writing that not only alerts the reader to vital issues but offers personal testimonies to living harmoniously with other species in urban, rural, and wilderness communities.

MILKWEED EDITIONS publishes with the intention of making a humane impact on society, in the belief that literature is a transformative art uniquely able to convey the essential experiences of the human heart and spirit. To that end, Milkweed publishes distinctive voices of literary merit in handsomely designed, visually dynamic books, exploring the ethical, cultural, and esthetic issues that free societies need continually to address. Milkweed Editions is a not-for-profit press.

Join Us

Since its genesis as *Milkweed Chronicle* in 1979, Milkweed
has helped hundreds of emerging writers reach their readers.
Thanks to the generosity of foundations and of individuals like
you, Milkweed Editions is able to continue its nonprofit mission of publishing books chosen on the basis of literary merit—
of how they impact the human heart and spirit—rather than on
how they impact the bottom line. That's a miracle our readers
have made possible.

In addition to purchasing Milkweed books, you can
join the growing community of Milkweed supporters. Individual contributions of any amount are both meaningful and
welcome. Contact us for a Milkweed catalog or log on to
www.milkweed.org and click on "About Milkweed," then
"Supporting Milkweed," to find out about our donor program,
or simply call (800) 520-6455 and ask about becoming one
of Milkweed's contributors. As a nonprofit press, Milkweed
belongs to you, the community. Milkweed's board, its staff, and
especially the authors whose careers you help launch thank you
for reading our books and supporting our mission in any way
you can.

Interior design by Christian Fünfhausen.
Typeset in ACaslon 11.5/15
by Stanton Publication Services
on the Pagewing Digital Publishing System.
Printed on acid-free, recycled
55# Natural Odyssey Hibulk paper
by Friesen Corporation.